"You Can't Fire the Bad Ones!"

"You Can't Fire the Bad Ones!"

*And 18 Other Myths About
Teachers, Teachers' Unions,
and Public Education*

. . . .

WILLIAM AYERS, CRYSTAL LAURA,
and **RICK AYERS**

BEACON PRESS, BOSTON

Beacon Press
Boston, Massachusetts
www.beacon.org

Beacon Press books
are published under the auspices of
the Unitarian Universalist Association of Congregations.

21 20 19 18   8 7 6 5 4 3 2 1

This book is printed on acid-free paper that meets the uncoated paper
ANSI/NISO specifications for permanence as revised in 1992.

Text design and composition by Kim Arney

Library of Congress Cataloging-in-Publication Data

Names: Ayers, William, author. | Laura, Crystal T., author. | Ayers, Rick, author.
Title: "You can't fire the bad ones!" : and 18 other myths about teachers,
    teachers' unions, and public education / William Ayers, Laura Crystal,
    Rick Ayers.
Description: Boston : Beacon Press, 2018. | Includes bibliographical references.
Identifiers: LCCN 2017025652 (print) | LCCN 2017049877 (ebook) |
    ISBN 9780807036679 (e-book) | ISBN 9780807036662 (paperback)
Subjects: LCSH: Teachers—United States. | Teaching—United States. | Public
    schools—United States. | Education—United States. | Education—Aims and
    objectives—United States. | BISAC: EDUCATION / Teaching Methods &
    Materials / Social Science. | EDUCATION / Inclusive Education. |
    EDUCATION / Research.
Classification: LCC LB1775.2 (ebook) | LCC LB1775.2 .A95 2018 (print) |
    DDC 371.1—dc23
LC record available at https://lccn.loc.gov/2017025652

Contents

"ROTTEN APPLES"

In 2014, *Time* magazine ran a cover story entitled "Rotten Apples," with the subheading "It's nearly impossible to fire a bad teacher. Some tech millionaires may have found a way to change that."[1]

Several years earlier, *Time* had run a long feature on Michelle Rhee, the public face of the newly energized corporate school reform forces and then chancellor of the Washington, DC, schools, with the headline "How to Fix America's Schools."[2] The article praised Rhee for rapidly making more changes than other school leaders had, "even reform-minded ones." In a year and a half on the job, Rhee had closed 21 schools (15 percent of the total) and fired 270 teachers, 100 central office personnel, and 36 principals. Rhee argued that teachers are the key to school improvement and made her case by publicly scrapping with teacher leaders and championing zealous campaigns to "fire the bad ones and reward the good ones." Or as Joel Klein, former New York City schools chancellor, said, "If we don't change the personnel, all we're doing is changing the chairs."[3]

Newsweek's cover of March 15, 2010, consisted of an artist's nostalgic rendering of a classroom cliché: a blackboard with colored chalk and an eraser on the shelf beneath, the board covered with a single phrase in the style of a child required to atone for misbehavior by writing the broken rule over and over until it finally sinks in: "We must fire bad teachers." The bright-yellow text in the center underlines the message: "The Key to Saving American Education." No one could possibly miss the message, and yet the article itself would hardly warrant a passing grade as a college essay: it's filled with assertions disconnected from evidence ("Some educational experts have noticed an uptick in the academic quality of new teachers."), and it makes sweeping and unexamined claims ("In recent years researchers have discovered something that may seem obvious, but for many years was overlooked or denied. What really makes a difference, what matters more than the class size or the textbook, the teaching method or the technology, or even the curriculum, is the quality of the teacher.").[4]

On March 7, 2010, the *New York Times Magazine* ran a cover with the heading "Building a Better Teacher," which portrayed a teacher-as-Wonder-Woman-in-motion, wearing black horn-rimmed glasses labeled "Behavior-Monitoring Glasses" while holding a piece of chalk ("Smart Chalk—Never Writes a Wrong Answer") in one hand and a cup of coffee spiked with a supplement ("Instant Command of Authority") in the other.[5] Several weeks later, May 23, 2010, the *Times Magazine* used a familiar image—the front of a modern classroom with a whiteboard, markers, and erasers; a table with papers and a coffee cup; and an assignment posted on the board in red script: "Are Teachers' Unions the Enemy of Reform? Discuss."

On August 31, 2009, the *New Yorker* ran a lengthy story called "The Rubber Room: The Battle over New York City's Worst Teachers," which opens with a pithy quote from an anonymous principal claiming that the head of the teachers' union was so single-minded and corrupt that she "would protect a dead body in the classroom."[6] The article focuses on a site in the central bureaucracy where teachers who've been removed from their teaching duties report while awaiting arbitration that will settle their teaching status permanently. It's a thick description of a kind of purgatory for fifteen teachers, and it invites a bit of lip-smacking fascination with an oddly compelling collection of outcasts. But it is, after all, fifteen teachers in a system of forty thousand. And it turns out that there's no battle at all, only a nod to due process, an exercise that is a little clumsy on all sides but completely common in employment and labor disputes in all areas. Buried deep within the quasi-ethnographic piece is this: before teachers got organized, they "endured meager salaries, tyrannical principals, witch hunts for Communists, and gender discrimination against a mostly female work force." Still, it's those fifteen "bad teachers" and their awful, self-interested union that wreak havoc on the schools and must be the core of reform efforts. The conservative commentator Bill O'Reilly gleefully broadened that focus on October 12, 2010, offering his opinion that unruly students, lazy and incompetent teachers, and apathetic administrators together destroy an adequate academic environment.

These are all examples of a common frame and a stuttering refrain: "Rotten teachers and their reactionary unions are killing the schools and hurting our children." Listen to almost any politician at a microphone responding to the question "How would you improve public education?" Without missing a beat, and in a rising voice, the first answer seems programmed and rehearsed from a repeating loop in everyone's stump speech: "I'd get the lazy, incompetent teachers out of the classroom." The assumptions are questionable, the evidence nonexistent, but the frame is airtight: who, after all, is advocating for the lazy or the incompetent?

Of course, if we were to get to the microphone first, we'd change the frame and flip the script: all public school students deserve a well-resourced and fully functioning school right in their own community or neighborhood, and that school must be staffed by thoughtful, intellectually grounded, morally awake, caring and compassionate, well-rested and well-paid teachers who know their students well and are committed to their growth and full development. That's a truer frame than the one that says lazy teachers are ruining schools, because it reflects a more honest and compelling look at reality, and a more hopeful goal. So, in part, the problem is about who gets to set the agenda and who sets the frame?

And that's what this book is about: changing the frames and challenging the myths about teachers teaching, diving into the details, and setting the record straight.

Our focus is intentional—we are thinking and writing about teachers and teaching specifically, not education policy and not research on teaching. Teachers, their individual and collective voices, their lived experiences and particular perspectives, are too often ignored or dismissed in the larger narratives about teaching and schools, education and reform. Teachers are too often talked about but not listened to. We come from an entirely different place: teachers are the ones who do the work that needs to be done—again and again—under conditions that are always demanding and many times demeaning and dehumanizing as well. We turn to teachers to shatter the myths about teaching from the bottom up, and from the inside out. We turn to the wisdom of the assembled teachers to call out what isn't working—in policy, in politics, and, yes, even among their colleagues in the schools—and commit to a mission of repair.

In the continuing public conversation and boiling political debates, education is increasingly cast as a commodity like any other—a washing machine, say, or a laptop—something to be bought and sold in the marketplace. Picture a gigantic distribution center with floor-to-ceiling shelves; steer the warehouse bot or helpful drone down the "E" aisle where it will find "Education" squeezed in between "E-books" and "Eggs." Pick one up, toss it into the cart, next-day delivery guaranteed.

It's a commanding metaphor: schools become businesses run by CEOs. Teachers, then, get cast as the pieceworkers toiling on the assembly line, and students are the raw materials bumping along the factory floor as information is incrementally stuffed into their empty, up-turned heads. Neat and rational and efficient—with this metaphor, it's rather easy to suppose that closing and downsizing the least productive units or outsourcing and privatizing a space that once belonged to the public are naturally occurring events; that developing a simple, standardized metric and relentlessly applying state-administered (but privately developed and quite profitable) tests to determine the "outcomes" are rational proxies for learning; that the organized and collective voice of teachers is irrelevant at best and more likely a self-serving and destructive chorus of whiners; that centrally controlled standards are sensible; that "zero tolerance" for student misbehavior as a stand-in for child development or justice is sane; that crude competition is an effective motivator for learning; and that a range of sanctions on students, teachers, and schools in the name of "accountability" is logical and level-headed.

But what if the metaphor is a fraud—insistent, yes, pervasive and persistent, but a racket nonetheless? What if education is a universal human right and not a product at all? That would lead necessarily to a wide range of options and a different set of goals and demands.

All metaphors are imperfect, of course, but their task is always the same: advance interesting and important insights by providing a lateral perspective and a unique or unexpected point of view. This metaphor—education as commodity production—adds nothing of value to our understanding of public education and its real (or potential) role in a free society. Instead, the metaphor commandeers the discussion about schools and school improvement; yanks our attention away from the real issues we need to face; forces us far afield on every important dimension; misunderstands how human beings learn; misreads teaching and how teaching actually works; finesses the central place of inequality, racism, and poverty in student outcomes with pseudoscientific notions of objectivity; and dismisses the crucial role communities must play in the effective education of the young. But the metaphor is indeed what a range of notably powerful philanthropists, politicians, and pundits have embraced and christened "school reform."

It's as clear as ever that the public schools and classrooms are contested spaces and arenas of struggle as well as of hope.

We all need to ask ourselves a couple of simple, straightforward questions: What if this school/classroom/experience was for me or for my child? Are these the schools a free people require? This is a clarifying starting point for discussion: If it's not OK to cut the arts or sports programs, the clubs or libraries or science labs for the children of privilege, how can it be OK to cut those things for the children of the poor? If the privileged want teachers for their kids who are thoughtful, caring, compassionate professionals—well-rested and well-paid—how can they advocate for teachers who are little more than mindless clerks for the children on the other side of town? We should be highly skeptical of reformers who claim to know what's best for other people's children when those same conditions and experiences would be unacceptable for them or for their kids. It's worth noting that the major voices for the current corporate model of reform—including the two most recent US secretaries of education, Betsy DeVos and Arne Duncan—never attended or sent their kids to public schools.

In the current sweep of public school reform, it may seem that the privatizers and the marketeers hold all the cards and wield all the power, but that's simply not the case. True, they have a lot of money and resources, foundation endorsements, an amen chorus from the for-profit media and the chattering class, and the acquiescence of major players in the two dominant political parties. That's a lot, and it can seem overwhelming, but look more closely at what the corporate reformers are missing, even after decades of dangling the sweet golden carrot and wielding that super-sized big stick: they have not won over a majority of teachers and students, or parents and community members, and they have not quelled the opposition or resistance to their "reform" initiatives, which is only growing.

Most important, there is no compelling or coherent moral argument for destroying the public education system and replacing it with a string of privately managed profit centers. This is where we begin.

"Teachers' Unions Are the Biggest Obstacle to Improving Education Today."

There is a near-unanimous view in the national narrative that teachers' unions are public enemy number one—*the chief culprits*—when it comes to underperforming schools: they've consistently protected low-skilled and low-performing teachers; they've been intransigent and obstructionist when local school systems have attempted to implement innovative or ameliorative strategies such as altering schedules or offering financial incentives to exceptional teachers for good work; and they've blackmailed school boards into granting compensation packages for union members that far exceed what the school districts can bear. The excessive wages paid to union members are bad enough, but combined with their iron-clad job protections, the teachers' unions have managed to ruin public education. Furthermore, union membership does teaching itself a disservice, casting teachers in the role of mid-twentieth-century industrial workers rather than twenty-first-century white-collar professionals.

As Donald Trump argues,

It's a straightforward clash of issues:

The Brotherhood of the Blackboard Workers wants to keep the door closed to competition. That way they can run things as they choose, without review.

And we've got to bring on the competition—open the school-house doors and let parents choose the best school for their

children. Education reformers call this school choice, charter schools, vouchers, even opportunity scholarships. I call it
competition—the American way.[1]

The big national unions—the National Education Association
(NEA) and the American Federation of Teachers (AFT)—are special interest groups that use their excessive wealth to manipulate
politicians and buy support for their narrow, self-serving agendas.
Their vast influence undermines effective improvement in the nation's schools.

Many politicians have been direct and clear in their courageous
opposition to the stranglehold of the labor bosses and their mindless followers: Governor Chris Christie of New Jersey, for example,
has argued, "The single most destructive force for public education in this country is the teachers union. It is the single most destructive force."[2] And he has repeatedly asserted that leadership in
teachers' unions "deserve a punch in the face."[3] Elaborating on his
reasoning, Christie said, "They're not for education for our children. They're for greater membership, greater benefits, greater
pay for their members."

Many others have been waking up to the disastrous consequences of allowing the teachers' unions and their special interest bosses to hold sway over future generations. *Los Angeles Times*
columnist George Skelton wrote, "The biggest thugs in the Capitol
these days are not the tobacco lobbyists, Teamster bosses or Texas
gougers. The biggest thugs seem to be schoolteachers."[4] Fox Television's Sean Hannity noted that teachers' unions have "destroyed
our school system, and we don't do anything. The parents—why
there aren't people rising up against it is unbelievable."[5] Andrew
Sullivan, the conservative author and pioneering blogger, offered a
possible solution: "Until we really do bust the teachers unions, the
next generation of kids in public schools is at risk."[6]

Busting the unions is a relatively modest proposal, and for many
a necessary correction, but it's just a start. In 2004, then secretary

of education Rod Paige called the National Education Association a "terrorist organization,"[7] which was followed by the radio host Neal Boortz arguing that teachers' unions were destroying a generation and that that made them much more dangerous than terrorists. "Look, Al Qaeda, they could bring in a nuke into this country and kill 100,000 people with a well-placed nuke somewhere. OK. We would recover from that," Boortz said. "It would be a terrible tragedy, but the teachers' unions in this country can destroy a generation."[8] Now we're in the territory of apocalyptic war and pending annihilation. The teachers' unions must be stopped.

REALITY CHECK

In current public discussions about education and schools, teachers' unions loom as the biggest, brightest, and apparently most convenient target for the champions of market-based reforms. Fortunately the repeated assertions that the teachers' unions are hindering student performance or acting as the main obstacle to school improvement is a theory that's quite easy to test. Here goes: Collective bargaining for public school teachers is prohibited in Georgia, Texas, Virginia, and the Carolinas and is severely limited in "right-to-work" states that disallow binding contracts for teachers. These states are consistently ranked at the bottom in national comparisons of student achievement according to the standardized tests favored by the anti-union forces. Those at the top? States like Massachusetts, with the strongest teachers' unions.[9]

Nine out of the ten states with the highest average achievement scores on the National Assessment of Educational Progress (NAEP) tests were states with the largest number of teachers covered by union contracts.[10] Further, teachers at the prestigious University of Chicago Laboratory Schools (among others) all belong to a strong teachers' union. This fact-based reality holds true internationally as well: Finland and Canada, for example, where teachers' unions are strong and where practically every teacher is a member of the union, have among the highest average achievement scores on the Program for International Student Assessment (PISA) tests.[11]

So, the theory that teachers belonging to a union equates with school failure turns out to be utter nonsense from top to bottom. The dominance of this myth has much more to do with the frequency of its repetition and the ferocity of its messengers than with any evidence whatsoever.

In terms of political clout, the combined political action spending of the National Education Association (NEA) and American Federation of Teachers (AFT) amounted to $56 million over the two decades from 1990 to 2010,[12] a drop in the bucket compared to the hundreds of millions spent by the leading anti-union forces (Rupert Murdoch, the Koch brothers, Eli Broad, Michael Bloomberg), most of whom also have a stake in making profits in the education "market."

The anti-union myth making has a range of short-term and long-term costs. One insidious toll is the undermining of public confidence in teachers and schools, and another is discouraging people from entering the profession altogether. The myth encourages a split between teachers and families, falsely casting teachers as standing in opposition to the interests of children and communities, when in reality their interests largely overlap: Smaller schools and smaller class size are good for teachers, true, and they're also good for student learning. Sustained time to prepare helps teachers teach, true, and it also helps students engage in classroom activities as well.

Social priorities are contested and established through the push and pull between those who wield power at any given time and those who effectively resist or reconfigure power in order to influence policy and planning. Through the nineteenth century, teachers had no power. Neither did students, parents, or communities. Only the ruling group of wealthy white men determined school policy, pay, and curriculum. The shifting balance of force and authority between different interests has always been part of the struggle for a more robust and participatory democracy. The development of unions was an important piece. We do not, however, reflexively advocate uncritical support for teachers' unions—the two major ones have a mixed history to be sure—and we can and should judge the impact of unions, not only by how effectively they represent the interests of teachers but also by how well they advance meaningful education and the broader interests of communities.

In the mid-nineteenth century, there was a developing consensus in the United States that states should provide a free, basic education to all children. Business interests needed a disciplined work force as well as more literate workers, and social reformers wanted to socialize immigrants into the existing social order and "lift up" the underclass. Some saw education as a way to reduce social ills like public drunkenness and crime, and many others followed the initiatives from Black Reconstruction in the South and amplified an old and basic argument: democracy requires informed citizens and thoughtful voters who can participate equally in the polity, people who are capable of considering the common good above short-term, personal interests. It's worth remembering here that W. E. B. Du Bois famously said, "Public education is a Negro idea."[13]

The prospect of mass education was daunting, and the expense constituted a major obstacle, but a convenient solution was at hand: women. At the turn of the twentieth century, the face of teaching was changing dramatically: women were staffing the classrooms in larger and larger numbers, and earning a fraction of what their male counterparts made, while men were moving into administrative and supervisory positions in an increasingly bureaucratized enterprise. And this feminization and consequent perceived cheapening of the profession had required a "rethink" of who could teach and why they should teach. For example, Horace Mann, the leading voice of the Common School (or public school) movement, had campaigned in favor of women as teachers in the public schools, arguing that "her head [would be] encircled with a halo of heavenly light, her feet sweetening the earth on which she treads, and the celestial radiance of her benignity making vice begin its work of repentance through very envy of the beauty of virtue!"[14] Clearly this overblown rhetoric was meant to obscure the ugly reality of pay discrimination and impossibly difficult working conditions.

A typical Chicago classroom held sixty children, many of them poor immigrants from southern Europe who spoke no English. Hours were long, and an elementary school teacher made less than a clerk or a streetcar conductor.[15] In 1897, primary school teachers Margaret Haley and Catherine Goggin established the Chicago Teachers Federation (CTF), the first teachers' union in the country. Haley, now known as the founding mother of teacher unionism, was a sixth-grade teacher who had organized an investigation into the school system's shady budget process and then successfully sued several of the wealthiest corporations in the city for holding hundred-year, tax-free, and below-market-value leases on land owned by the public schools. Not surprisingly, Haley was despised by corporate power—one Chicago business leader called her "a nasty, unladylike woman."[16] Another nasty woman who persisted! Haley and Goggin formed the CTF after leading a walkout of the male- and administrator-dominated National Education Association conference, and through their determination and activism attracted other like-minded teachers to their cause.

One of Haley's allies for several years was Ella Flagg Young, a high school teacher who earned a PhD at the University of Chicago and eventually became the city's superintendent of schools. A student of John Dewey, Young worked with the CTF to develop a broad curriculum designed to educate the whole child—physically, emotionally, intellectually—and a pedagogy constructed on projects and performances. Young believed in empowering teachers, arguing, "In order that teachers may delight in awakening the spirits of children, they must themselves be awake."[17] Haley and Young helped create "teacher councils" within each school. They resisted attempts to push working-class children toward narrow vocational training, and they fought against corporate efforts to pay lower school taxes.

Fast-forward to 1960 in New York City and the creation of the United Federation of Teachers (UFT) out of an amalgamation of smaller teacher groups. Before the UFT existed, teachers received miserable salaries and endured despotic tyrants as principals who disciplined and fired them without due process or any appeals process whatsoever. Racial prejudice was widespread, and gender bias was also an accepted fact—wages were unequal, and there were several discriminatory rules. At one point, for example, women teachers in New York City were forced to take a two-year unpaid leave for the violation of becoming pregnant. And, of course, communist witch hunts and the blacklisting of liberals were widespread in the 1950s. The UFT engaged in political organizing and deployed the threat of strikes to become a forceful organization that could contest the exclusive power of the boards of education.

The story of the New York teachers' union contains other, more troubling, chapters. In 1968, for example, the power of the teachers' union stood in direct opposition to the explicit interests of Black and Puerto Rican communities, and activists initiated a campaign for community control of the schools. New York public schools acted, the activists believed, as hostile sites of control over poor students, failing to educate or even engage them in any meaningful way. In response, parents, inspired by the Black Panther Party and the Young Lords campaigns for community control of police, housing, and jobs, saw the possibility of transforming neighborhood schools by creating local school boards and taking leadership. As with the best of teachers' unions, the community control project was focused on expanding participatory democracy.

At the time, the teachers' union, under the race-baiting leadership of Albert Shanker, turned against the community because these union leaders saw local boards as a threat to their positions and called a teacher strike. Doubling down on the anti-community bias, UFT publications described the students as an ongoing danger

and threat—turning teacher demands into calls for more policing and repression of students. While many teachers supported
the community demands and even staffed strike schools, the UFT
leadership positioned itself as hostile to their own students.[18]

The New York City teachers' strike was settled in November
of 1968, and slowly the community-control school boards were
phased out. But distrust and tension between the Black and Brown
communities of the city and the AFT continued for years afterward.

A more hopeful and positive aspect of teachers' union organizing has emerged recently in New York; Chicago; Portland, Oregon;
Milwaukee; and other places. Breaking from the business unionism of the old guard (craft unions and service-model associations),
whose main activity had been economic service to members around
contractual grievances and pushing for better salaries, insurgent
caucuses with deep connections to the communities they serve have
won the leadership of many teachers' union locals. These emerging unions consider themselves social justice unions—aligned with
other workers in a broad sense of class struggle and powered by a
sense that the union must fight oppression—white and male supremacy, inequality, and discrimination—in the broader society,
as well as in any particular school or classroom. What characterizes
successful union struggles today is an unstinting commitment to
robust public schools—adequately staffed, fully funded, inclusive,
forward-looking, well-resourced—in every community and overall
better conditions *for students as well as teachers.* The best teacher
leaders position themselves and their struggles in solidarity with—
rather than in service to—the community.

Teachers' unions will necessarily make salary and wage demands; these are essential to building a viable and sustaining
profession. Demands will also always address issues of working
conditions—after all, good working conditions (limits on class
size, access to adequate materials) are in fact good teaching conditions, and good teaching conditions allow for the creation of better
learning conditions. The road to good working conditions includes

the wisdom of teachers, and that means that the strong and collective voice of teachers must be fully represented.

Imagine setting the basic standards for a city fire department concerning what to bring into a burning skyscraper in, for example, downtown Chicago. The process would involve accessing a working knowledge of the anatomy of modern buildings—geography, architecture, aesthetics, plumbing and electrical systems—thinking through questions of personnel, training, and working conditions; making an inventory of available supplies and considering what's necessary and affordable; and drawing on the latest thinking and experiences from firefighters across the country and around the world. There is obviously a range of considerations—cost, accessibility, equipment, standards, state-of-the-art practice—and in any serious conversation about fire and firefighting, elected officials would necessarily have a seat at the table. But no one who's thinking clearly could possibly want those standards and policies set by a committee of Chicago aldermen only, possibly meeting in one of their notorious smoke-filled back rooms trading favors. If the discussion is to be realistic and useful, the collective experience and thinking of firefighters must be fully and powerfully present.

Just so with teachers. They are the ones who bring practical classroom experience and knowledge to the conversation. Without that, the exchange is abstract and largely meaningless. Positive learning experiences depend on teachers.

The new social justice unions have also demanded more libraries and laboratories in schools, better transportation options, smaller class sizes, the end of school closings, and the right of community members to be consulted in all the affairs of the school. The 2014 strike of the Chicago Teachers Union (CTU) pitted the considerable power of Mayor Rahm Emanuel against just such a progressive, community-based union, led by the formidable Karen Lewis and her progressive caucus. At the end of the day, the union, with its deep community support, won.

In the face of a long list of Emanuel's repressive measures—massive school closings in Black and poor neighborhoods, a rescinded negotiated pay raise, increased class size, a plan to evaluate teachers based on student test scores (more on that later), the closing of libraries and arts programs across the city—the teachers were determined to reframe the agenda of reform, to champion the needs, desires, and demands of children and communities. The state hit back with a law of questionable constitutionality that required 75 percent of the union's membership to authorize a strike vote and then set the voting deadline in the middle of the summer when many teachers might not be available. Through extensive organizing, the CTU got a 95 percent vote to authorize a strike.[19]

Though the mayor and most politicians in the state, along with powerful business people, major foundations, and all the major media outlets, declared that the teachers were harming Chicago students and forcing taxes up, Lewis and the CTU maintained and increased community support. The Chicago strike demonstrated that perhaps the debates over education reform and education equity would best be led not by policy makers and academics but by the unions. As Elizabeth Todd-Breland of the University of Illinois at Chicago explained, "With this . . . strike, Chicago teachers are once again challenging the status quo by reasserting their voice in the national debate on education reform. By striking, teachers have not 'abandoned the children' that they have committed to serve. Instead, teachers are rising to fight for the children of Chicago by advocating for a slate of reforms that, if implemented, could transform the status quo in urban education."[20]

Teachers' unions have taken the lead in other cities by supporting families who opt out and refuse to participate in standardized testing, organizing for the right of students and teachers to wear Black Lives Matter shirts, and demanding greater representation of teachers of color in their ranks, among other efforts.

Corporate and market-based reformers spend time and money demonizing union members as armies of lazy, incompetent teachers who are mostly self-interested bureaucrats protected by life-time tenure. While raising the alarm that the sky is falling, these reformers also claim that capable and confident teachers don't need unions and that union contracts are massive and impenetrable, imposed by union bosses on naive teachers and hapless boards of education.

In reality, contracts are negotiated between boards of education and teachers' associations, and are the result of dialogue, conversation, and give-and-take discussions. In fact, they are not "union contracts" at all but, rather, union-board agreements. They typically cover wages and working conditions, true, as well as plans to evaluate teacher performance and improve learning. In most school districts, there is little conflict in negotiations. The crunch comes when funding is cut and the local boards shrug their shoulders, claiming that the state—a distant and inaccessible player—is the only entity that can help with funding. Much of the energy that goes into attacking teachers' unions, and indeed, much of the money behind measures to weaken these unions (for example, to end tenure or to create non-union charter schools) comes from wealthy foundations that are not remotely interested in education. Billionaires such as Bill Gates, Eli Broad, the Koch brothers, and the Walton family absurdly paint themselves as heroic underdogs in a fight against greedy and predatory teachers. They are, however, ideologically committed to ending trade unionism altogether, rolling back the remaining accomplishments of the New Deal of the 1930s, and shifting the blame for a global economic collapse from themselves to the main victims of the rolling crises. With the deindustrialization of America, many of the strong unions of the past—steel, automobile, and other heavy manufacturing—have been weakened or even disappeared. The largest remaining national unions are public sector teachers' unions, which are overwhelmingly women's organizations. Along with unionized nurses, unionized teachers have the potential to not only protect members and strengthen the overall enterprise; they also hold the hope of

uniting and organizing other workers and impacting political debates in favor of workers, the exploited, and the oppressed.

Strong union activists have driven deep reforms in several districts. For example, the activist teachers at *Rethinking Schools*, the
widely respected educators' journal from Milwaukee, developed a
platform for what they called "social justice unionism":

1. Defend the rights of its members while fighting for the
   rights and needs of the broader community and students.
2. Recognize that the parents and neighbors of our students
   are key allies and build strategic alliances with parents,
   labor unions, and community groups.
3. Fully involve rank-and-file members in running the
   union and initiate widespread discussion on how education unions should respond to the crises in education
   and society.
4. Put teachers and others who work in classrooms at the
   center of school reform agendas, ensuring that they take
   ownership of reform initiatives.
5. Encourage those who work with children to use methods
   of instruction and curricula that will promote racial and
   gender equity, combat racism and prejudice, encourage
   critical thinking about our society's problems, and nur-
   ture an active, reflective citizenry that is committed to
   real democracy and social and economic justice.
6. Forcefully advocate for a radical restructuring of American education.
7. Aggressively educate and mobilize its membership to
   fight for social justice in all areas of society.[21]

This manifesto is fiercely opposed to market-based reform, but
it's also light years away from whatever some bureaucrat might be
thinking. It defends public education while simultaneously work-

ing to transform it. It advocates for significant parent and community involvement on local school governing bodies, seeks to unite all staff members at a school, and argues for taking up other issues affecting students, such as job programs, housing, health care, recreation, safety, and antiviolence and antiracism initiatives. The platform goes on to reject a "service model" of unionism—in which inactive members are passive recipients of services provided by a paid staff—in favor of a social justice model of democratic engagement and mobilization.

Finally, this approach foregrounds teaching and learning, highlighting classroom- and school-based practices that promote better education and equity for all students. The Milwaukee teachers affiliated with *Rethinking Schools* have fought consistently against the overuse of standardized tests and in favor of alternatives to tracking and ability grouping; they've advocated for and developed fully staffed two-way bilingual classrooms, so that each child's home language can be affirmed, honored, and respected while students also learn a second language; and they've partnered with communities in building programs that reduce prejudice and promote equity.

There are many other forces—parent and teacher groups, community organizations, student and youth projects—around the country that are neither market-based reformers nor plodding bureaucrats: the Baltimore Algebra Project, the Chicago Freedom School, the Black Youth Project 100, Teachers 4 Social Justice, and the Caucus of Radical Educators, to name a few. As children face deepening poverty and social dislocation, schools confront greater challenges and higher expectations, combined with declining resources. The fight back—against both the corporate reformers and the status quo—gathers new momentum.

This movement-in-the-making resists the preoccupation with standardized test scores and narrow conceptions of economic competitiveness. It focuses instead on equity and social justice, including high expectations and educational excellence for all, and a commitment to public education as a cornerstone of society's commitment to opportunity, equity, and democratic participation.

The fight for forward-looking, community-engaged, democratic teachers' unions in no way harms students or their families, or blocks the fight for good schools. Rather, it is itself a fight for decent public schools for all children, as well as for a stronger, more vital democracy.

"You Can't Fire the Bad Ones."

Incompetent teachers should be fired, period. That's the simple and straightforward bottom line, but their self-interested and bureaucratic unions never allow it. You simply can't fire the bad ones—ever. So criminals, drunks, pedophiles, and monsters continue to occupy the nation's classrooms. Or, in that rare instance when someone is actually removed from a school, the miscreant punches a clock and sits around in some shabby room—usually referred to as a temporary reassignment center, popularly known in New York City as a "rubber room"—and waits months or even years for the conclusion of a tangled adjudication process. The person draws a paycheck and builds up a pension the entire time. This is intolerable—terrible for the kids, bad for our society.

In an interview with Charlie Rose in 2014, former US solicitor general Ted Olson argued that all teachers are "granted tenure after eighteen months and then you can't fire them. And the oldest gets to stay and the youngest teacher gets to get fired if there's any contraction in the budgets."[1] This means, he went on, that "teachers who are incompetent—unqualified teachers—are kept in the public school system, and the students are subject to incompetence." Olson described what he claimed is a common arrangement in which inferior and bungling folks dodge the consequences of their inept performances as they are shuffled from school to school—"the parade of the lemons," in his words—often landing the rotten apples in troubled schools that in fact need the greatest teachers.

Olson, now a powerful Washington, DC, lawyer, was speaking to Rose about a lawsuit he'd filed in California in 2012 challenging the system of teacher tenure. The plaintiffs in *Vergara v. California* claimed that the tenure system was unconstitutional on the basis that teacher tenure harmed students.[2] The plaintiffs argued that students were deprived of the right to an education because of "grossly ineffective" teachers who were protected by California statutes regarding tenure and dismissal.

Indeed, when the plaintiffs won an initial victory and the judge ruled teacher tenure unconstitutional, "one group of critics [Center for Union Facts] went so far as to place a full-page newspaper ad claiming teachers unions are 'treating kids like garbage' and depicting a child's legs sticking out of a trash can. The ad advises people to file suits aimed at weakening state-level tenure laws because 'it worked in California.'"[3]

When Arne Duncan arrived in Washington in 2009 as secretary of education, one of his top priorities was to abolish teacher tenure. In remarks to the National Education Association, he asserted, "When inflexible seniority and rigid tenure rules that we designed put adults ahead of children, then we are not only putting kids at risk, we're also putting the entire education system at risk. We're inviting the attack of parents and the public, and that is not good for any of us."[4]

Duncan wanted to measure teacher performance, he said, so that good teachers could be rewarded and bad, lazy, incompetent teachers could be sanctioned. In order to qualify for federal funds, each state was ordered to close, "turnaround" (dismiss the entire teaching staff), reorganize its schools, or convert their worst-performing ones to charter schools. In February 2010, the school board in Central Falls, Rhode Island, fired every high school teacher. Ninety-three people—including the principal, three assistant principals, and seventy-seven teachers—were fired. The firings affected seventy-four classroom teachers, plus a number of other educators, such as guidance counselors and reading specialists.[5]

Duncan applauded the action for "showing courage and doing the right thing for kids," adding, "This is hard work and these are tough decisions, but students only have one chance for an education. . . . When schools continue to struggle we have a collective obligation to take action."[6]

Central Falls is the poorest city in Rhode Island, with 41 percent of youngsters living in poverty and two-thirds of the high school kids qualifying for free or reduced lunch. The high school graduates a dismal 48 percent of its students. President Barack Obama joined Secretary Duncan, immediately embracing the mass firing as an indication that the administration was serious about reform.

California governor Pete Wilson argued, "Good teachers don't need tenure."[7] The good ones should fear not, he assured everyone; they know who they are, and so do the school boards and the principals, and the tenure system's business is nothing more than obstructing progress by defending terrible, useless freeloaders. It has become by now a national disgrace. "We wouldn't tolerate a chef who can't cook, or a pilot who can't fly," Wilson said. "We shouldn't tolerate a teacher who can't teach."

And Governor Chris Christie of New Jersey went to the heart of the matter: "The time for a national conversation on tenure is long past due. Teaching can no longer be the only profession where you have no rewards for excellence and no consequences for failure to perform. . . . The time to eliminate teacher tenure is now."[8]

Michelle Rhee has emerged as a powerful voice for reform and has been for many years a prominent public face of market-based corporate school reform. After serving as chancellor of the Washington, DC, schools, from 2007 to 2010, she founded a nonprofit organization called StudentsFirst, which, among other things, champions the elimination of tenure.[9] Tenure, Rhee says, is teacher-focused instead of child-centered, places an unnecessary burden on districts, and hurts teachers themselves. Teacher tenure is also "harmful to children," she claims, because it rewards mediocrity: "Once [teachers] have [tenure], they have a job for life—regardless of performance."[10] But tenure is also harmful to teachers because it diminishes their sense of themselves as professionals, she says. "Tenure undermines teacher morale, because the good teacher who consistently works hard and makes every effort to improve her practice notices that the rotten ones are never held accountable. Good work is not rewarded; bad work is not penalized—mediocrity is the predictable end-point."

Rhee proposed abolishing tenure in DC public schools, claiming that teacher quality would improve quickly and dramatically. "Tenure is the holy grail of teacher unions," she said, "but has no educational value for kids." Tenure is the chief business of unions, in her view, because tenure protects adult jobs, and protecting jobs is the unions central and, in some cases, solitary concern; the problem is that tenure "only benefits adults."[11]

Finally, the process for removing an incompetent teacher, which is glacially slow, fuels a sense of futility—can school districts really be so feeble and completely impotent? As Donald Trump said in Milwaukee in August 2016, "On education, it's time to have school choice, merit pay for teachers, and to end the tenure policies that hurt good teachers and reward bad teachers."[12]

Get rid of tenure so we can fire the bad ones; fire the bad ones so our kids can have a future. It's the only answer: do it for the kids!

REALITY CHECK

When President Obama and Secretary Duncan saluted the mass firings in Central Falls, Rhode Island, they didn't know any more specifics about the actual situation than anyone reading the national press knew: Who were the good teachers? Who were the incompetent ones? What was being done about the various impacts of poverty on the kids? How equitable was state funding? What about firing the board itself? No, none of that apparently mattered; none of it was worth a conversation. School failure and school problems were reduced to a ready answer: we must fire the bad teachers.

After all the public humiliation and headline grabbing in Central Falls, eventually the teachers were rehired. Administrators admitted that other factors, such as the economic and social challenges the students face, had contributed to the low-proficiency test scores. After three years, federal funding for the "turnaround" effort ($1.3 million a year) ran out and extra programs to support student learning were cut.[13]

If one argues that tenure is the holy grail of the teacher unions, one might also argue that eliminating tenure appears to be the holy grail of the corporate, market-based school reformers. But evidence does not support the conclusion that teacher tenure is the ruin of public schools or even a major culprit in poor school performance. If this were true, Mississippi, a state with no teacher tenure, should have wonderfully successful schools, while Massachusetts, a state with strong teacher tenure, should have miserably failing ones. But it's exactly the opposite. States with established and strong provisions for teacher tenure consistently rank near the top on traditional measures. We won't make any causal claims here: correlation, as everyone knows by now, is not causation. But let's be skeptical of every causal claim, whatever the source, and let's get smart about every argument. Most important, let's break our ideological lenses—always fact-free and faith-based—and look squarely at the evidence.

There's simply no evidence that teacher tenure causes low student test scores, and there's no evidence that children have higher scores when teachers work without tenure. The strongest predictor of low test scores is poverty, and student test results on every standardized test—SAT, ACT, NAEP, state or international—correlate with family income. But, again, correlation is not causation, so we'll hold our judgment on that for now as well.

Furthermore, though tenured college and university professors are guaranteed lifetime employment, typically after six or more years and with demonstrated proof of productivity in scholarly work, this is not true for elementary, middle, or high school teachers. In fact, the term "tenure" is misleading because administrators remove ineffective grade-school teachers every year, regardless of their tenure status. For K–12 teachers, tenure simply means they are protected by an agreement that binds a board of education or an administration to due process procedures for discharging ineffective teachers. Every teacher contract includes these kinds of agreements, and they amount to nothing more nor less than a road map for dismissals with cause, rather than firings that are arbitrary or capricious or unpredictable.

The evidence in the *Vergara* case was weak since the plaintiff children had done quite well in school and one of the teachers they identified as ineffective had been named a Teacher of the Year in Los Angeles. But Judge Rolf Treu in 2014 ruled that tenure was unconstitutional.

As Diane Ravitch argued:

> How did [Treu] define "grossly ineffective" teachers? He didn't. How did these dreadful teachers get tenure? Clearly, some grossly incompetent principal must have granted it to them. What was the basis—factual or theoretical—that the students would have had high scores if their teachers did not have the right to due process? He didn't say.[14]

The argument of the plaintiffs was the typical one: bad teachers create low test scores. This is the reasoning behind the No Child Left Behind legislation, as well as the claims of the Race to the Top update: test scores can and should be used to evaluate and dismiss bad teachers. Ravitch pointed out that this is a typical example of the blame-shifting strategy of those who want to privatize education. For if they admitted that poverty is the greatest predictor of school failure they would have to, Heaven forbid, develop social policies to alleviate poverty. How much easier, and cheaper, it is to argue that education ends poverty and to blame the teachers. The backers of the case, therefore, set their sights on teachers but do not advocate for fair and generous funding, fully resourced schools, smaller classes, comprehensive arts programs, sports and clubs, health clinics and libraries, counselors and social workers, and attractive incentives that will encourage a stable corps of talented teachers. After all, those measures would cost actual money. Better to wipe out due process rights for teachers and quickly move on.

The *Vergara* case was overturned by the California Court of Appeal in 2016, but the struggle to retain teacher tenure is far from over.[15] Teacher tenure is sure to make its way to the US Supreme Court under a Trump administration.

Relatedly, there's little evidence that terrible teachers are clogging the schools. For example, the notorious "rubber rooms" of New York City's public schools are populated by 0.0005 percent of teachers—too many to be sure but not the zombie apocalypse one might have imagined. And the fact is, tenured teachers who are inadequate to the task are fired all the time, and appropriately so. Schoolteachers are perhaps assessed and formally evaluated more than any other profession, and the contractual road map provides predetermined opportunities to remove bad teachers. No tenure agreement can prevent criminal prosecution, and none will prevent dismissal for cause; when administrators or boards complain that a contract prevents them from getting rid of bad teachers, they are really only exposing their own incompetence or laziness— behind every teacher who shouldn't have a job is an administrator who's not doing hers.

In New York City, teacher tenure was first established almost a century ago, in response to a good government reform movement. It was initially instituted as a protection against political patronage, and the pattern nationally has been consistent: after a set number of years (often three years) in which teachers are on probation and can be dismissed at will, teachers are protected against termination without just cause. That is, teachers cannot be fired for personal retribution, for racial or religious or gender or political objections, for blowing the whistle or speaking out on the issues of the day, for writing blogs or letters to the editor, for advocacy on behalf of students or families, for fighting for school reforms, for showing up at a rally or posting on Facebook. In the past, teachers and school employees were routinely fired for personal and political reasons. A principal might want to hire a relative or the daughter of a friend, or perhaps he didn't like Jewish people or Italian people. He might not have cared for a teacher's looks or, perhaps more commonly, he wanted to save money by getting rid of experienced teachers who had become more expensive. But tenure guaranteed that those things could not happen, ensuring that personnel decisions would be reviewed by a neutral third party and that they would be grounded solely in educational matters.

Without some form of teacher tenure, a veteran educator—experienced and proven, admired and supported by successive administrations over decades—could be dismissed by the newest principal in an effort to cut the budget and make way for a novice or a short-term, a "tourist teacher," a young person taking a gap job between college and graduate school.

Without tenure, every teacher would be the puppet or pawn of every nomadic administrator. Without tenure, outside pressures and political expediency would assert themselves more powerfully into classroom life, and because teachers could be fired due to something as simple as a conflict over teaching style, a culture of fear would embrace schools—"Do as you're told, or you're out!" Without tenure, innovation would suffer, and authentic critical exchanges between teachers—the lifeblood of improvement—would cease. Teachers would be even more subject to the whims of whoever happens to be the most powerful person in the building on any given day with whatever educational fads or fancies she or he brought along. They would teach under a cloud where their best professional judgments were easily dismissed and their advocacy for students and families simply suppressed. Conformity and compliance would become even more firmly the order of the day.

The whole uproar about tenure and the elimination of "bad" teachers, moreover, serves as a smokescreen that deflects attention from a much more serious crisis. Instead of looking for the few miscreants at the back end, we should be focusing on the crisis at the front end, with new teachers. Teaching can be so frustrating—teachers are hemmed in by mandates and surveillance, are overloaded and overworked and often underpaid—that many are leaving the profession. In fact, after three years on the job, about one-third of new teachers have given up. After five years, it is fully half.[16] Here we are, bleeding out new teachers—passionate, caring, idealistic teachers—and no one from the corporate reform crowd highlights or foregrounds that fact. These new teachers are the ones who would be replacing those veteran teachers who retire or are burned out, and they would be reinvigorating the profession. But they just can't stay. It's too painful to their lives and their psyches.

The biggest problem with eliminating teacher tenure, then, is not that a handful of teachers would lose their jobs or that a few less-than-satisfactory teachers have been protected because due process procedures must be followed before these individuals can be removed. No, the biggest problem with destroying tenure is that all teachers will lose the freedom to do their jobs well, and our attention will have been turned away from the real needs of schools and classrooms.

Tenure doesn't so much help teachers keep their jobs as it protects a teacher's freedom to do an excellent job. Alan Singer describes teaching in poorly resourced New York City schools, where he organized student clubs that testified at public hearings against budget cuts in education and in favor of condom availability in schools, and where he organized classroom debates on reproductive freedom and informational meetings on the meaning of Islam, equal rights for LBGTQ people, and the importance of the census.[17] Sometimes, Singer says, these activities brought him into conflict with administrators—so be it. Great teachers have developed student-driven inquiry projects focused on school tracking, immigration, war, inequality, segregation, sexuality, and policing. In these and countless other instances, tenure was there to protect inspired and exceptionally good teachers from being undermined and possibly even removed.

Assessing teacher effectiveness is complex; it's labor-intensive and time-consuming. Performance is more than a score on a paper-and-pencil test and more than accumulated student test results; assessment requires close observation of both context and flow. This calls for a major commitment of resources from the start—time and focus of administrators, possibly peer evaluation and release-time—so that those first years are productive and accurate. Fixing a business model onto teacher assessment and developing an operational definition of effectiveness tied to the simple metric of student achievement on standardized tests may be tempting, as it has the ring of objectivity and the promise of certainty. But it's complete nonsense.

Tenure assures teachers that they will have protection from the consequences of incompetence; it allows them to know that some administrator or powerful school board member can't arbitrarily interfere with their good work.

"Teachers' Unions Represent a Flock of 'Go Slow/Status Quo' Sheep."

In 2015, David Leonhardt, a liberal editor with the *New York Times* who had attended the progressive Horace Mann School in Riverdale, New York, as a youngster and graduated from Yale University, dismissed the growing opposition to high-stakes standardized testing by parents, students, and educators: "Some of [their] frustration stems from the fact that accountability isn't fun."[1] The blogger Ruben Navarrette Jr. listed "a resistance by teachers to accountability and criticism" as one of the top three obstacles to serious school reform.[2] The liberal columnist Jonathan Alter offered this advice to President Obama in 2008: it would be "wrong to give teachers 'ownership over the design of better assessment tools'" because "the teachers unions, for all their lip service, don't believe their members should be judged on performance."[3] Juan Rangel, a charter school champion and former head of the influential United Neighborhoods Organization in Chicago, said that those opposed to Mayor Rahm Emanuel's plan to evaluate teachers "just don't want to be held accountable to standards." And Marcus Winters of the Manhattan Institute remarked in 2012 during the Chicago teachers strike: "All this week, public school teachers in Chicago have refused to show up for work unless they get a 'fair' contract—by which they mean one that pays them even more without meaningfully changing the status quo. The Chicago strike reflects the resentment many teachers feel about accountability and choice reforms, which undermine the teachers union's once-ironclad hold on the school system."[4]

In a flattering 2010 portrait of former secretary of education Arne Duncan for the *New Yorker*, Carlo Rotella mapped out the "two major camps" dominating contemporary school reform battles.[5] The first camp consisted of what Rotella calls the "revolutionaries" and "free-market reformers," the powerful forces mobilized to storm the heavens. They champion higher standards and more rigorous teacher accountability linked to high-stakes testing; they support an end to teacher tenure; they oppose teachers' unions; and they advocate closing public schools in favor of non-union and privately managed charters. This camp is characterized by zest and spark, and it's where the energy and the excitement live.

The second camp is draped in duller shades of gray—bureaucrats and old-timers who rally around the colleges of education and the teachers' unions, or, as Rotella refers to them, "the liberal traditionalists." These are the go slow/status quo folks who resist any innovations whatsoever, and this is where we can find most teachers, gathered close together in the teachers' lounge. Teachers are generally lazy. They want smaller class sizes simply so they can work less.

"The teachers' unions are the clearest example of a group that has lost its way," according to candidate Mitt Romney during the 2012 US presidential campaign.[6] "Whenever anyone dares to offer a new idea, the unions protest the loudest." There has been a broad, bipartisan consensus around this characterization. Progressive Antonio Villaraigosa, the former mayor of Los Angeles, quoted a former president in his assessment of teachers: "John F. Kennedy said, 'Change is the law of life. And those who look only to the past or present are certain to miss the future.' This message has apparently been lost on some people in our teachers unions who used their . . . national conventions . . . to argue against desperately needed changes in our public schools."[7]

REALITY CHECK

Carlo Rotella's revolutionaries (who have included Arne Duncan, Barack Obama, George W. Bush, and the former US education secretaries Margaret Spellings and John King, and now include Donald Trump and Betsy DeVos) are powered by a merry band of billionaires: Bill Gates, Michael Bloomberg, Sam Walton, Eli Broad. Note that the only reason the superrich have these massive billions, and hence a major voice in policy, is because of the unfair tax laws that allow them to keep the vast wealth their employees have created. In a democratic society, this socially produced wealth would be distributed by the government with at least a semblance of public input. Wielding their large checkbooks, the superrich have created a cogent and captivating narrative for the national school reform conversation. This narrative is predicated on a few fundamental points: we need to disrupt the system and turn around low-performing schools by reinforcing rigorous academic standards, improving data collection, bolstering teacher quality, enforcing scrupulous accountability measures, and crushing the go slow/status quo unions. That neutral-sounding language has gone a long way toward creating a consensus among the two major political parties, the mainstream media, and the biggest foundations. The talking points are reiterated—and extended—in virtually every policy discussion: failing public schools must be closed or replaced by charter or contract schools; school boards must be replaced by emergency managers; teachers must be subjected to tougher and much more exacting accountability measures based on the performance of their students; and if teachers and their associations impede educational progress and block rational, commonsense proposals for change, they must be swept aside.

All right: "accountability" and "achievement"—who in their right minds would oppose accountability in our public schools, and who would stand hard against student achievement? No one. Zero. So it's unanimous, and we can all cheer wildly in unison.

Well, not so fast. Let's step back and take a hard look at what accountability has come to mean in recent years. George Orwell coined the terms "newspeak" and "doublethink" and taught the world how politics corrupted language, and how the English language was routinely deployed by ideologues to pervert politics. Our current newspeak epidemic would not surprise Orwell a bit: spy organizations call mass surveillance "bulk data collection" and rebrand torture to the more congenial "enhanced interrogation."

With President Trump, newspeak has gotten a powerful new lease on life. "Alternative facts" create an auxiliary universe in which the "fake news media" is "the enemy of the people," and the only true source of information is the powerful leader himself.[8] Autocrats and dictators of every stripe showed long ago that repetition is a key to doublespeak. When the echo chamber operates at full speed, the meaning of any word or phrase can be manipulated and bled dry, as an entirely different meaning is hastily infused into the dead shell of the old.

"School reform" is a phrase that's become untrustworthy as its casing is intact but its meaning refigured. When powerful market-based reformers initially spoke of "high expectations," "school improvement," and "reform," each seemed like a good thing on its face. It took a minute to determine what was actually meant by those benign words: "high expectations," a practice of exclusion through suspensions and expulsions; "school improvement," a strategy of school closings; and "reform," a policy of widespread teacher dismissals. It might be difficult to rally widespread support for exclusions, dismissals, and closings, but since normal folks would naturally assume that "high expectations" means, well, high expectations, it's a sweeter sell.

To be accountable is to be responsible, answerable—that much is clear. An emergency room doctor is responsible for the care of her patients; a bus driver is responsible for the safe transport of her passengers—each is answerable to the entity that employs and engages them, as well as to a public that depends on them. But, wait: neither is solely responsible; neither is working in a social, cultural, economic, or political vacuum; neither is a Lone Ranger. If the bus driver accomplishes her task every day, it's not because of her good work alone in isolation from the work of the manufacturer, the mechanics, the road builder, the dispatcher, and others. If she breaks down one day because a mechanic failed to replace a valve, she may feel bad for the residents who rely on her, but she should not be held solely accountable.

Imagine a young person arriving in the ER with a life-threatening head injury from a motorcycle accident. Our doctor is accountable for a quick and smart intervention, bringing to bear her skill and knowledge and training, and deploying all the resources at hand. The patient survives and recovers, hooray! But is the doctor the only one who deserves credit? Don't the technicians and residents, the medical students and nurses, in attendance get a little love? And how about the university that built the hospital, the tax monies that supported it, the researchers who studied head injuries and published papers on best practices, and the administrators who saw to it that the latest equipment was readily available? How about the maker of the state-of-the-art helmet that the youth was wearing? Without that helmet, the head injuries would have been far worse. OK, the doctor did her job, and a lot of other people did too. Credit can, and should, be shared.

We can turn the scene upside down and imagine an opposite conclusion: the patient does not survive. Now accountability takes a turn. How do various actors justify their roles, and who or what is to blame for an unwanted outcome? Perhaps the wound was simply too severe and there was no real chance of surviving it; perhaps the ER was overcrowded, filthy, and lacking in necessary support personnel; perhaps chronic underfunding left the hospital without the basic resources needed to treat this kind of injury; perhaps the ambulance was outdated and the EMTs incompetent; perhaps the doctor made a mistake. One thing is certain: a myopic focus on the doctor, and the doctor alone, is foolish in either scenario. The ecology of the situation is the essential starting point in order to understand responsibility, answerability, justification, praise or blame—and improvement.

Just so with teachers and teaching. Even teachers who wish to close their doors and do their jobs in isolation find that they cannot create a tightly sealed vacuum. Life is leaky; classrooms are porous places; and the real world has the inconvenient habit of pouring through the transom, pressing uninvited into the classroom with family issues, community problems, disturbances and distractions from every direction. Every student walks in with a language and a culture, a family and a community, experiences that will not be safely deposited inside a locker in the hallway until class is done. There is no platonic ideal in classroom teaching, with the scholar-teacher sitting in a lotus position on a fluffy cloud with an attentive ten-year-old at her feet. Nice image. Never happens. We are never alone.

Furthermore, every teacher enacts teaching amid concentric circles of context: cultural surround and social situation, historical flow and economic condition, administrative circumstance and political setting. This means that some teachers work with a dozen students at a time, others with thirty-five, forty, or even fifty students; some teachers have complete sets of books and up-to-date materials, including laptops and tablets, and others have thirty-year-old textbooks and no access to computers. Some teachers can rely on special education and English-language-learner support as well as a routine in which their students will participate in library and art and physical education every day, others will be without any support whatsoever. Some teachers have rooms of their own, others move from one space to another six or eight times a day. Some teachers work in modern facilities, others in broken-down buildings with leaky roofs, opaque windows, and busted furnaces; some teachers teach privileged kids from well-resourced communities, others teach kids who are contending with poverty and other forms of structural violence on a daily basis. We could go on, but the point is clear: the range of teaching contexts is vast and varied.

So let's turn to teacher accountability, and as with our doctor, let's insist on full accountability—no excuses—from every teacher and from every other actor in the immense ecology and wide, wide universe of childhood. All children and youth deserve healthy, robust environments in which to survive and thrive; they need safe spaces physically and psychically; they need support and recognition, access to the colossal human cultural carnival and also freedom to breathe and stretch and reach; they need nourishment and security, and they need and deserve a quality education.

Let's remember, too, that there is contention over the question of who our educators should be accountable to. Are we only expected to satisfy the demands, the constructed requirements, of the elite officials and overseers in the education world? Why not have schools be accountable to communities, to the articulated needs of oppressed and marginalized families? Might not families have an interest in the kind of education the students are getting or in how the kids might emerge from school with skills and tools useful in advancing the interests of the community? Who anointed the powerful ones to be able to declare what knowledge is important? Indeed, knowledge, economic reality, and the world as we know it will be totally transformed in ten, fifteen, or twenty years. Would the education forecasters in 1997 have been able to know what an educated person needed to know in 2017?

In the end, the US government, the state, the city or county, and the community (not to mention the corporate class) all have a huge measure of responsibility for the condition of public education today, and each entity has a lot to answer for. Governments must be held accountable, and we should join hands and demand that they justify their practices and priorities in regard to public education, including taxing and spending, equity and access. Each is also answerable in some part for public safety in our neighborhoods, for healthy environments, for accessible transportation, for clean water and access to healthful foods, for adequate sanitation, for stable and affordable housing, for employment and useful work, and more. Wall Street should be held accountable for economic crises and inequality; the White House, Congress, and the Pentagon for the waste of war; Big Oil for catastrophic climate change; Big Pharma for heath costs, and on and on. Yes, let's talk accountability *for real*.

In contrast, corporate reformers offer an anemic sense of what accountability actually means, drawing a thick, tightening circle around individual teachers and demanding "no excuses"—poverty is no excuse for low test scores, and neither is chronic asthma, lead poisoning, homelessness, unstable housing, insufficient diet, or living amid gun violence. These reformers flatly refuse to consider the ecology of teaching or the universe of childhood. And when they repeatedly chant "no excuses" at teachers, they are playing a sophisticated game of misdirection, using an overemphasis on teacher accountability as an excuse for doing nothing about public health, street violence, or, most important, about poverty itself. Recognizing, as everyone should, that external factors can have an outsize impact on student learning, researchers and reformers— some surely sincerely, others opportunistically—have pursued teacher evaluations that attempt to measure an individual teacher's contribution to each student's learning while "blocking out" noise from the larger environment—poverty, parental involvement, tutoring, whatever.

Enter value-added assessment, or value-added modeling (VAM). By comparing the standardized test scores of students in any given school year to the scores of those same students in previous years, as well as to the scores of other students in the same grade, VAM's champions claim the method can isolate a single variable, that is, the teacher's impact, her "value added," with some precision. To say it another way, VAM practitioners operate on the assumption that any student will generally score as well in any given year as he or she has in the past, so that when the student's actual score is recorded and compared to the predicted score, the difference between them is posited to be the result of a teacher's teaching. Common sense, but only if you can convince yourself that nothing else can have influenced the student's life in the intervening year.

The Obama-era Race to the Top program required states and districts seeking federal assistance to make some attempt at a rigorous assessment of teachers, and Secretary Arne Duncan singled out VAM for special praise. Major school districts, including New York, Chicago, Los Angeles, and Washington, DC, all bought into and adopted some version of the value-added approach, each of them tying the results to policies like teacher bonuses and even retention. This is a staple of the corporate reformers, and most are pushing hard for value-added methods. The Bill and Melinda Gates Foundation, for example, is funding a multiyear study of value-added modeling, and many academic researchers are dutifully falling in line. VAM is a step toward the holy grail of teacher accountability.

This accelerating frenzy of activity taps into a widely accepted conviction that we also share: good teachers make a positive difference in student success (and bad teaching has a negative impact). But the step—or is it a lurch?—from that sensible bit to VAM as a way to understand and measure good teachers is considerably more than a hop, skip, and jump—it's a giant leap of faith. And, given the generous resources poured into it, VAM is a god that fails.

Journalist Michael Winerip tells a story of how value-added assessment tilted one New York City public school, in Brooklyn.[9] PS 146 is by all traditional and standard measures a good school: 96 percent of fifth graders proficient in English, according to standardized tests; 89 percent in math; parents uniformly happy with the school; a veteran principal with enormous confidence in her teachers, especially the hard-working team of fifth-grade teachers, whom she considers among the most creative, energetic, and collaborative she's ever worked with. One of the fifth-grade team had run her own theater company and won an award from the Guggenheim Museum for a drama program she developed in the schools before becoming a teacher. Another teacher had gone to Peru and Mexico on a Fulbright scholarship and later developed a fifth-grade curriculum on Mayan culture. Another instructor taught education classes at Teachers College, Columbia University, and the Bank Street College of Education.

Working to win a federal Race to the Top competition in 2010, New York agreed that 20 percent of a teacher's evaluation would be based on students' scores on high-stakes standardized tests. Soon after that—in the name of accountability and rigor—the state's Board of Regents doubled that number: now test scores would account for 40 percent of a teacher's evaluation. And in the name of transparency and motivation, the teachers' evaluations would be released to and published by the *New York Times* and other corporate media.

A lot of this process is worth wondering about and digging into a bit more deeply, but before we do, let's return for a moment to PS 146 and those fifth-grade teachers. It's natural to think that the three mentioned above would receive positive assessments and rave reviews, but when assessment results were released, two of them scored a 7 out of 100 in math, and the other got a score of 1 in math and 11 in English. Seemingly the cream of the crop, they were, according to the numbers, near the bottom of the barrel. Why?

One knee-jerk reaction—from the test-and-punish crowd, for example—could be to insist that numbers don't lie and that all the accolades were superficial and missed the larger point about teacher effectiveness. But, in fact, as Winerip points out, numbers *do* lie—often and sometimes with dire and unjust results. In the case of PS 146, that 89 percent proficiency in fifth-grade math scores turns out to be a problem, because as fourth graders, these students scored at 97 percent. Scores went down as the result of three students scoring a 2 instead of a 3 out of 4 on the math test. "This," Winerip writes, "resulted in the worst thing that can happen to a teacher in America today: negative value was added."

As noted above, correlation is not cause, and no worthwhile research makes that first-order error; students are not (and cannot be) randomly assigned to teachers across a city, a district, or a state, making VAM bad science. VAM incentivizes test preparation above deeper teaching and learning, while measuring yearly progress with abstract mathematical formulas and excluding professional judgments concerning a particular child's needs and abilities. In addition, it leads to cheating and student dumping—those with more power in a school might seek the most easily reached students and pass on those who have challenges, in a dog-eat-dog struggle for survival. Most egregiously, VAM assumes that learning is a linear, plodding, and predictable process rather than an idiosyncratic and often unpredictable carnival of light and action.

On this last point, anyone who has watched a young child learn to play piano or add numbers or speak or spell (or a struggling English-language learner to finally *get* English) can testify that it would be a fool's errand to judge a parent (or a teacher) on annual progress. As the old saying goes, education is not the filling of a pail, but rather the lighting of a fire. It could be a year, or two, or five, or more before we can see the results of any teacher's work in any one learner—and those results may come from a swirling vortex of intermingled influences not possibly isolated or distinct.

Say the teacher created a language-rich environment, worked hard to construct activities that creatively engaged and challenged the learner, motivated and nourished the learner in a thousand ways, and so on. A dramatic leap in learning noticed on a test in year four may obliterate the real work of teachers (or parents) in years one, two, and three, while it dramatically inflates the contribution of the teacher in year four. The teaching in the earlier years would be judged—wrongly—ineffective, while the current teacher would be considered—wrongly again—brilliant.

Each of these is disqualifying in its own right, and yet there are two even deeper structural flaws at VAM's foundation that make us wonder how anyone who knows anything about schools, teachers, or children can take VAM seriously as a tool for improving teaching and learning. Assuming that teachers work outside the myriad concentric circles of context is absurd, and equating learning or student achievement with the score on a high-stakes standardized test is ridiculous. Researchers and scholars uniformly agree with these criticisms, and those who continue to participate in the faulty work knowing that it's wrong typically respond with some variation of these replies: "The testing is flawed, but it's all we've got, and better measures are constantly emerging"; "We always advise school people to use the results cautiously and never to rely on any score or test as a sole measure"; "The measures are wrong up to 40 percent of the time, and we always explain that"; "These measures are more reliable when we use ten or fifteen years of data"; "The method is most reliable when identifying teachers who are consistently in the top 5 percent or the bottom 5 percent and should not be used to determine whether a teacher is slightly above or slightly below any other teacher."

Well damn! VAM seems little more than a punitive cat's paw swiping at the fabric of public education. So why is the education policy world so enthralled with it?

Accountability, yes, and "no excuses" as well. But if improvement is our goal, we must reject the false notion that casts a harsh light on the teacher as an isolated variable in the education of students while politicians, government officials, foundations, or corporations escape even a glance. Every actor in the universe of public education must be fully accountable.

"GOOD TEACHING IS ENTIRELY COLOR-BLIND."

The United States has become at long last a postracial society. True, slavery was terrible, and it was followed by a sorry time in America when Black people endured the humiliation and pain of second-class citizenship, held back and put down on the basis of race. Racial segregation was law and policy and habit for a hundred years after the abolition of slavery, especially in the states of the old Confederacy, and there were some racist white people who made things even worse. African American life was constrained and restricted, and Black people were forced, for example, to attend separate, inferior schools.

But that difficult racial experience has been relegated to the dustbin of history and is now a thing of the dark and distant past. In 1954, the Supreme Court delivered a unanimous decision in *Brown v. Board of Education*, overturning *Plessy v. Ferguson* along with the century-old doctrine of "separate but equal" and heralding the termination of racially segregated schools. The language of *Brown* includes the language of justice—it repudiates racial segregation and states unequivocally that separate schools are *inherently* unequal.

Brown also unleashed massive energy toward doing away with segregation and the vestiges of racism in all areas. The Reverend Martin Luther King Jr. emerged two years later to lead the Montgomery bus boycott that successfully desegregated the public bus system. He later delivered his iconic "I Have a Dream" speech at the great 1963 march on Washington; witnessed the signing of the Civil Rights Act of 1964 outlawing discrimination based on race, color, religion, sex, or national origin, as well as the 1965 Voting Rights Act, which prohibited racial discrimination in voting; and won the Nobel Peace Prize before he was assassinated at the age of thirty-nine in 1968. King's tragic death doesn't diminish or overshadow his vast accomplishments—he changed the nation, and he made all of us better people. Thankfully, Martin Luther King Jr. lived long enough to see his dream became a reality: people can now be judged exclusively by the content of their character, not the color of their skin. Some individuals still hold backward and bigoted ideas, but the solution to that is to foster values that ignore rather than emphasize race.

Today, African Americans are CEOs of major corporations, college presidents and professors in every field, senior partners in law firms, foremost brain surgeons, network news anchors, acclaimed fine artists, prize-winning journalists and columnists, preeminent scientists and well-known astrophysicists, influential entertainers, and dominant athletes—the list goes on and on. Further, the American people elected an African American president in 2008 and reelected him in 2012, breaching the last institutional barrier to full equality for African Americans and proving once and for all that people are judged by the content of their character. We do, indeed, live in a postracial world.

"The way to stop discrimination on the basis of race," wrote Chief Justice John Roberts in a 2007 Supreme Court decision "is to stop discriminating on the basis of race."[1] The majority opinion in *Parents Involved in Community Schools v. Seattle School District No. 1* rejected noncompulsory racial integration efforts in Seattle, Washington, and Louisville, Kentucky. Both school districts had voluntarily used racial classifications in assigning students to schools in order to avoid racial isolation and achieve racial diversity. Writing for the majority, Roberts held that the school systems could not take race into account, even in a small minority of cases. "Simply because the school districts may seek a worthy goal does not mean they are free to discriminate on the basis of race to achieve it," he wrote. The majority constructed a moral equivalency between old-style Southern school segregation and current attempts to remedy ongoing patterns of racial separation, writing that, "Before *Brown*, schoolchildren were told where they could and could not go to school based on the color of their skin. The school districts in these cases have not carried the heavy burden of demonstrating that we should allow this once again—even for very different reasons." A year earlier, Roberts had written in a voting rights case that, "It is a sordid business, this divvying us up by race." True.[2]

The law of the land once supported and defended the institution of slavery and, later, Jim Crow segregation; the law evolved to outlaw segregation and the dreadful doctrine of "separate but equal." Today the law is entirely color-blind.

Teachers in particular, should take this to heart: Kids are kids, and the best teachers don't see race at all. Teachers simply need to apply more rigorous discipline on students who are not applying themselves and earning good grades. If these students are going to have a hopeful future and decent employment, they need to learn basic skills, as well as how to follow directions. Too many teachers coddle their students in the name of cultural relevance. Teachers need to catch up with reality and get color-blind!

REALITY CHECK

James Baldwin, in his "talk to teachers," famously said,

> The paradox of education is precisely this—that as one begins to become conscious one begins to examine the society in which he is being educated. The purpose of education, finally, is to create in a person the ability to look at the world for himself, to make his own decisions, to say to himself this is black or this is white, to decide for himself whether there is a God in heaven or not. To ask questions of the universe, and then learn to live with those questions, is the way he achieves his own identity. But no society is really anxious to have that kind of person around. What

societies really, ideally, want is a citizenry which will simply obey the rules of society. If a society succeeds in this, that society is about to perish. The obligation of anyone who thinks of himself as responsible is to examine society and try to change it and to fight it—at no matter what risk. This is the only hope society has. This is the only way societies change.[3]

In the spirit of James Baldwin, let's look at reality, gather a few of the relevant pieces of information, and attempt to remove the blinkers of fact-free, faith-based thinking concerning race and education and the myth of colorblindness:

· In the wake of the *Brown* decision, the percentage of Black students in majority white Southern schools went from zero to a peak of 43.5 percent in 1988, before the trend reversed itself— by 2011 that figure was back to 23.2 percent, just below where it stood in 1968.

· Seventy-seven percent of Black students attended schools with a Black majority in 1968–69; in 2014, it was 75 percent.

· Thirty-eight percent of schools experienced "intense segregation" in 1980–81; in 2014, that number was exactly the same: 38 percent.

· From 1968 to 1980, racial segregation in schools steadily de- clined, with school integration peaking in the 1980s and heading downward ever since.

· Data drawn from a survey by the US Education Department of more than fifty million students, and nearly every one of the nation's 95,000 public schools, show that though the nation's high school graduation rate has risen, many students lack ac- cess to college-preparatory classes in math and science—a mere 48 percent of the nation's high schools offer calculus, but among schools with majority Black and Hispanic populations, that num- ber drops to 33 percent.

· While 24 percent of the nation's elementary schools and 42 percent of high schools have police officers in the buildings,

51 percent of predominantly Black and Hispanic high schools have assigned law enforcement officers; approximately 1.6 million students attend a school that has a police officer on campus but no school counselor.

· Majority Black schools have fewer resources, including funds, facilities, books, and other learning materials, as well as fewer highly qualified or experienced teachers, than majority white schools. Majority Black schools experience higher levels of teacher turnover, tend to have less challenging curricula, and offer far fewer Advanced Placement courses.

· Nationwide, 2.8 million students were suspended from public schools during the 2013–2014 school year, representing a nearly 20 percent decline from the 2011–2012 school year. But Black students were four times as likely as white students to be suspended and nearly twice as likely to be expelled. Black children represented 19 percent of all public preschoolers but accounted for 47 percent of suspensions.[4]

West Oakland, California, is the home of the devastatingly low-resourced McClymonds High School, which is rodent infested and lacks laboratory equipment, counters, stools, and chemical vents. McClymonds is 96 percent Black and Brown, and 95 percent of its students qualify for free or reduced lunch.[5] A mere six miles away is beautiful, over-resourced Piedmont High School with a student body that is 70 percent white and 17 percent Asian. At Piedmont, 96 percent of students are not economically disadvantaged, and 99 percent of students graduate, with 93 percent eligible for the California university system. Everyone—radical/progressive teachers and conservative teachers, parents in Piedmont and parents in West Oakland, kids in both schools—goes about their business day in and day out, seemingly accepting that these distinctions are normal, as natural as rain. But desegregation efforts were never fundamentally about the imagined (in the minds of white people) delights of students of color sitting next to white people, nor were they about the need to "attain" white middle-class knowledge. They were and are struggles over resources. Teachers work their butts off teaching the students at McClymonds, but that's quite a different matter from demanding or attaining justice for them. It is a wonder that no one marches for justice from McCly-monds to Piedmont, just to expose the hypocrisy. Will America ever decide to educate youngsters who are Black, Brown, immigrant, or "other"? It's an open question, and it's entirely a question of political will. We know it can be done, but will it be done? The evidence says that we're stuck, that wishing race away doesn't make it go away—it turns out that race still asserts itself, still distorts, still exerts its terrible drag on human progress. For example, ideology and wishful thinking aside, Black unemployment in 1960 stood at 10 percent (white unemployment was 5 percent); in 2016, it had climbed to 14 percent (7 percent for whites).[6] You see, race matters.

The myth of color-blindness is indeed blinding. It glibly erases the experience of two and a half centuries of legal slavery based on color, of its physical torture, psychological torment, economic exploitation and impoverishment, rape, social obstruction, and cultural genocide. It obscures the fact that, in America, Black families were transformed into reproductive units designed solely to produce more enslaved workers, and that people were subjected not only to the whims of their white enslavers but also to the mercy of every white person they encountered. When slavery was at last abolished, formerly enslaved people were forced to survive and adapt to multiple forced migrations, rampant disease, unstable living and working conditions, Black codes, chain gangs, and, for all but the last few decades, a Jim Crow regime that included legal exclusions from jobs, housing, and property owning. Indeed, the US government shaped housing segregation throughout the twentieth century and deprived Black and Brown families of access to middle-class resources.[7] The racial hierarchy was cemented by the constant threat of terrorist mobs bent on ritualistic human sacrifice designed to keep the descendants of formerly enslaved people in subservience. Color-blind wishful thinking asks us to accept that race is obsolete and white supremacy a thing of the dim past. True, race is a social construction, not a biological fact, but race is also a marker that defines the boundaries of a system of domestic colonial oppression. Color-blindness as ideology is oblivious to the afterlife of slavery as a living wound in our body politic and an ongoing blight on our shared social life. It's grossly insensitive to ongoing injustices visited upon people every day because of skin color, including in isolated, majority-Black schools that act as little more than conveyer belts for mass incarceration. And in its less brutal expression—that is, in its self-styled beneficent, philanthropic, and charitable forms—the idea of color-blindness is at best patronizing and universally unseeing, denying folks the deeper truths of their common experience, both their suffering and their accomplishments. It's out of a history of hardship and triumph that people have constructed a powerful identity replete with a distinct language, unique cultural expressions, and highly visible artifacts. People want and deserve recognition for that.

Color-blindness fails to take aim at the institutional and societal structures of privilege and oppression based on race but encourages instead an exclusive and narrow focus on the targets of those structures: Black and Brown people, and Black and Brown youth in particular. There's talk in philanthropic circles of a "culture of poverty" and "cultural deprivation," and there are well-financed programs of research into what makes Black and "Hispanic" children tick, what qualities might make them tick better, what accounts for the "racial achievement gap," and what qualities make for "effective teachers" of "those students," but there's little or no research (or action) on how structures and institutions police the borders of privilege. There are no high-powered research programs structured to study the issues that marginalized or disadvantaged people speak of with excitement, anger, fear, or hope, none to explore the local experiences people already have that can point the way toward solutions to their own self-identified problems. There are few (if any) projects that uncover the narratives missing from the "official story" that will make the problems of the oppressed more understandable, and there are no well-funded research projects focused on why the beneficiaries of white privilege are blinded to the suffering of others. Nor are there studies that examine the ways that current or proposed policies serve the privileged and the powerful and how they are made to appear inevitable, nor studies about how the public space for discussion, problem posing and problem solving, and fuller and wider participation in a revitalized democracy can be expanded. Upton Sinclair noted, "It is difficult to get a man to understand something, when his salary depends upon his not understanding it!"[8] True, so while the single-minded and backward approach to educational research is outrageous, it's not surprising: educational research is an industry founded on chasing federal dollars after World War II, and it's still largely powered by government and foundation funding streams that themselves follow a set and relatively narrow embankment.

The well-worn rut leads to an unnatural blindness with predictable narrative clichés concerning lazy and incompetent teachers, failing schools, achievement gaps, rotten apples, dreadful families, and kids who are either mad, sad, bad, or can't add. Note: in every such cliché, society is completely off the hook for the existence of poverty and oppression. Be skeptical whenever someone repeats another well-worn trope: "We need more research." We really don't. What we need is action against poverty and white supremacy.

One dominant trope in contemporary school reform is the racial achievement gap. "Across the US," declared the National Governors Association in 2005, "a gap in academic achievement persists between minority and disadvantaged students and their white counterparts."[9] Once again, whether heartfelt or self-satisfied, the narrative never mentions the monster in the room: white supremacy.

It's true, of course, that standardized test scores reveal a difference between Black and white test takers: twenty-six points in one area of comparison—fourth-grade reading—twenty points in another, twenty-three in a third.

But the significance of those differences is wildly disputed. Some argue, as Charles Murray and Richard Herrnstein did in their popular and incendiary 1994 book *The Bell Curve*, that genetic differences account for the gap, and there's little that can be done to lift up the poor inferior Black folks. An alternate theory—popular since the 1960s—holds that Blacks are not inherently inferior to whites but merely culturally deprived, and that fixing the "massive pathologies" in the Black family and African American communities will require social engineering on a grand scale.

Each of these explanations has its large and devoted following. The first, while difficult for many whites to endorse publicly, carries the reflected power of eugenics and the certainty that what they'd always secretly suspected is true: whites are indeed superior beings by some measure or another. The second has the advantage of pretending to give a bit more than a pig's eye for the well-being of Black people while blaming—overtly or slyly—lazy Black welfare mothers, criminal and chronically absent African American fathers, or terrible families, all the while disturbing none of the pillars of white privilege. Either theory can exist comfortably within the obsessive focus on the so-called achievement gap.

The belief in our meritocratic system assumes that this achievement gap is simply a measure of the failure either of students themselves or of poor communities—a failure that is the result of cultural pathologies, lack of grit in students, and ineffective teachers. Those who work hard and apply themselves will necessarily succeed, and, therefore, those who don't succeed failed to work hard and apply themselves. Moreover, the tests that generate the achievement gap have grown out of social constructions designed by eugenicists to reinforce racial hierarchies. As in all racist constructions, the premise that the tests rest on is that white knowledge, white ways of expression, and white values and experiences are the gold standard, against which everything else must be measured. The first IQ tests were developed by psychologist Lewis Terman at Stanford University, where they are devising ever more sophisticated tests today. Princeton University psychologist Carl Brigham furthered the testing culture to create the first SAT tests, in 1926. Both Terman and Brigham were convinced that their work demonstrated a biological, immutable hierarchy of intelligence, with white people at the top.

The racist conclusions of their beliefs are hardwired into the construction of these tests today. Cultural values, ways of expression, types of argument, and discursive styles are all part of these tests. And the tests drive a kind of instruction that is remote, hostile, and inaccessible to the majority of students of color in the United States. Students resist instruction that too often feels alien and bewildering, and hold back their full engagement with an institution that seems to have only a tenuous and contingent commitment to them. Then they confront tests that are unfamiliar and distrusted. Many of these students just check out on test day. And when the results come back, foundations and government bureaucrats draw wild conclusions from the so-called data.

Those who argue for a colorblind curriculum are themselves demonstrating blindness to the hegemonic values found in and the Eurocentric bias of the knowledge that is ratified as "high quality," rigorous, and important. This means that local knowledge, cultural practices, and community discourses are banished from the assessments—and that the whole project is aligned with dominant, white practices and culture. The wonder is that so many students from marginalized communities do in fact succeed— even if they have learned that they can only climb the rungs of academic success by becoming conversant in dominant values and discourses. While these successful students may go along to get along, generally they know the game they've been forced to play, and they still represent subversive (that is to say, more learned and brilliant) knowledge because they maintain what W. E. B. Du Bois called "double consciousness."

Django Paris and Samy Alim describe powerful and effective "culturally sustaining" knowledge—not just culturally relevant to get the attention of students from oppressed communities but culturally sustaining in order to support and carry forward the vital cultural practices of these communities.[10] Carol Lee talks of "cultural modeling" in supporting African American students to approach a text from their own framework and schema.[11] Good teachers have the courage to explore learning with their students on their own terms. Because most official curricula do not support or acknowledge this approach, these teachers are setting off into unknown territory with their students on a voyage to a curriculum of discovery.

It takes courage because one never knows if this will lead to success—either in the dominant testing regime or even on its own terms. But by trusting the students and the community, teachers set out on this voyage. Ultimately, it is a risk worth taking and one that benefits students, our sworn priority.

Gloria Ladson-Billings, a leading researcher and professor of education at the University of Wisconsin, upends all of this with an elegant reversal: there is no achievement *gap*, she argues, merely a glancing reflection of something deeper and more fundamental: the United States has a profound education *debt*. The educational inequities that began with settler colonialism, the genocide against and attempted annihilation of First Nations people and the enslavement of Africans, the conquest of a continent and the importation of both free labor and serfs transformed into apartheid education—something anemic, inferior, inadequate, and oppressive. Over decades and then centuries, the debt has accumulated and passed from generation to generation, and it continues to pile up. The education scholar Jonathan Kozol documented the way the

debt grows year by year based on spending: Chicago serves 86 percent Black and Latinx students and spends around $8,000 per pu-
pil per year, while a few miles away, in the tony suburb of Highland
Park, 90 percent white, the school district spends $17,000 per stu-
dent; New York City, 72 percent Black and Latinx, spends around
$12,000 per pupil annually, while suburban Manhasset, 91 percent
white, spends over $22,000.[12] In most states, the highest-poverty
districts receive far fewer resources, and, according to Ladson-
Billings, in thirty states, "high minority districts receive less money
for each child than low minority districts."[13]

Though oppressed peoples have always valued education and
have always taught their young the cultural and literacy practices
that matter, state-sponsored education has played a troubling role
in maintaining educational apartheid. Though public schooling has
been nominally offered to all children, the options for students of
color were always and still are—limited and distorted. Poor funding, inadequate infrastructure, and overcrowding all contribute
to the educational debt, resulting in a failure to provide authentic
educational opportunities.

Many of the powerful corporate reformers assume literacy is
an abstract, context-free skill that the working class should learn
so they can follow directions. But in actuality, literacy is always
a social practice, and meaning is always negotiated between the
writer and the reader. The oppressed demand the right to read
the world—to define their reality and change it—while reading
the word. Thus framed, literacy can help people define the world
and devise ways to make it more livable. Schools can contribute to
meaningful literacy practices for communities or they can actually impede and hold back the human right to literacy. Imagine
the possibilities.

Race matters, then, and in education it matters desperately.
Young people from Black communities in our cities, from Latinx
neighborhoods, from the agricultural fields and the factories, con-

tingent communities, often with a mixture of the globalized citizens on the move, are themselves creating and constructing cultures out of their circumstances. It is an act of violence against their creative struggle for survival to deprive these students of teachers who know them, who know their struggles and dreams. While the majority of students in the United States are students of color, the number of teachers of color has actually been dropping—and now stands at 18 percent.[14] Though Black youth comprise 16 percent of public school students in the United States, only 7 percent of all teachers are Black, and only 2 percent of all US teachers are Black men.[15] In New Orleans, after Hurricane Katrina, an influx of charter schools taught by mostly white Teach for America and new-hire teachers meant that the existing teaching force consisting largely of African American women was mostly fired. The number of Black teachers in Chicago has fallen from 40 percent to 23 percent since 2000, and in San Francisco, the Black composition of the teaching force dropped 20 percent from 2003 to 2012.[16]

Students need to see teachers who look like them, teachers who have similar life experiences and cultural references. Strong relationships between teachers of color and students of color support a positive learning environment, and they also invite new kinds of inquiries and new directions in the curriculum that can serve their communities better than the more traditional body of school knowledge.

Teachers committed to social justice find themselves with different responsibilities in different situations. More and more teachers of color are banding together to resist institutional assaults and to strategize how to build community power. As for white social justice teachers, too often the image one conjures is a white teacher doing powerful work in inner-city, colonized communities. But if white teachers want to fight racism, at least some of them need to be in more privileged schools, more white spaces.

After all, this is where racism is coming from for the next generation. The hard organizing work for social justice has to take place
here too. Wherever white teachers are, it is incumbent on them to
challenge racial privilege.

White teachers in communities of color cannot come as charity workers, must not imagine they are simply bringing the good-
ies that the powerless desperately need. They need to recognize the
centuries-long struggles these communities have waged to survive
and thrive; their job is to act in solidarity, to recognize the beauty
and strength that is already there.

Ladson-Billings imagines what could be done if the political powers took the "achievement gap" seriously: smaller classes
and smaller schools, a Marshall Plan–type effort to rebuild school
infrastructure, create a massive influx of resources, immediately
reassign the best teachers in the country to schools for poor children of color, guarantee places for those students in state and re-
gional colleges and universities, and more. Use your imagination
and discover what we might accomplish, virtually overnight, if we
mobilized the political will to get it done.

Ladson-Billings argues that the United States also owes a moral
debt to African Americans, a debt that "reflects the disparity between what we know is right and what we actually do."[17]

W. E. B. Du Bois posited that the Black struggle for education
was about decent and well-resourced schools, not about sitting
next to white students:

> Theoretically, the Negro needs neither segregated schools nor
> mixed schools. What he needs is Education. What he must re-
> member is that there is no magic, either in mixed schools or in
> segregated schools. A mixed school with poor and unsympathetic
> teachers, with hostile public opinion, and no teaching of truth
> concerning black folk, is bad. A segregated school with ignorant
> placeholders, inadequate wretched housing, is equally bad.[18]

And early on, in 1933, Carter G. Woodson exposed the problem of hegemonic control of the minds of the oppressed in *The Mis-Education of the Negro*, noting:

> When you control a man's thinking you do not have to worry about his actions. You do not have to tell him to stand here or go yonder. He will find his "proper place" and will stay in it. You do not need to send him to the back door. He will go without being told. In fact, if there is no back door, he will cut one for his special benefit. His education makes it necessary.[19]

Woodson had in mind the way education serves the social order, the way American schools satisfy a society with identifiable structures of privilege and oppression based on race and how they reflect and promote that racial stratification perfectly. When there is, for example, a pervasive sense that there is nothing about the presence of African American youngsters, especially Black boys, that is deemed valuable or desirable or important—their presence always being a problem, a deficit, an impediment—that sense and assumption will be manifested on the street and in the classrooms.

Education, of course, is never neutral. It always has a value, a position, a politics. Education—teaching and schooling—either reinforces or challenges the existing social order. The largest, most generous purpose of education is human enlightenment and human liberation, and the driving and undergirding principle is the unity of all humanity: every human being is of incalculable value, entitled to decent standards concerning freedom and justice and education, and any violations, deliberate or inadvertent, must be fought against, testified to, and resisted.

But because schools serve societies—in fact, in many ways all schools are microcosms of the societies in which they're embedded—every school is both mirror and window onto a specific social reality. If one understands the schools, one can see the whole of society; if one fully grasps the intricacies of society, one will know something about how its schools must be organized. In a totalitarian society, schools are built for obedience and conformity; in a kingdom, the schools teach fealty; in a racialized society, educational privileges and oppressions are distributed along the color line. In an authentic democracy, schools embody a spirit of cooperation, inclusion, and full participation—they honor diversity while building unity.

On October 26, 1992, the US Congress designated one of the segregated Black schools in Topeka, Kansas, the Monroe Elementary School, a National Historic Site because of its significance in the famous *Brown v. Board of Education of Topeka* decision, an icon in the popular story America tells itself about its inherent goodness and its inevitable upward trajectory.

Brown occurred in the wake of World War II, in the wash of that global, reenergized sense of freedom. The decision followed incessant and increasingly intense demands by African Americans that the country live up to the promise of the Fourteenth Amendment. And, importantly, *Brown* coincided with clear white interests that had nothing to do with Black well-being: avoiding a revolution led and defined by subjugated African Americans, transforming the feudal South and integrating it into a repositioned capitalist juggernaut, removing a blatant and embarrassing fact of American life that was effectively wielded against the United States in the escalating Cold War. White people needed *Brown*—but only a bit of *Brown*.

To take *Brown* to heart would require a hard look at the racial reality we inhabit: a system with institutions operating at every level to attempt to construct Black "inferiority" and deny full participation in social, political, and economic life. The hard look would hopefully lead to an iron commitment, then, to smash the institution of white supremacy. No such luck with that—yet.

Brown embodies a fundamental, even a fatal flaw that runs deep in the American racial narrative as well. The argument in the case turns on the harm suffered by Black children and the feelings of inferiority that are a result of segregation, rather than on the despicable, immoral, and destructive system of white supremacy itself. Black people—not racism—were the acknowledged concern; Black pathology instead of white privilege was the focus of action.

And so *Brown*, the widely celebrated and lofty statement of principle, was followed immediately by its lesser-known brother, the betrayer and assassin *Brown II*. *Brown v. Board of Education of Topeka II* was the implementation, or remedy phase, of the decision, and here again—consistent with the long tradition of all things racial in the United States—the remedy fitted neither the crime nor the injury. In fact, *Brown II* gave the local school districts, the parties defeated in *Brown*, the power and responsibility to construct the solution—to desegregate their schools *"with all deliberate speed."* The fox, far from being banished from the hen house, was given the only set of keys.

Lewis Steel, a civil rights lawyer, noted that the Supreme Court had never in its history issued an order to implement a constitutional right that was so vague. The court made clear that it "would protect the interests of white America in the maintenance of stable institutions" and that it "considered the potential damage to white Americans resulting from the diminution of privilege as more critical than continued damage to the underprivileged."[20]

"With all deliberate speed" turned out to mean "never." The activity in the courts over the decades following *Brown* went decidedly South: racially isolated communities of color were denied the right to draw students from adjoining white suburbs; children were denied the right to equal school funding; and the concept of "neighborhood school" was reinforced and strengthened, even if the result was resegregation. On and on and on it went. More than six decades after *Brown*, school segregation is alive and well, more firmly entrenched than ever, and each year schools are more segregated. The original impact of *Brown I* is all but dead, and the structure of white supremacy rules.

As usual, white supremacy is hiding in plain sight. The most dissembling hypocrites argue that anyone who sees race is a racist, that race-conscious integration is the equivalent of Black-hating segregation—because both are based on skin color. This is an invented and wholly fictitious symmetry. The problem in America is not and has never been race consciousness per se; the problem has always been white supremacy in fact. Anything that undermines white supremacy and fights for equality, self-determination, and the power to control one's own life sides with humanity; anything that excludes, segregates, or subordinates is on the side of oppression and exploitation. And so, using the lofty language of *Brown*, ordinary white supremacists continue to herd Black children into unnatural and inferior schools, build walls, and lock the gates.

Monroe Elementary—that iconic temple in Topeka elevated as a National Historic Site—may as well have been turned into a mausoleum, for it was one more place where African American aspirations and struggles for decent and equal education were laid to rest.

"TEACHERS HAVE IT EASY."

Appearing on Fox News's *Follow the Money*, Keith Ablow was blunt about how easy being a teacher really is, saying that two thirty in the afternoon is quitting time for teachers, and they don't work summers. For the hours they put in and the work they do, teachers are overpaid. Teaching is in reality a part-time job, the system is failing miserably, and still we coddle these entitled part-timers.

Teachers have it easy. They make a lot of money for only a little work. Their benefits are overly generous. They're incredibly lazy and unmotivated. And in spite of all their advantages and good fortune, they lay about in a union-enabled bubble that encourages endless whining and a narcissistic culture of complaint.

John Kasich, the governor of Ohio and former presidential candidate, captured this last point succinctly at a 2015 event leading up to the New Hampshire presidential primary: "If I were, not president, if I were *king* in America, I would abolish all teachers' lounges, where they sit together and worry about 'woe is us.'"[1]

Jason Richwine, a researcher at the Heritage Foundation, and Andrew Biggs of the American Enterprise Institute buttress the overpaid argument with some data. Workers who go into teaching see their wages increase roughly 9 percent, Richwine and Biggs claim, while teachers who leave for non-teaching jobs see their wages drop 3 percent. Even where teacher salaries are comparable with similarly skilled private-sector workers, more generous benefits for teachers (Richwine and Biggs include "job security" as a benefit) means that total compensation is 52 percent greater than "fair market levels," which amounts to "more than $120 billion overcharged to taxpayers each year."[2]

Instead of complaining steadily about their woeful lives, "teachers should be happy!" insists Matt McCall, Penn Financial CEO. "I hate to get, you know, down on the teachers right now, but this [teacher debate] is about the public sector unions, where it's the teachers that are complaining. . . . They have a pretty darn good job, working nine months a year, amazing benefits, salaries not bad . . . [and] they're not happy with it!"[3] This may not be entirely their fault, however, because, as Ruben Navarrette Jr. points out, teachers can't help but complain. "It's in their professional DNA," he says. "Everything is always someone else's fault."[4] All that whining is largely out of teachers' control; it's an inherited condition, like ectodermal dysplasia or freckles.

Besides, teaching is mainly instruction, partly performing, certainly being in the front and at the center of the classroom for several hours a day. How hard could it be?

REALITY CHECK

In the first place, such claims ignore the actual hours that teachers are in the classroom or doing work. Visit any public school at 5 p.m. or 7 p.m. or even 6 a.m. and you will find teachers hard at it, refining plans, responding to student work, setting up activities. Check their computers at 9 p.m., 10 p.m., and later and you will see that they are sending e-mails to colleagues, students, and parents, and that they are studying their own disciplinary content and working on lesson plans. Teachers have required classes to keep up their skills, as well as workshops and conferences they attend at their own expense because of their passion for getting better and their understanding that knowledge about teaching is ongoing and never finished. They take additional courses, study source materials, and travel during days when school is closed—all to improve their craft. And, yes, after months of sixty-hour weeks, they do take some downtime.

In the real world of schools and classrooms, simple instruction turns out to be the least of the responsibility. Teaching includes a wide range of activities demanding a greater set of skills, including counseling, organizing, assessing, modeling, coaching, disciplining, persuading, observing and recording, inspiring, and, well, a lot more. Teachers must be experts and generalists, psychologists and social workers, judges and gurus, and, paradoxically but critically important, they must become astute and attentive students of their students.

One thing becomes clear enough: teaching as the direct delivery of some preplanned curriculum, teaching as the orderly and scripted conveyance of information, teaching as clerking, is simply a myth. Teaching is much larger and much more alive than that; it contains more pain and conflict, more joy and intelligence, more uncertainty and ambiguity. It requires more judgment and energy and intensity than, on some days, seems humanly possible. And yes, many more hours and more days than can be deduced from a school schedule. Teaching is spectacularly unlimited.

There are many reasons not to teach, and none can be easily dismissed. Teachers are, in fact, often badly paid, so badly that it's a national disgrace. Teacher pay nationally still hovers around the mid-$40,000s nationally, which means they earn on average a quarter of what lawyers are paid, half of what accountants make, less, in many cases, than truck drivers and shipyard workers.[5] Economic appeals aside, wages and salaries are one reflection of relative social value; a collective, community assessment of worth. There are no other professionals who face so many demands and receive so little in financial compensation. The state compensates teachers sparingly, while stipulating extensive and specific educational requirements. Slight improvements in pay and benefits in some districts serve only to highlight how out of step we really are when it comes to valuing and rewarding teaching.

Journalist Alissa Quart has documented the growing number of teachers who drive for Uber, taking passengers around at night simply to make ends meet financially.[6] Uber even promotes the idea as part of their "teacher/driver initiative," but in spite of the cheery face they put on it, the thousands of teachers who pick up second jobs are clearly doing so because they're underpaid.

Teachers also suffer low status in many communities, in part as a legacy of sexism. Teaching is largely women's work, especially in the lower grades, and it's constantly being demeaned in the public discourse, described as something to be performed mechanically, without much thought or care, covered over with layers of supervision and accountability and bureaucracy, and generally patronized. Low pay is part of that dynamic. So is the paradox of the movie cliché of holding teachers up as paragons of virtue (the traditional pedestal) while constraining real choices and growth.

Teachers are being driven out of the profession in record numbers. Poor salary and poor retirement benefits, followed by class size and workload, top the list of reasons that teachers leave.[7] If we had this level of failure in any other profession, medicine or law, say, it would be deemed a national crisis. But we blithely skip along, ignoring the loss to our schools—and the pain inflicted on these young teachers and the communities they serve—while repeating clichés about the bad teachers.

Add to that the fact that fewer and fewer people are willing to go into the profession at all—applications for teacher education programs are down as much as 53 percent in some states—this at a time when tens of thousands of baby boomer teachers are retiring, leaving districts in a crisis of overfilled classrooms.[8] With a national narrative that denigrates the profession and a salary that is unsustainable, who would even go into the profession?

In our highly charged and contentious society, where racial hierarchies and hatred, sexual violence and gender oppression are built into the very DNA of the larger world, teachers often find themselves confronting issues of justice in the classroom and fighting for equity and social equality on behalf of their students. The hopes and dreams of youth are in teachers' hands; their goals and aspirations are shaped through their encounters with us. Positive memories of teachers are reserved for particular and special people: the teacher who touched your heart, the teacher who understood you or who cared about you as a person, the teacher whose passion for something—music, math, Latin, kites—was infectious and energizing. Teachers are a large presence in the lives of students, and that responsibility is something teachers shoulder as part of the job.

Teachers are asked hundreds, perhaps thousands of times why they choose teaching. The question often means: "Why teach, when you could do something more profitable?" "Why teach, since teaching is beneath your skill and intelligence?" The question can be filled with contempt and cynicism or it can be a simple request for understanding and knowledge: "What is there in teaching to attract and keep you?" Either way, it's a question worth pursuing, for there are good reasons to teach and equally good reasons not to teach. Teaching is, after all, different in character from any other profession or job or occupation, and it is not for everyone.

It's true that teachers often work in difficult situations under impossible conditions, isolated from other adults yet with no privacy and no time for themselves. Teachers work with young people who are compelled by law to attend school, many of whom have no deep motivation or desire to be there. Teachers sometimes work in schools that are large, impersonal, and factory-like; sometimes in schools that resemble occupied territories, with regular police patrolling the halls and metal checks at the doors. Teachers are subject to the endless and arbitrary demands of bureaucracies and distant politicians. Teachers are expected to cover everything without neglecting anything, to teach reading and arithmetic, for example, but also good citizenship; basic values; drug and alcohol awareness; AIDS prevention; dating, mating, and relating; sexuality; maybe how to drive or parenting skills; and whatever else comes up.

The complexity of teaching can be excruciating, and for some, that may be a sufficient reason not to teach (for others, it is one of teaching's most compelling allures). Teachers must face a large number of students: thirty or more for typical elementary school

teachers, a hundred and fifty a day is average for high school teachers. Each youngster comes to class with a specific background,
with unique desires, abilities, intentions, and needs. Somehow,
teachers must reach out to each student, to meet each as the one of
one, entirely unique, with specific skills and abilities, hopes and
dreams, needs and desires. A common experience of teachers is
to feel the pain of opportunities missed, potential unrealized, students untouched. Add to this the constancy of change and the press
of time, the lack of support and the scarcity of resources, and some
of the intensity and difficulty of teaching becomes a bit more apparent. It's no wonder that many teachers retreat into something
certain and solid, something reliable, something we can see and
get our hands around—lesson plans, say, or assertive discipline
workshops—because we fear burning out altogether.

These are some of the reasons not to teach, and they can add up
to a pretty compelling case. So, why teach? Is it the imagined country club–appointed teachers' lounge? No one who works in schools
has ever seen one, and no one really believes these places exist.
The real answer is romantic but true: teachers share in the lives
of young people; teachers are privileged partners who are invited
to touch the future. For that reason, the difficulties and challenges
must be faced and engaged, with courage and compassion.

Smart educators work to figure out concretely how to meet and
overcome (at least partially) the difficulties and obstacles peren-
nially faced by teachers teaching. One such educator is Deborah
Loewenberg Ball of the University of Michigan. Ball has done important research on teaching and the process of learning to teach,
and she and her colleagues have built a teacher education program
on the foundation of that work.[9] Ball herself was a French major
in college who was not entirely comfortable with math when she
began teaching, and yet her research and her subsequent insights
about learning to teach were based in the mathematics classroom.

Teaching math, whether to a class of eighth graders or third
graders, requires an extraordinary range of skills and math knowl-

edge to be sure, but it also requires much more than content and subject knowledge. "Mathematicians need to understand a problem only for themselves," explains Elizabeth Green, while "math teachers need both to know the math and to know how 30 different minds might understand (or misunderstand) it."[10] Teachers need to step out of their own heads and into the heads of others, says Ball, because "teaching depends on what other people think, not what you think."[11] A bad math teacher will simply mark an error wrong and give it a zero; a good math teacher will follow the student down the rabbit hole of her own reasoning, working to figure out what went wrong, and then walk her back out. This leads to deep mathematical knowledge, not just winner or loser games on our quizzes and tests. From this insight, Ball and her colleagues developed a technique she calls Mathematical Knowledge for Teaching, which includes the everyday math most adults know as well as more specialized mathematical knowledge, teaching skills and familiarity with a wide range of material, and, most important, a sense of common math errors and misunderstandings that new learners are likely to experience and present.

Teacher education at Michigan revolves around nineteen practices every candidate must master in order to graduate, practices that include content and teaching skills as well as methods to create a positive, purposeful, and joyous environment with young people. Ball believes that teaching is "decidedly not about being yourself" and that learning to teach is strenuous work.[12] It takes more than personality and confidence, good intentions and enthusiasm, high test scores or good grades in college—it takes effort and commitment and time and more effort. And more effort. But it is possible to do it well.

Leaders at the University of Chicago Laboratory Schools (Lab) also believe that learning to teach is an arduous affair: tough, expensive, time-consuming, and complex. They invest heavily in the process, though, because they don't want to see good people fail at teaching or potentially good teachers get away.

Lab is an elite school founded over a century ago by John Dewey, then a professor at the University of Chicago. It's an extravagantly privileged place with a full arts program, small classes, state-of-the-art facilities, more than a dozen librarians, a curriculum based in part on inquiry and student interest, a well-respected and unionized teacher corps, and the list goes on. It's the school the Obama children attended when the family lived in Chicago, and it's the school the children of Mayors Richard M. Daley and Rahm Emanuel as well as Arne Duncan attended; Duncan graduated from Lab, and his wife is an admissions officer there.

By design, the top administrators at Lab are all educators and former teachers because, they argue, school leaders must pilot the school from the deck of classroom experiences. Their jobs include guiding and supervising teachers, and so they must be able to collaborate on questions of curriculum and instruction, pedagogy and assessment, academic content and courses of study. They need to know more than how to read a spreadsheet—they need to know what they're talking about.

An integral part of the Lab School culture is a palpable sense of respect for good teaching. But what is good teaching, and how do we know it when we see it? Those questions are implicit in everything the school does, and they're questions the school explores explicitly as well. They're the focus of faculty meetings, parent gatherings, student assemblies, guest speakers, and educational conferences.

The result of that singular focus is that a conversation about teaching—what it entails, how it's done well, how it can be supported, and where it needs to be improved—is always ongoing. It means that no one is settling for a reductive one-size-fits-all definition of goodness in teaching, and it means that the continuous efforts at improving teaching are everybody's business, all the time.

Over several years, Lab teachers have outlined, rethought, and refined several expectations that they call "domains," with accompanying indicators that are used for faculty evaluations and that together point to the school's definition of goodness in teaching. The field is necessarily dynamic, always growing in elaboration and idiosyncrasy, and always subject to change. The domains, the teachers argue, simply provide useful guideposts for an intricate and ongoing conversation and revision. The domains include Preparation and Planning; the Classroom Environment; Instruction; Communication, Collaboration, and Reflection; and Professional Responsibilities. Under "Preparation and Planning," for example, indicators include markers such as "designs coherent instruction," "designs lessons with substantive and significant outcomes in mind," "chooses instructional outcomes that are appropriate to the students' prior knowledge, skills and level of development," "responds to individual differences," "actively observes students' response to planned instruction," "demonstrates flexibility in planning and makes reasonable choices," and "adaptations in instruction to promote engagement and learning by all students." Together they demonstrate a clear focus on students and multiple pathways for student success.

When a new teacher is hired, she is assigned a mentor who meets with her regularly and becomes a reflective guide and support. The veteran teacher is paid and given time off to commit to the novice, and the new teacher is expected to do ongoing self-evaluations in order to identify areas of strength and areas that need improvement. In the first year, and again in the second year, the principal visits the novice teacher's classroom two times and does a lengthy formal appraisal; she then meets with the veteran teacher in a lengthy conference to discuss the evaluation. In the third year, the new teacher is either released or given a three-year contract. That first contract is golden, because before that is signed, the teacher can be let go without any elaborate reasons or complicated justifications. The contract will be renewed automatically unless an incident or complaint triggers a reevaluation; at that point a due-process mechanism kicks in and the teacher is given multiple opportunities to improve.

All teachers are expected to attend professional conferences and workshops, take classes at colleges or universities, and engage in other activities to improve their practice—and they are paid to do so. One administrator told us that the goal was to create an environment of trust throughout the community and encourage the entire community to embrace a collective commitment to greatness. "It's hard work," one administrator told us, "and anyone who thinks it's easy has never seen the inside of a classroom." She added, "We have a hundred teachers here with an average of ten years in the classroom—that's a thousand years of experience, and I'd be nuts if I missed opportunities to tap into that vast pool of wisdom."

When asked how much student test scores counted in evaluating teachers, the administrator looked bewildered: "What do test scores have to do with good teaching?" she asked. Excellent question.

"High-Stakes Standardized Tests Improve Student Achievement and Effectively Detect Inferior Teachers."

Reformers base their initiatives on organizational-change models developed by nonprofit and for-profit managers. These frameworks are sound and have been widely tested. Modern management science, combined with these successful prototypes of change, have worked in these sectors, but government typically resists such efforts. Yet data-driven accountability is the foundation of success, and business leaders work hard to measure the right things because they know that what gets measured is what counts. Moving the performance metrics that have broad agreement in the education community as being crucial to student success in the wider world is the only sensible way we will achieve success in our schools, and know when we've done so. Scholastic Aptitude Tests began to be administered after World War II in order to evaluate college applicants outside the context of the grading system of applicants' schools. More recently, testing at all grade levels has been important in objectively evaluating student, and therefore school, performance. Tests provide extensive data that allow administrators to plan instruction and recognize areas that need improvement.

Standardized tests have been scientifically proven to provide the best available metric for comparing students to one another, and for finding out which teachers are effective and which are falling down on the job. Defenders of the status quo simply complain about testing, but we all know tests are never going away. Teachers and their unions hate the standardized tests because they reveal their own weaknesses.

REALITY CHECK

The Steinway people proudly describe to the world that each one of their legendary grand pianos is unique, that no piano is exactly like any other. The wood from one tree is subtly different than the wood from another tree, and questions of age and humidity, growing conditions, light, and temperature all come into play. Moreover, constructing a piano is a labor of love and a creative if practical art—there is no assembly line, and there are no robots or autopilots that can get the job done properly. Each baby grand piano is the one of one, the assemblage of an astonishing twelve thousand parts, fondly fabricated. Prospective buyers visit the showroom and typically sit at one keyboard after another, sampling several before deciding which one to purchase, and owners display genuine affection toward their own unique baby grand.

Moving on to children and schools, it's worth noting that the number of neurons in a third grader's head is quite a bit more than twelve thousand. There are, in fact, upward of a hundred billion neurons in that kid's brain.[1] We know that no child is exactly like any other—each is unique, one of a kind. Teaching and raising children is a labor of love and both a creative and practical art. There is no assembly line, and there are no bots that can get the job done properly. Practicing and prospective teachers might want to keep that in mind as they develop authentic affection for the human beings before them, and a touch of awe toward the mighty profession they're a part of.

Oddly, in our society, people who think and care about Steinways are pretty certain that each one is unique, while people who make policy about children and schools seem pretty sure that kids aren't one of a kind and that, in fact, there's a uniformity that can be discerned from (or imposed by) a test. Policy makers tend to talk about "the third grader" or "the third-grade level" as if third graders were a thing—a bounded identity—or as if the platonic ideal of

"Third Grader" exists or resides somewhere high above the clouds up there with the gods on Mount Olympus. That may be where the trouble begins.

Testing harms everyone. Most outrageously, those who learn differently are marginalized and perhaps most punished by the testing regime. As Boston special education teacher Sean McAdam points out, "I see so many of the strengths my students possess. Many of my students are more organized, mechanically inclined, or able to listen and respond thoughtfully to others than the average person in America. . . . Many of my students' futures hang in the balance because of this one assessment. Simply put, they will not be able to get a high school diploma without passing [the Massachusetts Comprehensive Assessment System test]."[2]

Testing also discriminates. Standardized test results have been shown repeatedly to be most strongly correlated with family income and the educational levels of parents, which means that they are first and foremost a measure of zip codes and a test of class backgrounds. Therefore, to ask everyone to act as if students "earned" their scores in an objective, context-free world is a kind of massive fraud. The students most harmed by high-stakes standardized tests are the least standard among us. It would be more honest and transparent (not to mention more efficient and much less expensive) to simply survey kids about those two facts—family income, parental educational level—and label them "winners" or "losers." The tests do that in any case, but they come cleverly wrapped in mystification and disguised as scientific, unbiased, and fair.

In response to proposals to evaluate teachers based on the test scores of their students, the American Statistical Association, the largest organization in the United States representing statisticians and related professionals, released an analysis that demonstrated that such measures were "useless."[3] But the reformers soldier on, glibly rejecting the evidence provided by statisticians and happily eschewing the very "scientific skills" they purport to want for our students.

Moreover, while teachers have the demanding and dizzying task of constantly monitoring and evaluating students, standardized test results have been shown many times over to be of no practical help to teachers. Results are aggregated, general, and delivered to schools after students have left a teacher's classroom, so high-stakes standardized tests typically fail to link back to teachers in any meaningful way. They're useless, then, as tools that might help teachers teach better, and because that's so, they misdirect and mystify and entirely miss the point—that is, if the point is student growth, learning, and achievement.

Testing has been a convenient hammer in the hands of the market "revolutionaries," but it has unleashed a forceful opposition from parents and communities as well. The Opt-Out Movement—parents electing to have their children skip the tests, stay home, or sit in the auditorium during test time—is one expression of dissent that speaks to a deep discomfort with and mistrust of the dominant testing regimen. One of the worst things about the testing system—and parents and teachers witness this up close—is the "winner" or "loser" label that becomes attached to very young kids. That's a tragedy for all of them, and over time, the labeling becomes a catastrophe for the larger society. Many families and entire communities have been labeled deficient and pathological, and many have concluded that the tests are expensive and disruptive but have no authentic educational benefit. Many parents and education activists are becoming more sophisticated in analyzing and critiquing the relative value of high-stakes standardized testing.

One of the clearest objections to our collective metric madness is that gaming the system, fudging and cheating, is now inevitable because of the emphasis placed on measurement (testing) combined with the huge consequences (high stakes). And this is because of a simple principle that is well known in business, social research, and science but is not practiced—and is even suppressed—in education. In economics it's called Goodhart's law, after the British economist Charles Goodhart, and it holds that a performance metric is only useful as a performance metric as long as it isn't used as a performance metric.[4] That paradoxical concept simply means that announcing a policy with significant rewards and punishments tied to a specific measure—a measure meant to stand for an entire universe of interest—will result in people working exclusively on that particular designated measure to the detriment of larger and more comprehensive goals, and the universe itself will be ignored or undermined.

For example, a charter school in Chicago called Urban Prep built a reputation as a good school (the universe of interest being "good schools") by pointing to a single performance metric: it sent 100 percent of its graduates to college every year. Everyone in the school focused on that one goal: all graduates go to college! And yet, Urban Prep is not a good school—the curriculum is anemic; the instruction is "drill and skill" morning to night; marginal students are pushed out of school before graduation; "college" is an elastic category that includes sketchy, for-profit trade schools; and retention in college has been terrible. But as long as the school focused on this one thing—college attendance—it ignored a thousand other factors that could help to create a good school. Using college attendance as the sole performance metric meant that it didn't work as a useful performance metric after all.

Goodhart's law explains why cheating scandals on student standardized tests have become ubiquitous—from Seattle to San Diego, and from Lake Tahoe to Lake Forest. The Department of Education barked up the wrong tree when it hired former FBI director Louis Freeh to protect the test answers "at all costs." The department would have done better to circulate and study Goodhart's law.

Rather than exploring the knotty problem of what constitutes an education of value, or what we collectively think the wild diversity of educated persons ought to look like, we bow low to the test and say that, in effect, an educated person tests well, and we can line up educated folks, best to worst, on a linear scale. And since the testing machine can test only specific, relatively narrow things, those constricted and testable things become glorified as the things-most-needful, the markers of value in education. This is a through-the-looking-glass world, everything upside down and everyone acting as if the Mad Hatter is completely sane. Sociologist William Bruce Cameron noted that not everything that can be counted counts, and not everything that counts can be counted. Think about it: How do you create a test for kindness or compassion? We may know those qualities when we see them; we may practice them as best we can and experience them in our lived lives; we may create spaces for their enactment, but how—and why—would you test for them? There are a zillion other positive qualities and powerful dispositions that count but are not counted in school: initiative, curiosity, commitment, effort, interest, awareness, imagination, a sense of humor, honesty, self-confidence, respect for others, and . . . keep going, and keep counting.

Testing, and especially high-stakes standardized testing as a central aspect of schooling, is a relatively recent phenomenon, and its history is enlightening if not particularly admirable. Testing is not immune from social, political, or economic factors, and it's worth noting that the testing movement began in earnest in the early twentieth century and rapidly expanded due, in part, to an unbounded faith that modern science and measurement in all areas were the keys to progress and prosperity.

Testing drew on a belief in the "science of eugenics," the movement to sort humanity into complex systems of superior and inferior races and ethnicities. During World War I, IQ tests were widely administered to soldiers in an attempt to discover who should be elevated to the officer corps. The social commentator Walter Lippmann said at the time that the tests were a form of "quackery in a field that breeds quacks like rabbits."[5] The SAT tests were a close cousin of the IQs, and their inventor, the psychologist Carl Brigham, who never intended them to be used beyond counseling and advising, later denounced them as misused and misleading. He also pointed out that the scores were not neutral or particularly useful since they measured "schooling, family background, familiarity with English, and everything else."[6]

The high cost of testing could be ended immediately by simply lining the kids up in the schoolyard from richest to poorest, and sorting them out from there, but without the fig leaf of objectivity offered by those high-priced tests. Further, no matter what kids learn, how or what their teachers teach, or how difficult or simple a norm-referenced test is, precisely 10 percent of kids will score in the top 10 percent, and exactly half the kids will fall below the median—not because a kid is weak or a teacher terrible, but because of the definition of median. As the education scholar Wayne Au has argued, "If all the students passed the test . . . that test would immediately be judged an invalid metric, and any measure of students which mandates the failure of students is an invalid measure."[7]

Twenty years ago, the College Board, the corporation that owns the SATs, acknowledged that the tests had little to do with "aptitude" and dropped that word from its title, changing the name to the Scholastic *Achievement* Test. That wasn't quite right either, and so the name was changed again—it's now simply the SAT. Journalist Elizabeth Kolbert pointed out that "the letters 'SAT' stand for nothing more (or less) than SATs. As the Lord put it to Moses, 'I am that I am.'" In looking more deeply at, studying for, and taking the tests herself, Kolbert concluded: "As befits an exam named for itself, the SAT measures those skills—and really only those skills—necessary for the SATs."[8]

The "testocrats," as the educator Jesse Hagopian calls them, are the test and textbook publishers who profit extravagantly from our national obsession, as well as the corporate reformers and banksters who push an agenda of hypercompetition and privatization of public education in direct opposition to cooperation, collaboration, critical thought, and the expansion of the public space. Hagopian compares our testocracy to any run-of-the-mill theocracy: "a deity—in this case the exalted norm-referenced bubble exam—is officially recognized as the civil ruler of education whose policy is

governed by officials that regard test results as divine."⁹ The tes-
tocratic elite, he writes, is "committed to reducing the intellectual and emotional process of teaching and learning to a single
number—a score they subsequently use to sacrifice education on
the altar devoted to high-stakes testing by denying students promotion or graduation, firing teachers, converting schools into
privatized charters, or closing schools altogether." Hagopian bris-
tles at the idea of "data-driven reform" and argues for schools and
classrooms that are both student-driven and data-informed.

Vast numbers of the thousands of PhDs and graduate students
in the American Educational Research Association are "working
on" the achievement gap created by the testing game. Researchers wring their hands, try new studies, create brilliant models,
but never seem to wrestle the gap monster to its knees. If we simply declared the gap over, all those researchers would be out of a
job, destroying what's become in effect an "achievement-gap-
industrial-complex."

The most honest and effective way to deal with the achievement gap is to just declare that it is a non-problem, a problem constructed by those in power to inscribe the very elements of their
defined privilege. The problem in education should be redefined
as one of engagement, community needs, school resources, student agency, genuine inquiry in curriculum, and the full development of free people.

John Dewey observed long ago that you can get caught up in a
logical fallacy by asking questions that trap you into only narrow
choices for what the answer could be. But, he pointed out, "intellectual progress usually occurs through sheer abandonment of
questions together with both the alternatives they assume. . . . We
do not solve them, we get over them. Old questions are solved by
disappearing, evaporating, while new questions corresponding to
the changed attitude of endeavor and preference take their place."¹⁰

In the best of all possible worlds, schools would focus on the
educational and social experiences that matter and would dispense

with standardized testing altogether. We would stop asking the question about the "achievement gap" and would instead address what Gloria Ladson-Billings calls the "educational debt," the reparations owed to poor communities for decades of underfunding, marginalization, and soul-crushing attacks on student dignity.[11]

In the 1990s, a mandate for strict "accountability" and higher test scores swept the nation, and seemingly overnight, standardized test scores were being held up as the new—and sole—measure of progress for students and schools. Simultaneously, a strict, structured, and much more prescriptive curriculum, narrowed to little more than reading and math, slipped into place. In many places, the tests became the curriculum, and the impact on both students and classroom teachers was palpable. For students, this meant markedly less time to think, reflect, or participate in the arts and dramatically more time on test preparation; for teachers, this meant reduced autonomy, increased stress levels, and decreased job satisfaction.

One example of the hustle to avoid facing reality: *Newsweek* offers an annual list of the "best high schools" in the country.[12] The rating system is based on six variables: on-time graduation rate (25 percent), college acceptance rate (25 percent), Advanced Placement (AP) and International Baccalaureate (IB) tests per student (25 percent), average SAT and ACT scores (10 percent), average AP and IB scores (10 percent), and AP and IB courses per student (5 percent). Sounds like science—fair and objective, all neatly arranged with engineered precision. Yet here, as elsewhere, the interpretation of these figures depends on how one weighs the variables—40 percent of the data relies on AP data, and a school that doesn't offer AP will never make the grade, even though many excellent schools reject those classes as a waste of resources and time.

And a close look at the schools reveals a lot—of the top fifty schools, for example, thirty-seven have selective admissions, and among the open-enrollment public schools are Bronxville, New York (number 40) with a median household income of $166,000, and Jericho, New York (number 41) with a median of

$128,000—compared to $54,000 for New York State as a whole. At one charter school in Arizona, the school population is 41 percent Asian in a state with 2.8 percent Asian residents, and 2 percent Hispanic in a state with 33 percent Hispanic people. The lesson is clear: to make a "best school," bring in the "best kids" and don't let the "unbest" near the place.

If you believe market models and competition are the best way to measure and improve education, if you expect schools to mimic the capitalist marketplace, then you are going to have the very practices that characterize corporate life in America, and that means cheating. After all, virtually every corporate annual report cooks the books, and almost every engagement at the marketplace involves some form of deception or distortion of the truth. So we are finding across the country that some educators, under tremendous pressure from state authorities and administrators, are cheating on the tests—erasing wrong answers and filling in correct answers on answer sheets. Even when there has not been overt cheating, such a system encourages corruption and undermines teacher collaboration.[13]

One of the most spectacular cases of such cheating was in Atlanta, where eleven educators went to prison, charged with criminal conspiracy, a law designed to go after mobsters. Their crime? Allegedly changing test scores under pressure from school superintendent Beverly Hall, who was on her way to winning awards for record improvement in student test scores. The entire district had created a "culture of fear, intimidation, and retaliation" for teachers and staff to push up test scores, according to Richard Rothstein.[14] And the administrators themselves were facing fear, intimidation, and retaliation in the form of competition for federal monies.

Rothstein adds, "Certainly, educators can refuse to cheat, and take the fall for unavoidable failure in other ways: they can see their schools closed, their colleagues fired, their students' confidence and love of learning destroyed. That would have been the legal thing to do but not necessarily the ethical thing to do."

Similar cheating has been uncovered in Baltimore, Houston, Toledo, El Paso, and Philadelphia, while even in Washington, DC, where Michelle Rhee claimed to have made great advances, circumstantial evidence points to success through cheating.[15] While bankers who were caught cheating for billions of dollars or car manufacturers who created software to deceive smog-monitoring devices did not go to prison, the teachers in the Atlanta scandal were led off in chains. The visual in this case says a thousand words about the anti-teacher narrative that has gripped the public discussion. Rachel Aviv's 2014 *New Yorker* article, "Wrong Answer," captures in excruciating detail the agonies the teachers faced in trying to protect their students and keep their schools open in the test-and-punish regime.[16]

As Monty Neill of FairTest points out, high-stakes testing troubles teachers because it narrows the curriculum and is of no use as a practical guide to teaching.[17] Teachers find themselves limited to narrow test prep, to coaching students as to how to outsmart the test writers, reinforcing the assumption that the world is made up of right answers, settled truths. However, the best education involves the pursuit of an expansive and exploratory curriculum that encourages students to take chances and forge new directions. Such testing masks the real problems we have in our schools, which is, as you could expect, a reflection of real problems in the larger society: structural racism and white supremacy, entrenched poverty, inequality, brutal class distinctions.

The Department of Education acknowledges that tests don't tell us everything that's important about a child and that they're consistently used for purposes for which they were not designed. Nevertheless, the DOE is now in the business of making tests more efficient and more intense, handing them over to private firms such as Pearson to turn a profit. And they pledge absolute fealty to the underlying ethos of the contagious metric madness: intense competition and individualism, the privatization of the public sphere, and tying teachers' fates to kids' test scores.

"WHILE TEACHERS AND THEIR UNIONS USE POVERTY AS A CONVENIENT SMOKESCREEN FOR THEIR OWN FAILURES, IT'S BECOME OBVIOUS THAT GRIT AND MERIT CAN OVERCOME EVERY DISADVANTAGE."

Eva Moskowitz, the founder and CEO of Success Academy charter schools in New York City, argues, "We . . . can't fix poverty unless we fix education, and we can't fix education if we keep telling ourselves our schools are 'good enough.'"

She's right. Poverty is a result of poor schooling, and fixing poor schools is the key to improving lives for the next generation. As long as teachers and their self-serving unions dodge responsibility by passing the blame for poor student performance onto external factors like poverty, schools will remain "lifeless houses of detention." Good schools need to become "lifelines out of poverty," and in those places, teachers make no excuses—their expectations are consistently high, their energy steady, their standards and demands elevated. The fallacy, as Moskowitz explains it, is that "poverty and race are overwhelming barriers to a child's ability to learn." It's simply not true. We sell kids short when we promote poverty as a justification for school failure.[1]

It is common sense that students must learn grit and perseverance, even in the face of obstacles, in order to succeed. It does not serve low-income students to coddle them and tell them they are victims. They need teachers and schools that challenge them to be successful in our competitive marketplace and world.

Public schools in poor communities are often failing, it's true, but poverty is an intractable social problem and, one must note, an age-old phenomenon. Poor schools, on the other hand, will respond quickly and easily to the "magic of the market" and should, therefore, be turned over to the private sector and run like businesses—with competition, big data, standardization, evaluating teacher effectiveness according to student test scores, and so on. Our country is exceptionally prosperous, and the secret is letting the market do its work. The watchword in schools, as in all areas, must be "market accountability."

We need to think outside the box to solve the problem of poor kids failing in schools. Ideas that might have seemed far-fetched once—tax-payer supported religious schools or home-schooling options, a range of for-profit cyber-schools, a fully vouchered system where parents take their publicly funded check to any school they like—are entering the mainstream, and nothing should be beyond consideration.

Former House majority leader Newt Gingrich, for example, was ridiculed when he proposed to an audience at Harvard in 2011 that schools should hire poor students to mop the hallways and bathrooms: "You say to somebody, you shouldn't go to work before you're what, fourteen, sixteen years of age, fine. You're totally poor. You're in a school that is failing with a teacher that is failing. I've tried for years to have a very simple model. Most of these schools ought to get rid of the unionized janitors, have one master janitor and pay local students to take care of the school. The kids would actually do work, they would have cash, they would have pride in the schools, they'd begin the process of rising."[2] According to Mr. Gingrich, and he's right on this, child-labor laws and unions keep poor students from bootstrapping into the middle class.

"This is something that no liberal wants to deal with," Gingrich said, but his approach would have all the advantages he described, and it would counter the habit and culture of laziness by creating a culture of work. "Really poor children in really poor neighborhoods have no habits of working and have nobody around them who works," Gingrich said. "So, literally, they have no habit of showing up on Monday. They have no habit of staying all day. They have no habit of I do this and you give me cash—unless it's illegal."[3]

Schools can teach proper work habits, as well as skills young people need to get good jobs. Generating enough good jobs will bring an end to poverty.

REALITY CHECK

The American myth of meritocracy is a clever way that schools preserve class and racial hierarchies, year after year, without ever taking responsibility for the reproduction of privilege and oppression. After all, goes this story, if you work hard and show grit, anyone can make it. There are always a few exceptions, the students who do succeed despite the odds, and those examples perpetuate the illusion that the opportunities are there for all. But no one argues that poverty "justifies" failure. Rather, critics point out that school success correlates powerfully with poverty and that willful ignorance of this demonstrable fact leads to a range of magical proposals, missteps, and false moves leading to non-solutions. As Mike Klonsky points out, "It's a matter of fact that hungry and often homeless children aren't as successful in the classroom as those who are well fed, clad and housed."[4] A closer look at the data, as well as the mechanisms of failure and marginalization, shows that the game is fixed for the vast majority of kids. Let's look at the extent of poverty in the United States and its effects.

The Southern Education Foundation (SEF) released a report announcing the passing of a shocking and inexcusable benchmark: in the 2012–2013 school year, more than 50 percent of students attending public schools in the United States came from low-income families, that is, they received free or reduced-price lunch. Mississippi had the highest rate of poverty, at 71 percent; New Hampshire had the lowest, at 27 percent.[5]

Growing up in poverty is unambiguously bad for you and a prime predictor of school failure: data from the National Assessment of Educational Progress in 2011, for example, showed that fourth graders who were eligible for free lunch scored twenty-nine points lower on reading tests than other students, and that eighth graders eligible for free lunch scored twenty-five points lower than their non-poor peers.[6] Poverty is one of the most appreciable impediments to a child's academic development and ability to learn.

In 2012, 46.5 million people were living in poverty in the United States—the largest number in all the years the census has measured poverty.[7] The poverty rate in 2015 was found to be 13.5 percent for all Americans, and 19.7 percent for children under age eighteen.

So, just over 21 percent of all children in the United States—nearly fifteen million children and six million under six years old—live in families with incomes below the federal poverty level, itself an inadequate measure of real needs. In order to meet basic necessities and cover essential expenses, a lot of credible research says that families require an income of about twice the federal poverty standard to meet basic necessities and cover essential expenses.[8] By that measure, closer to 42 percent of children live in low-income families.

The United States has one of the highest relative child poverty rates in the developed world, according to UNICEF, which says that children's "material well-being is highest in the Netherlands and in the four Nordic countries and lowest in Latvia, Lithuania, Romania and the United States."[9]

Most children in poverty have parents who work, but low wages, inadequate child support, and unstable employment leave families struggling. Poverty impedes a child's ability to learn and contributes to poor health and to social, emotional, and behavioral problems.[10]

Research is clear that poverty is the single greatest hazard to a child's well-being and that effective public policies, including higher minimum wages for workers, high-quality child care, and robust learning experiences for children, can make a demonstrable difference. Investing in vulnerable children pays off.

The trends are stunning, and yet the national debate over public education and school reform is practically silent on the question of poverty and its impact on student learning or achievement. The school reformers have shouted down anyone who dares mention the adverse impacts of poverty, leaving limited space for a serious discussion. But ignoring poverty is to close one's eyes to "the elephant in the room," according to American Federation of Teachers president Randi Weingarten.[11]

Compared to high-performing nations, the United States does not direct its education funding toward poor communities and low-income families. High-performing countries "spend their money in highly equitable ways," explains Linda Darling-Hammond of Stanford University. "If you spend more in schools on the education of children who have fewer socioeconomic advantages, you do better as a country. Other countries invested more money and that is what shot them up in the rankings."[12]

Poor communities are the result of a long and living history that includes government policy, law, and traditions of white supremacy, hierarchy, privilege, and oppression. Stereotypes, negative overgeneralizations, act as justification—well after the fact—for the reality of inequality based on race, class, and any number of other identity markers visible in the real world. Paul Gorski has done brilliant research on the impact of stereotyping, particularly around poverty and poor families in relation to schools.[13] He argues that stereotypes are dangerous, even deadly, because meaning-making is causal for human beings; that is, we act on our self-constructed beliefs, perspectives, and attitudes. If one imagines, for example, that poor people are unintelligent, that attitude itself can lead to lowered expectations and less attention in legislatures and city halls to reducing poverty or reducing its harmful impacts, as well as less effort by school personnel to craft an appropriate and successful classroom experience. Stereotypes about poverty can lead policy makers and educators to some bad places: lowered expectations, to be sure, but also fear, blame, and "solutions" that in no way meet the real problems.

In his research, Gorski names and examines common stereotypes about poor people: they're ineffective and inattentive as parents; they communicate poorly; they don't value education; they're lazy; and they wildly abuse drugs and alcohol.[14] He systematically demolishes each of these false perspectives, drawing on mountains of data to make the case. To cite just two of his research-based conclusions: low-income people are *less likely* to use or abuse alcohol than their wealthier counterparts, and, in fact, greater wealth correlates with greater substance abuse. There is absolutely no credible evidence (beyond "I know a guy who . . ."), Gorski found, to indicate that poor people are lazier or have weaker work ethics than non-poor people. Indeed, low-income workers tend to work much longer hours and often hold down two or three jobs, compared to well-paid workers. The stereotypes linger as justification for unearned privileges, and the "lazy" stigma in particular has devastating impacts both on the morale of poor communities and the misplaced interventions that are putatively designed to uplift poor kids.

The reality is that the "poverty-is-no-excuse-for-failure" rhetoric has a staggering amount of mythmaking at its heart. It allows corporate reformers to perpetuate the illusion of meritocracy while driving privatization of the public space under the rubric of "improving schools" and ignoring deeply entrenched inequities that exist in our society and are perpetuated by our public school systems.

The late scholar/activist William Watkins pointed this out in 2012 when he wrote, "The consequences of school reform are earthshaking. The restructuring of public schools will most likely dismantle universal public education as we know it and 'de-school' significant populations of Black, Brown and poor people. School closings and reconfigurations are now a fact of life in major American cities. This book provides a deep critical examination of the attack on universal, open and free education now called school 'reform.'"[15]

The market is not magic and it's not free; the market is constructed and calibrated to create designated winners and losers and is, therefore, a terrible fit with the goals of public education. Teachers want all their students to learn, and the market demands that "the best and the brightest" move ahead, while everyone is sorted on a scale of "best" to "worst," and many are left behind.

The fact that a few people move up in the system or escape grinding poverty is simply an exception that proves the rule of nonmobility. Indeed, finding a few success cases every year only creates cover for the overall game of maintaining class privilege and, while those few cases are heartwarming, they leave the system unchallenged. And those few who succeed do little to shake up the fundamentals of a highly segmented and hierarchical economy.[16] In fact, the capitalist market is the cause of tremendous wealth and massive poverty, and pretending that the market only creates winners is to misread reality. Since the market causes winners *and* losers, it expands poverty. It's a naked lie to pretend that the market will "save" schools from the effects of poverty.

Schools are complex social organizations, and changing schools is no easier or harder than changing societies themselves. Furthermore, good public schools, successful schools, are not "market driven." Rather, they typically exist in communities of privilege, and like all schools, they mirror the societies that create them.

Many policies promoted under the slogan of "no excuses" actually hurt children living in poverty: standardized tests are riddled with cultural and racial biases, for example, and a focus on testing takes away opportunities for a more robust and rich curriculum; the framing of school subject matter and discourse is aligned exclusively with the white master narrative; charter schools disproportionately underserve special needs students, English-language learners, and children of color; school closings force children out of their communities and put teachers of color out of work more frequently than their white counterparts.

Moreover, parental wealth and income largely determine educational access, and students attending "low performing" schools are more likely to be low-income students of color. These schools are not funded equitably, and as a result, schools in high-poverty areas are more likely to have outdated and/or dilapidated facilities; overworked administrators and staff; fewer resources for art, libraries, and social workers; larger class sizes; and teachers who are either new, working on emergency licenses, or cycling in and out of the profession. These are school-based factors that are constructed on unfair policies, but there's more. Because of housing and job discrimination, poor students have higher mobility and absentee rates, and they obviously suffer the concentration effects of poverty disproportionately: hunger and malnutrition, homelessness, incarcerated or deported parents, and being witnesses to violence or crime.

In this context, to ignore the deeply ingrained inequalities in our society and the structural realities of school, which tend to sustain that inequality, is to perpetuate a crime. To focus on "accountability," firing teachers and closing schools, is to reify the myth. What can firing this or that teacher do toward creating equitable funding? What can one more standardized test do to reduce class size or fix the dilapidated building?

Rather than closing schools and firing teachers, Randi Weingarten calls for "wraparound services."[17] "The schools would be a place to go for children to get the entire range of services they need—and that their families need too. And then let's put in an accountability system, not just testing, to ensure the services get to the kids and that they work."

The latest buzzword in educational reform is "grit," the invention of Angela Duckworth, an Ivy League psychologist whose marketing skills and timing are tip-top but whose research agenda doesn't deviate a hair from conventional orthodoxy. "Grit" in Duckworth's world is essentially self-control and stick-to-itiveness, and it is, according to Duckworth, the key predictor of success in school and in life.[18] Grit is interior, an individual quality lacking in unsuccessful people but abundant in . . . well, in us successful people. And—good news—poor and Black kids can be taught to be more "gritty" through a pedagogy of "tough love" and "no excuses." Not a word about structural racism—grit is separate from society, morality, economics, and history—nor about critical thinking, independent reasoning, curiosity, or initiative, all the qualities foregrounded in schools for the privileged. So, grit aims to fix Black kids on the inside, rather than to disrupt and revolutionize the powerful forces, structures, traditions, and policies that attack African Americans from the outside.

Gloria Ladson-Billings points out that Black folks have boatloads of grit. If they didn't have an abundance of resilience and stick-to-itiveness, they wouldn't have survived the last four hundred years. What they lack is not *grit*, she writes, but access, equality, and justice.[19]

Schools need adequate resources and teachers need support to be successful. Beyond this, there must be larger community revitalization initiatives and programs that really tackle the root causes of poverty. Anything else is a fraud.

"Teachers Are Made More Visible and Accountable in Charter Schools, More Competitive Through Voucher Programs, and Irrelevant with the Advent of Teacher-Proof Cyber Schools."

Donald Trump has distinguished himself as a champion of school "choice," pushing charters and vouchers in place of public schools. He wrote:

> What will public school officials do if they're confronted with school-choice programs? Will they compete to see which system can offer the best education to kids?
>
> They'll sue.
>
> That's what the public education establishment did in Milwaukee, where the country's first-ever school-choice program was established in 1990. The teachers' unions' lobbyists fought tooth and nail to keep the program from getting through the Wisconsin legislature. When the lobbyists lost, the lawyers came in—and sued to stop a thousand low-income Milwaukee parents from claiming the school-choice voucher the state had voted to give them.[1]

While campaigning for president, Trump called school choice "the civil rights issues of our time."[2] He proposed earmarking

$20 billion in federal education funds for vouchers that would al-
low parents to use tax dollars to pay for schools of their choice. This
single move would break the government monopoly on education,
introduce real market competition into the system, and increase
participatory democracy by allowing consumers of education to
vote with their feet. In the education market today, school choice
is the clearest and most effective way to save those who've been left
behind—children of poverty.

REALITY CHECK

Charter schools, vouchers, privately run alternative schools, cyber
schools, and other schemes of that type have no relation to civil
or human rights whatsoever. There is no link between so-called
choice schools and ensuring equity or civil rights.

Ground zero for voucher schemes has been Milwaukee, the
poorest district in Wisconsin and a test case for the new privatizing
schemes. The Milwaukee case is glaring proof that the school-choice
scam has simply taken public money and increased inequity. The
Wisconsin Policy Research Institute, funded by big business, ush-
ered in a massive charter and voucher program in the early 1990s.
For twenty-five years, the state legislature has allowed tax dollars
to be channeled into private schools—schools that are virtually
unregulated—in the name of choice. The marketplace was supposed to drive school improvement, but between 1991 and 2015,
41 percent of schools (102 schools) set up to spend voucher money
failed. They didn't just do badly; they no longer exist.[3] An independent evaluation by Patrick Wolf of the University of Arkansas
found no academic improvement for students participating in the
Milwaukee or Washington, DC, voucher programs.[4] Political economist Gordon Lafer demonstrated in detail that these projects have
been driven by financial and ideological considerations, not by the
interests or needs of children and that by whatever measure, they
don't improve student experience or student outcomes.[5]

In 2016, delegates to the convention of the National Association for the Advancement of Colored People (NAACP) voted overwhelmingly for a complete moratorium on new charter school development, underlining and strengthening the organization's stance against charters, which dates back to 2010.

The NAACP resolution states plainly that the organization "opposes the privatization of public schools and/or public subsidizing or funding of for-profit or charter schools" and "calls for full funding and support of high quality free public education for all children." The resolution also opposes tax breaks to support charter schools and calls for new legislation to increase charter school transparency.[6]

Julian Vasquez Heilig, education chair of the California and Hawaii NAACP chapter that proposed the anti-charter resolution, argues that the goal of the "choice schemes" floated by the corporate reformers is not choice at all. The reformers' unvarnished aim is to replace public schools with privatized charter schools or to channel public money to private academies and parochial schools—exactly what's being done in US-occupied Puerto Rico. Public tax money designated to helping students learn becomes another profit center for the wealthy.

The earliest charters in the 1990s were proposed as community-based efforts to build deeper student engagement in schools, something the teachers' unions saw as laboratories for innovation.[7] Soon, however, social conservatives and private investors jumped on the opening for a chance to create unregulated publicly funded schools. They saw an opportunity to strike a blow against the powerful teachers' unions, as well as a chance to turn a profit with public money.

Though the charter school cheerleaders claim that choice has improved student achievement and gotten countless students into college as the first generation in their family to attend, deeper dives into the research have led to a refutation of these claims. As Gary

Miron, William Mathis, and Kevin Welner of the National Education Policy Center at the University of Colorado point out,

> [The] most rigorous study, and by far the most expensive, commissioned by the US Department of Education, . . . undertaken by Mathematica, examined a sample of oversubscribed (i.e., popular and thus presumably better on average) charter schools and compared students at those schools to students who were on the waiting list but did not get a place. This longitudinal study showed no overall effect for charter schools. Mathematica's large-scale study identified a large pool of students who applied for charter schools. It then compared charter school students who received a place with students who didn't and enrolled instead in their district school. The study found no overall difference between the two groups of students. It did find that urban charter school students did slightly better and suburban charter school students did slightly worse. The clear answer that appears repeatedly is that after controlling for student demographics, charter schools show test-score results at levels that are not meaningfully better or worse than district schools.[8]

It is well known that the private-charter proponents have attracted venture capital money, paid themselves enormous salaries, and done everything they could to game the system. Some of these schemes include pushing out students who are not true believers in their approach, thus assuring that only compliant students will be skimmed from communities. Moreover, many charter schools actively keep special education students outside their doors and limit services to students with special needs, often with policies that violate state and federal laws.[9]

The call for "choice" gestures toward freedom and democracy, compelling core values for most Americans. We can pick Dawn or Joy dish detergent; we can watch any of hundreds of television channels and choose which freeway to drive on, so why can't we pick schools? And won't the marketplace thus improve schools, as it has made better detergent? The problem is that schools are public institutions designed to educate all students, regardless of background or circumstance. Market choice has the same impact in education as it does in any other market—it creates a few winners alongside many losers, and it favors those with resources, social capital, and connections. Remember, in fact, that when Governor Orval Faubus of Arkansas and George Wallace of Alabama stood in schoolhouse doorways and declared that Black students would never be allowed inside, they were invoking choice. Choice was the watchword in the racist uprisings in Boston against busing for integration. In the public sphere, we need an ethic that recognizes the rights of all for equal access to resources and that supports a constitutional right to a quality education for all students. The segmented marketplace cannot deliver that; *it is designed to create winners and losers.*

The pro-choice crowd—led by corporate heavyweights from Bill Gates and the Koch brothers to Michael Bloomberg and the Walton family—offers no evidence that its approach delivers success and relies instead on the suspect argument that a separate, parallel school system for poor Black and Latinx students will allow for a great leap forward in learning and achievement. The Supreme Court famously ruled in 1954 against the nightmare of "separate but equal" schools, saying separate is inherently unequal, and yet the corporate reformers persist. Business knows better.

The NAACP called the business world's bluff. It argued that people of color know that when poor children are separated from the rich kids, they don't have access to the same quality programs and funding. The NAACP call for integration, not segregation, is based simply on the demand for equitable resources. It is a demand for justice, not optics.

When asked specifically if school integration was important, Peter Cunningham, an aide to former secretary of education Arne

Duncan and a well-known advocate of corporate reform, re-marked, "Maybe the fight's not worth it. It's a good thing; we all think integration is good. But it's been a long fight; we've had mid-dling success. At the same time, we have lots and lots of schools filled with kids of one race, one background, that are doing great. It's a good question."[10] Really? Perhaps the speaker was referring to well-resourced, all-white private schools for the children of the rich and powerful, or maybe one or two all-Black charter schools where administrators handpick the best and brightest students and refuse to educate those most in need. Evidence, please, and thank you.

Donald Trump wholeheartedly embraces school-choice poli-cies. He favors the aggressive expansion of charter schools, and he supports school vouchers and other schemes to put public money in the hands of private entrepreneurs. This should come as no sur-prise; after all, he ran a private education scam—Trump University.

The liberal corporate reform advocates—Cunningham, Dem-ocrats for Education Reform (DFER), and others—brood about charters becoming clearly identified with a right-wing attack on public education. The liberal columnist Jonathan Alter worried that the NAACP argument could gain serious traction: "If it be-comes a social justice movement, doesn't that in some ways let, for lack of a better word or expression, Diane Ravitch's argument win? Which is, 'don't blame any of us, don't focus on schools; if we don't solve poverty, nothing is going to get better.' Isn't there a danger of falling away from the focus on at least some responsibil-ity on schools?"[11]

What is "Diane Ravitch's argument" that has Alter so uneasy? The renowned researcher and former education official in the ad-ministrations of both Ronald Reagan and George H. W. Bush be-came a high-profile apostate, turning forcefully against charters and vouchers once the evidence demonstrated that her original hopes that "choice" would improve schools were not borne out in practice.

Ravitch charges the federal government with massive deception and with running a racket against the public. Her comprehensive catalogue of the bipartisan swindle is an inventory of infamy:

- dispensed billions of dollars to promote a dual school system of privately managed charter schools operating alongside public schools
- encouraged the rise of an aggressive privatization movement seeking to eliminate public education altogether in urban districts where residents have the least political power
- failed to call attention to the fraud and corruption rampant in the fledgling charter school initiatives or to curb charter schools run by for-profit non-educators or to insist on charter school accountability or to require charter schools to enroll the neediest children
- pushed states to evaluate teachers by the test scores of their students, which caused massive demoralization, plummeting enrollments in teacher education programs including Teach for America, and sky-rocketing early retirement rates among veteran educators
- openly opposed "forced integration," a coded phrase from the old segregationist lexicon, all the while bemoaning the rising resegregation of the schools
- remained silent as state after state attacked collective bargaining and due process for teachers
- did nothing in response to the explosion of voucher programs that transferred public funds to religious schools
- loosened the regulations on the Student Privacy Act permitting massive data mining and looked away as exploitative for-profit colleges preyed on military veterans and minorities, plunging students deep into debt
- supported absurdly brutal tests that most students failed, even young people in schools that send high percentages

of students to four-year colleges, and the failure rates have
predictably been highest among students who are English-
language learners, students with disabilities, and students
of color

· unleashed a mad frenzy of testing in classrooms across
the country, treating standardized test scores as the goal
of education rather than as a measure, and brushed over
the fact that the high-stakes testing regimen has done
nothing to produce positive outcomes regarding student
achievement.[12]

In contemporary school debates, the corporate reformers
kick equity to the curb in order to focus on "data" (or, really, on
a single piece of preferred and often manipulated data), and this
focus overshadows and obfuscates deeper issues. Corporate reformers back charter schools with cash and elaborate fund-raisers
and then promote faulty comparisons and false equivalences. In
Washington, DC, for example, athletic programs, arts initiatives,
building renovations, and performance pay for teachers at public charters were all privately financed. It's fine to give to a public
school program, but it's underhanded to compare a privately financed program with one that is underfunded and gets no outside
or corporate support. And more than that, it would be unethical to
ignore the fact that the public is responsible for providing full and
open access to a nonprofit system of local, community-based high-
quality public schools for all children and youth; that state and local governments are responsible to fund them fairly and to keep
them accountable to the public; and that the federal government
has a key role to play in terms of taking responsibility to assure access and equity. The heart of the matter is that public schools must
be our community and collective responsibility.

Education activists fought to ensure that the 2016 Democratic
National Convention education platform would set forth a positive
vision of what public schools should and could look like. This led

to a tilt away from policies of school privatization and standardized testing. Immediately, DFER president Shavar Jeffries criticized the platform for turning against corporate education reform.[13]

Pedro Noguera points out, "Charter schools are frequently not accountable. Indeed, they are stunningly opaque, more black boxes than transparent laboratories for education."[14] And more and more research has pointed to the failure of the charters to improve education for children and to the wholesale hijacking of public funds to line private pockets.

It's becoming increasingly difficult for charter and voucher supporters to claim that these reforms are in the interest of poor, Black, or Latinx children, or to peddle the fraudulent notion that their work promotes civil rights—too many of us can document how their choice plans actually violate them.

"Anyone Can Be a Teacher."

George Bernard Shaw may have said it first: "People who are able to do something well can do that thing for a living, while people who are not able to do anything that well make a living by teaching." Thus, Shaw spawned the phrase that's a staple in every discussion of teaching, whether at a cocktail party or a policy institute: "Those who can, do—those who can't, teach." In *Annie Hall*, Woody Allen added his signature comical twist: "Those who can't teach, teach gym."

Teaching is a second-order profession if it's a profession at all, and in any case, it just isn't very complicated or difficult—it's easily learned and quickly remediated. Moreover, if someone possesses expertise, or some worthwhile knowledge or experience that would benefit children and youth, transmitting it to students is a straightforward affair: just instruct the kids to take notes, recount what you know, and inform them about what they need to know—simple.

California governor Pete Wilson railed against teacher education as a waste of money, time, and talent, bemoaning "a system that wouldn't let George Schultz [former secretary of state] teach history, or let John Steinbeck or Amy Tan [novelists and California natives] teach English, or let Bill Walsh [retired football coach] teach gym in our public schools."[1] Furthermore, "why, when confronted with a dearth of qualified teachers of science and math, do we ignore the talent and experience of retired or out-of-work aerospace and military personnel?"

REALITY CHECK

Every year in Chicago (and many other school districts coast to coast), a civic association sponsors Teacher for a Day as a display of low-stakes "community service," a program that brings political and business leaders, athletes, professionals, well-known personalities, and anyone craving the optic of themselves smiling among a group of happy students of color into public school classrooms in order to shine a spotlight on teaching and build community support for public education. The local news seems to relish the event, typically highlighting celebrities visiting poorly resourced schools and neighborhoods. Local TV played clips in a recent year of the mayor, a CEO, and a professional football player echoing one another as they noted that the experience was "a lot of fun" and the students were "just terrific" and "a lot of fun to be with."

So, a popular image of teachers as experts sharing their knowledge meshes neatly with the notion that teachers are clerks conveying the expertise of others: in each case, teaching is the mechanical and direct transmission of information and knowledge from the smart ones into the upturned heads of the passive and less smart ones. We must simply tell teachers: here is the literary canon; here is the truth of history; here is the skill of reading. Teaching is the efficient delivery of bundles of "teacher proof" knowledge called curriculum, and one person can deliver it as well as anyone else.

This view of teaching as a simple transaction in which the wise transmit knowledge to the ignorant has led agencies and organizations on a determined search to find innovative ways to recruit young folks and move them quickly from college graduation into brief tours of duty in troubled classrooms. Fast-track teacher-preparation initiatives have proliferated across the country in a wide range of programs geared to attracting college graduates to teaching.

Teach for America (TFA) is the most prominent and celebrated effort to test the hypothesis that academically successful, "smarter" people can quickly become great teachers. TFA recruits come mostly from Ivy League and other elite colleges and are placed in schools after a boot camp-like summer training program that lasts for just a few weeks. The program was purposefully designed around a notion that teaching is easily learned and quickly remediated. Of course, these young recruits were not expected to reflect on the complex project of teaching but to focus instead on test scores and the practice of test preparation. TFA is a real-world experiment under advantageous conditions for its proponents, and it has a track record to examine and analyze.

Wendy Kopp conceived of Teach for America as a Peace Corps–type program of national service, tapping into the natural idealism of young people, and recruiting them to work for two years in underserved urban schools. She had never seen a city school up close nor visited an urban classroom, and yet when she committed a vision of her proposed project to paper for her senior thesis at Princeton in 1989, the idea exploded and she knew she was onto something big. She met with and quickly impressed a group of corporate CEOs and steadily raised substantial funds from Union Carbide, IBM, Xerox, AT&T, and Mobil. Before long, she was a media mega-star, and TFA was an extremely hot player in school-reform circles. She launched the project in 1990 with 384 recruits working in urban schools in six regions. Twenty-five years later, TFA boasts almost half a million alumni and 8,800 corps members working in fifty-two regions. Kopp has branded her efforts as an inheritor of the 1960s freedom struggle: "My generation is insisting upon educational opportunity for all Americans. This is our civil rights issue."[2]

The title of Kopp's memoir, *One Day, All Children*, is a direct reference to the Reverend Martin Luther King Jr.'s 1963 "I Have a Dream" speech. Undoubtedly most TFA recruits are idealistic, smart, and hardworking, motivated by an earnest desire to make a positive difference for disadvantaged kids and communities. Surely, many are drawn by the notion that they can contribute to the challenges of today by channeling the inspiring spirit of the civil rights movement.

The TFA approach is consistent and essentially unchanged in twenty-six years: convince graduates from Ivy League and other elite universities to commit two years to teaching in a low-income urban or rural school before resuming their march toward future careers in law or business, train them in a quick but intensive summer experience and require them to take courses while teaching, throw them into the most challenging classrooms in the country, and remind them that their commitment and passion and good intentions can overcome any obstacle. This approach rests on two powerful assumptions: first, young people with privileged backgrounds and elite educations will have a significant and immediate impact on the underprivileged students they'll be teaching for two years, and second, after they leave the corps, these same young people will have an even greater effect on society as they become leaders in their communities and continue to draw on their TFA experience as education-reform advocates.

By telling the recruits that their knowledge and skills are wonderful, and that the communities they are working in are dysfunctional, even pathological, TFA assembles and brings forth teachers who are discouraged from being reflective, who are disincentivized from getting to know the families of their students, and who are actually often quite remote from the young people themselves. Under these circumstances, it's possible for a TFA teacher to do their two years' time and never have their negative assumptions about the community challenged, to finish their stint and get high-fives for their courageous and sacrificing work. Well-trained teachers are squeezed out of schools in favor of the cheaper TFA teachers, and social inequity is not challenged. Indeed, it is exacerbated.

Stanford University's Linda Darling-Hammond led a six-year longitudinal research project in Houston public schools and found "no instance where uncertified Teach for America teachers performed as well as standard certified teachers of comparable experience levels teaching in similar settings."[3] Her conclusion was based on student standardized-test score results, which, while dubious from a range of perspectives, is the measure that TFA and corporate reformers prefer.

The critiques of TFA have come not just from educators but from alumni of the program itself.[4] A 2004 Mathematica study using the Iowa Test of Basic Skills and involving seventeen schools, one hundred classrooms, and nearly two thousand students, found that TFA teachers "had no substantial impact on the probability that students were retained in grade or assigned to summer school."[5] The control group for the TFA teachers in this study consisted of other teachers in the same schools and in the same grades—teachers with "substantially lower rates of certification and formal education training" than a nationally representative sample of teachers. In addition, the study said that many of the control group teachers had no student-teaching experience at all and were less prepared than the TFA recruits. This prompted Barbara Miner, a journalist who has written extensively about TFA, to wonder why the TFA people were promoting the study at all—what did it prove? Miner laughingly imagined how the satirical *Onion* might headline the results: *"Teach for America goes up against the worst teachers in the country—they're both awful!"*[6]

An extensive review of research on Teach for America in 2010 by Julian Heilig and Su Jin Jez concluded: "Thus, a simple answer to the question of TFA teachers' relative effectiveness cannot be conclusively drawn from the research; many factors are involved in any comparison. The lack of a consistent impact, however, should indicate to policy makers that TFA is likely not the panacea that will reduce disparities in educational outcomes."[7] *Non-Profit Quarterly* came to the same damning conclusion in 2015.[8]

TFA claims that, given its relatively small size, it has an outsized impact on improving schools. Its most famous alumni are surely influential: Michelle Rhee, former chancellor of the Washington, DC, public schools, and Mike Feinberg and David Levin, founders of the KIPP Schools, a charter network led by Wendy Kopp's husband, Richard Barth. TFA points to these and other alumni to say that an overwhelming majority continue to labor in "the field of education." That "field" turns out to be quite wide and essentially borderless: working with a nonprofit advocacy group, getting a job as a foundation officer, running for political office, studying for a graduate degree, becoming an associate in a law firm that does education work, plugging away as a journalist on the education beat for a local paper. TFA also claims that half of its alumni are teachers, but Barbara Miner challenges that conclusion, noting that the contention is based on self-reported data—in 2007, 57 percent of the alumni network responded, leaving 43 percent of the alumni unaccounted for.[9]

Further, the data only counts those who completed the two-year commitment, and so the alumni network doesn't include the dropouts—13 percent or higher. It's also unknown whether the alumni who responded to the survey were a year or two beyond their initial commitment and more likely, then, to be in graduate school, teaching for a third year, or older alumni who had moved on to other careers. Miner ran the numbers more carefully and concluded, "The only thing one can say with certainty is that [in 2007] at least 16.6 percent of those recruited by Teach for America were teaching in a K–12 setting beyond their two-year commitment." A modest claim, indeed.

In 2010, a Stanford University study found that TFA alumni had lower rates of civic involvement than college graduates who'd been accepted by TFA but declined to join and lower rates than those who'd dropped out before their two years were completed.[10] So the Teach for America experience fails to support the claim that anyone can teach well, or that recruiting the "best" will result in quick school improvement, or that replacing experienced career teachers from the most demanding classrooms with a steady parade of short-timers specifically in urban and low-income areas—all "reforms" that the schools of the privileged manage to avoid—does anything to improve education for each and for all. The TFA experience challenges the claim that teaching is easily learned, and it undermines the idea that a two-year trip into an underserved area will lead to a lifetime of good work.

Indeed, it is possible and even inevitable that a privileged TFA recruit will go into Black and Brown communities, work for two years, and never have to question or reevaluate their negative assumptions about the community. They may be appalled (and frightened) by the students whose reality is so far from theirs. With no encouragement for reflection, with no education in the social foundations of education, they can return to law school or business school without ever understanding or knowing the communities they briefly ventured into. The *Onion* satirizes the whole idea of inner-city teaching as a heartening if brief tourist destination for recent college graduates in one of its "Point/Counterpoint" features: in the first photo, a perfectly privileged young woman smiles happily into the camera and the headline announces "My Year Volunteering as a Teacher Helped Educate a New Generation of Underprivileged Kids;" the Counterpoint is represented by an exasperated-looking fourth grader of color asking, "Can we please, just once, have a real teacher?"[11] Critics sometimes call TFA "Teach for Awhile."

The underlying idea driving TFA (and many other initiatives and programs including KIPP) is this: smart, good-hearted, and well-intentioned individuals are best positioned to solve difficult problems, and they don't need to work in concert with or consult the people who will be impacted by their interventions. More than TFA's missed targets or failed goals, more than its public relations efforts and inflated claims, this may be its most troubling legacy. This approach is not only antidemocratic and profoundly elitist; it has also failed repeatedly as a lever for social change.

Dilettantes and tourists will not solve the problems of public schools. It will take a deeper level of respect and engagement. In reality, problems in a democracy are best solved by more—not less—participation, as well as deeper and longer-term commitments, not drop-in charity. And the people with the problems are also the people who have the solutions. It takes a deeper level of engagement and struggle to unlock and build lasting results.

Teacher preparation—if accorded the attention it deserves—would be much more like medical preparation. In medicine, novices spend some years in coursework and background studies followed by years as interns, learning on the job next to experienced professionals. If we would commit the resources necessary for such preparation, certainly new teachers would be ready to go. As it is, teachers carry out their clinical practice while alone in the classroom, building the airplane while they fly it.

No first-year teacher gets it all right, or even mostly right. Take an activity such as group work, for instance. Dozens of considerations call out for attention: the dispositions and skills of each student, the social emotional architecture of the current group, the ways to engage each participant, the outcomes and products that will elicit commitment and pride from the students. Only after three, four, or five years in the classroom will a teacher have this down, or at lease provisionally ready. Good teacher-education programs recognize this and provide both social foundations and curriculum and instruction training; they also provide guided fieldwork that develops teachers as reflective practitioners, able to enter those first years with the tools to grow and develop, to learn and create, along the way.

The skills, dispositions, and qualities that make up an emerging teacher persona are all missing in the quickie teacher-preparation alternative pathways. The one thing that characterizes a solid, effective teacher is a commitment not only to the subject matter but also to motivating students, even discouraged or resistant students, to learn. If a teacher drops that responsibility and decides to "just teach" the material and fail those who don't step up and succeed, he has an easy job. But good teachers, and most teachers, claw and agonize and struggle through the weeks and months because they are determined to turn on and engage all students. Only through a deep teacher-preparation process will they be able to begin to do this work effectively.

"Teachers Follow Popular Fads and Political Correctness Rather Than Teaching the Basics."

Today, teachers refuse to teach the basics. Some of them are simply not up to the task, and some aren't bright enough or up-to-date enough to teach the essential subject matters. They don't focus their efforts on the skills and facts that are the necessary building blocks for future learning; they don't set strict standards; they don't demand proficiency or even minimal competency. Why? Glenn Beck offers a partial answer: "Teachers are too frustrated or too lazy or unmotivated to really get through to our kids, or they're too PC. . . . [They] correct the homework in purple ink because, you know, red may damage our kids."[1]

Teachers are so caught up in being politically correct and avoiding any possible misstep onto a student's extremely delicate toes that they won't even touch something as necessary and straightforward as the story of Columbus. Oh, dear, what if the Native Americans are offended? Better to teach "critical thinking," "personal essay writing," "interpretive history," "neofuturist art expressionism," or a thousand other airy and meaningless frivolities and distractions—anything to avoid teaching the basics and the facts.

A curriculum of facts is on order—uncontested and measurable, outside the purview of politically correct interpretations, inarguable and beyond dialogue or debate. Legislatures and school boards must move more decisively to stipulate the objective skills and knowledge students must obtain, and what teachers must teach. Students must more regularly be measured with a clear set of standards on precisely what they know and are able to do, and teachers must be held accountable for what students know and are able to do.

REALITY CHECK

In 2006, Florida passed the Florida Education Omnibus Bill, stipulating that "American history shall be viewed as factual, not as constructed, shall be viewed as knowable, teachable, and testable."[2] The bill called for an emphasis on the "teaching of facts"— facts and only facts will be permitted by the legislators to enter the schoolhouses of Florida; facts and only facts will guide instruction about, for example, the "period of discovery."

The Arizona legislature passed a law in 2008 called SB 1108 to deny state funding to schools whose courses "denigrate American values and the teachings of Western civilization" and teaching practices that "overtly encourage dissent" from those values, including democracy, capitalism, pluralism, and religious tolerance.[3] Schools are required to submit teaching materials to the state superintendent of public instruction, who can withhold state aid from districts that break the law. Another section of the bill bars public schools, community colleges, and public universities from allowing organizations to operate on campus if they are "based in whole or in part on race-based criteria."

In 2010, the Arizona legislature passed HB 2281, empowering the Arizona state superintendent of public instruction to fine a school district 10 percent of its state funding per month if classes are deemed to display any of these criteria:

1. Promote the overthrow of the United States government.
2. Promote resentment toward a race or class of people.
3. Are designed primarily for pupils of a particular ethnic group.
4. Advocate ethnic solidarity instead of the treatment of pupils as individuals.[4]

The Arizona legislation aims to counter local initiatives like the Mexican American Studies (MAS) Program in the Tucson Unified School District, which the legislators determined promoted "un-American" programs, racial separatism, and the overthrow of the US government.[5]

And in 2015, Wisconsin governor Scott Walker proposed to change the century-old mission of the University of Wisconsin system, known from the start as the Wisconsin Idea, by removing words that instructed the university to "search for truth" and "improve the human condition"—vague and open to any number of constructions, conflicts, contradictions, and interpretations—and replace them with "meet the state's workforce needs."[6]

Also, in a 2015 talk about the Common Core state standards, David Coleman, head of the College Board, said that teaching high school students personal-essay writing—the explanation of an opinion or the development of a personal narrative—was not particularly important. Students engaged in searching and questioning was beside the point, Coleman explained, and largely irrelevant to the task of forging young people into workforce-oriented adults. "People really don't give a shit about what you feel or what you think," he said.[7]

At the same time, the College Board revised its guidelines for teaching Advanced Placement History, which has broad influence in high school history courses. The concept of "manifest destiny" has become more benign in the retelling; the phrase "American exceptionalism" is used for the first time; and violence against Native Americans is downplayed.[8] Nevertheless, the Republican National Committee urged Congress to stop funding the College Board, saying it "emphasizes negative aspects of our nation's history while omitting or minimizing positive aspects."[9]

What counts as "subject matter" and "teachable facts," of course, depends. Teaching the "age of discovery" offers a clarifying example: Whose facts exactly? The facts of a Genovese adventurer in the pay of Spanish royalty; the facts of the "discovered" themselves with their complex stories of tribal rivalries, resistance, and accommodation; the facts of the First Nations residents overwhelmed, murdered, and enslaved; or a range of other facts and angles of regard altogether? Is the point to legislate a pep rally for Christopher Columbus—one particular *constructed* explanation and analysis of events and circumstances—or is the point to teach students a deeper lesson about what it means to be free people?

What percentage of people in the world are in the United States? About 4.4 percent.[10] That's a fact. Is it a fact worth knowing? Is it worth knowing what percentage of prisoners in the world are in the United States? Well, just in case it is, the figure is about 25 percent of the world's prisoners, more prisoners than in any other nation, and it represents a higher rate of incarceration than any other country—about 0.7 percent of the US population. According to the US Bureau of Justice Statistics, 2,220,300 adults were incarcerated in US federal and state prisons and county jails in 2013, along with 54,148 young people in "juvenile detention" and another 4,751,400 adults on probation or parole—that adds up to 2.2 percent of the US population.[11] Those are interesting facts, provocative and potentially meaningful. Should they be taught? Are they worthy of inquiry and debate?

Does the US have the longest life expectancy of any country on earth? Is that worth knowing? Here are the top twenty-five nations in the world in terms of life expectancy, in order, according to the World Health Organization: Japan, Spain, Andorra, Australia, Switzerland, Italy, Singapore, San Marino, Canada, Cyprus, France, Iceland, Israel, Luxembourg, Monaco, New Zealand, Norway, Sweden, Republic of Korea, Finland, Portugal, Ireland, Malta, Netherlands, United Kingdom.[12] Hmmmm? Where's the United States?

Should German schools teach how many people Germany killed in World War II?

Yes, of course. They should teach the facts: World War II, including war-related diseases and famines, killed some 80 million people.[13] Excluding some 30 million killed in Asia, the total comes down to 50 million. Excluding some 6 million Germans and Austrians and a half million Italians as having been killed by the Allies (though of course also by their own governments) brings the total down to 43.5 million. Of those, some 30 million were killed as civilians in the course of the war, including from war-related diseases and famines—the majority of them from the Soviet Union. The other 13 million were killed in German camps, including 6 million Jews, 3 million Soviet prisoners of war, 2 million Soviet civilians, 1 million Polish civilians, 1 million Yugoslav civilians, 200,000 Roma, and thousands of political prisoners, homosexuals, and people with mental or physical disabilities.[14] That's a lot of facts, but, yes, those troubling facts should be taught. And none are above or beyond analysis and critical inquiry.

Should US schools teach kids how many people the United States killed in wars on Native Americans, in the Philippines, in Vietnam, or in Iraq? Why not? Perhaps the same standard should apply: The biggest cause of death among Native Americans in the colonies that would become the United States was the spread of diseases brought by European people and their animals. At least ten million Native Americans died in the earliest years of colonization. From those earliest years up to the twentieth century, the intentional eradication of the remaining Native Americans was openly pursued by many politicians and European Americans, including through the intentional spreading of disease, starvation, ethnic cleansing, and violent murder. Certainly tens of thousands and probably hundreds of thousands of Native Americans were killed in wars waged by the United States. The Philippines, under attack by the United States, saw 20,000 combatants killed, plus 200,000 to 1.5 million civilians dead from violence and diseases, including cholera.[15] Over fifteen years, by some estimates, US occupying forces, together with disease, killed more than 1.5 million civilians in the Philippines, out of a population of 6 to 7 million—21 percent of its population.[16] There were an estimated 3.8 million violent war deaths, combat and civilian, north and south, during the years of US involvement in Vietnam. Between March 2003 and August 2007, there were 1.2 million violent deaths of Iraqi civilians in Iraq.

Facts. Just the facts.

Obviously, there's so much more to dive into and understand. The facts above are the start not the end of the matter. Free people learn how to investigate and interrogate the world, how to do research and discuss opinions, and how to form their own ideas based on evidence and argument. Free people deploy debate and dialogue, invoke independent inquiry and firsthand research, and insist on the right to think for themselves. They reject all dogmas and approach any claims with skepticism. All of this and more could easily be sacrificed in a scramble to paint a prettified picture of an intensely complex history in the name of "just the facts." Curriculum is complex, dynamic, and dependent on expanding modes of inquiry and on a teacher's, as well as the students', propulsive questions.

Further, dissent is an essential, foundational American value, etched into our consciousness from day one, and American history is nothing if not a long, unfolding story of defiance and refusal, protest and resistance, from the revolutionaries of 1776 onward: abolitionists, suffragists, anarchists, labor pioneers, civil rights and Black Power warriors, peace and environmental activists, feminists, heroes and sheroes and queeroes, Wounded Knee, Occupy, Standing Rock, Black Lives Matter! Wherever you look and whatever period you examine, questioning authority and taking it to the streets is as American as cherry pie, an apple-core American value, and the very engine of forward progress—that's a fact.

Charles Dickens's *Hard Times* offers a memorable portrayal of two school folks in Victorian England at the dawn of the contested argument about fact as the basis of a sound education: the aptly named Mr. Gradgrind, the owner of a school in an industrial city, and Mr. M'Choakumchild, his hired schoolmaster. Here, Gradgrind lectures M'Choakumchild on his philosophical orientation and a few of the finer points of curriculum and instruction:

> "Now, what I want is, Facts. Teach these boys and girls nothing but Facts. Facts alone are wanted in life. Plant nothing else, and root out everything else. You can only form the minds of reasoning animals upon Facts: nothing else will ever be of any service to them. This is the principle on which I bring up my own children, and this is the principle on which I bring up these children. Stick to Facts, Sir!" . . .
>
> The speaker, and the schoolmaster . . . swept with their eyes the inclined plane of little vessels then and there arranged in order, ready to have imperial gallons of facts poured into them until they were full to the brim.[17]

To deepen and illustrate his argument Gradgrind interrogates "girl number twenty" and, discovering that her father is a horseman, asks her to define a horse. When she stumbles, Gradgrind pounces: "Girl number twenty unable to define a horse! . . . Girl number twenty possessed of no facts, in reference to one of the commonest of animals!" He turns to a boy who obediently stands and recites: "Quadruped. Graminivorous. Forty teeth, namely twenty-four grinders, four eye-teeth, and twelve incisive. . . ." And on and on, at the end of which Gradgrind nods approvingly and notes, "Now girl number twenty, you know what a horse is."

Girl number twenty—Sissy Jupe by name—indeed knows quite a lot about horses, of course, and a number of other things as well. She's a three-dimensional person with agency and a mind and a spirit, a heart and a body, experiences and hopes and dreams just like every other human being. She has compassion for others and a fine sense of aesthetics, and she has a broad imagination, which she calls her "Fancy," all qualities Gradgrind finds irrelevant or repellant. Facts, Sir!

In these opening chapters (one appropriately called "Murdering the Innocents"), Dickens evokes the broad outlines of autocratic classrooms everywhere. He offers a kind of meditation on the power of these men of facts-without-feeling to crush or twist natural human dispositions and sympathies. Monarchies, of course, demand unquestioning allegiance first and foremost, whereas democracies, at least theoretically, are built on the active engagement and participation of free and enlightened people. And because schools no matter where or when are always mirror and window onto whatever social order creates and sustains them, we can easily imagine the society that the above-mentioned "imperial gallons of facts" are meant to sustain and reproduce. What's harder to reconcile is an inescapable feeling that Dickens's despotic classroom, with its imperious reasoning and its brute logic, is a bit too close for comfort.

Autocratic education disrupts what we know about human learning—from birth onward—and the natural human drive to explore, question, investigate, make sense, and become competent. It also undermines the foundation of being an educated person in a free and democratic society. Classrooms for free people note and even dive into contradictions. Take, for example, the following:

Greg Smith, a young, white high school history teacher in a Chicago public school, recently offered a standard lesson on the landmark Supreme Court case *Brown v. Board of Education*. The classroom was made up of twenty-four African American students and seven Latinx students. The lesson was taken from a textbook, and it pointedly illustrated our great upward evolution as a nation. A student who had appeared to be uninterested and inattentive spoke up suddenly, smiling broadly—class clown–style—as he forcefully addressed the teacher: "So, Mr. Smith, our class here against the law, right? We're breaking the law here in this segregated school. So can I call the cops?" Everyone yelped with laughter as the disruptive student beamed, pleased to be the center of attention and satisfied that he'd nailed an undeniable friction and a naked fiction: here was a segregated classroom in a segregated school in a country that had outlawed school segregation decades ago. *Brown* as myth and legend.

What should the teacher do? What do the facts demand? Obedience to a lie? Conformity and deference?

A gifted high school teacher in Baltimore city named Jay Gillen, who's found himself in similar territory again and again, has outlined a range of responses that might occur to any teacher who tries to teach the standard and expected *Brown v. Board of Education* lesson in a racially segregated space: patriotic ("Segregated schools no longer exist in America. This country is great."); ironic ("I have to mouth this official doctrine, but we all understand this doctrine is a lie."); devoted ("We must continue . . . making the promise of *Brown* more real in the coming decades."); moralizing ("You students of color should appreciate the advances that have been made by taking advantage of the opportunities offered to you to receive an education."); objective ("The . . . ruling was read May 17, 1954. Remember that for the test."); and Black nationalist ("We're better off in this segregated space.").[18] Gillen's list is far from exhaustive, but it powerfully lays bare some of the contradictions embedded in *Brown*.

It doesn't take perceptive young people any time at all to conclude that the lessons they're required to ingest at school are often half-truths, deceptions, misinformation, and outright lies—teachers lie, parents lie, and, in fact, the whole edifice of adult society lies incessantly. Many students choose to submit to the empire of deception, concluding that it's simply the price of the ticket; they wink at the massive hoax, promise to keep quiet and go along, and then pick up their rewards by-and-by. Many other students go in the opposite direction: their insights lead them to insurgent actions and gestures and styles, performances of self-affirmation, and hard-nosed refusals of complicity—flat-out rejections of a world that is determinedly not interested in their aspirations, perceptions, or insights. Schools, these students conclude, are asking them to discount their immediate experiences and their direct interpretations—and that proves to be a bridge too far.

There's a genre of jokes that all end with the same punch line: in one version, a man comes home unannounced and unexpectedly, sees his partner in the intimate embrace of another, and explodes in accusation. The accused looks up indignantly and says: "Who are you going to believe: Me? Or your own lying eyes?" Kids get it viscerally: schools are asking them to ignore their immediate experiences and their direct interpretations—to discount their own lying eyes. Who are you going to believe?

Too many schools and classrooms run along on the rails of indoctrination and propaganda: the hype that the curriculum is settled and complete, and the spin about children and youth who are regularly thingified—turned into objects—mistrusted and controlled, subjected to an alphabet soup of negative labels ("LD," or learning disabled, "BD," or behavior disorder, "EMH," or emotionally/mentally handicapped) that are putatively accurate and telling, and defined as lacking in many of the essential qualities that make one fully human. This cries out for re-imagination and resistance, rethinking and rebuilding.

In a free society, education must be public and democratic—these elements are essential to the creation of common spaces and cultures of community. The right to a free and public education, for example, is enshrined in every state constitution in the United States, a prestigious standing not granted other aspects we might include in our sense of life, liberty, and the pursuit of happiness—for example, housing, employment, or health care. The idea of free public schools has been such a fundamental aspect of democracy, even our limited version of democracy, that few have challenged it. But the trend in authoritarian education is toward utilitarian goals, the reduction of education to private businesses, profit-making projects aimed at narrow skill training.

Where do we see examples of nonauthoritarian schools, schools where student engagement is central to the design? Where might we find a curriculum of debate, deep inquiry, and history as contended space?

We know how to teach children well—the social science and the research are in—but in the United States (as in most places in the world), we do so unequally. Where do we find small classrooms providing opportunities for genuinely close relationships among teachers and students; an environment that provides a wide range of entry points into learning, including a full arts program, a focus on deep and critical thinking and authentic reasoning, as opposed to conventional thinking or rote parroting of the facts; the promotion of teachers who are intellectually grounded, compassionate and caring, well-rested and adequately compensated—all characteristics of good schools? Where do we find dazzling facilities and state-of-the-art materials, curricula that encourage engaged thinking and active curiosity, and great outcomes for students that are both anticipated and admirable? These schools are clustered in well-off communities where people have the economic/political capital to have them built, and where money is disproportionately showered on the already privileged. So we know what's possible, and we also know where it's likely (and where it is unlikely) to be brought to life in practice.

A visitor from Mars might conclude that we have a rather cynical policy regarding children, and it can be summed up quite simply: choose the right parents! That's it: if you choose the right parents, you'll have access to good food and excellent health care, adequate housing and well-resourced schools, police who act like public safety officials rather than an occupying army, clean air and sound neighborhoods, and decent recreational opportunities. If you pick the wrong parents, well . . . sorry. Bad idea. You're on your own.

Ultimately, the charge against social justice education, against teaching that is "politically correct" is a cover to attack deep, student-centered teaching, either implicitly or explicitly. It suggests that any teaching that involves inquiry, creativity, and open-ended design is dangerously subversive. The struggle is not between

PC teaching and objectivity; it is between generative, democratic education and authoritarian, single-note instruction. While such deep, exploratory education is always provided to the elite in the best private schools, such a pedagogy is considered dangerous if it is provided to the great unwashed masses.

"TEACHER ACTIVISTS
ARE TROUBLEMAKERS."

Good teachers never muddy the water by bringing their personal politics into school. They should not be social workers or activists. Teachers need to stick to imparting knowledge of the subject matter. Future teachers should just learn methods and focus on practice; no more of this feel-good stuff like values, emotions, or theory—student achievement should be their primary concern.

Consider the problems created for the young Black students in Jenna Lee-Walker's classroom at New York City's High School for Arts, Imagination, and Inquiry. Lee-Walker took it upon herself to create a curricular unit about the Central Park Five—young Black and Latinx men who spent their teenage years in prison after they had confessed under duress to a violent rape that they didn't commit. After more than a decade in prison, they were cleared on DNA evidence and the late confession of the actual perpetrator. The students would likely identify with the young men, get "riled up," and then look to Lee-Walker to help them process their insights and feelings—something she had neither the time nor the skill set to do. OK, she was teaching some factual material, true, but she was simultaneously and clearly spinning an activist agenda, and she could have taught better and more useful lessons without the controversy and all the drama.

It's irresponsible and reckless for teachers to upset their students, to distract them from the work at hand, and to undermine and distort the classroom learning environment with their personal political agendas and so-called "social justice" teaching.

Teacher activists are troublemakers. When they bring their activist politics into their teaching, they should be fired, as Jenna Lee-Walker was.[1]

REALITY CHECK

Galileo Galilei, the "father" of astronomy and physics, or of modern science itself, depending on who's summing up his life and contribution, is also the father of teacher activism. Galileo was born in Florence in the middle of the sixteenth century, and as a mathematician, engineer, philosopher, astronomer, and physicist, he played a leading role in the scientific revolutions rocking the world during the Renaissance.

In Bertolt Brecht's play about Galileo, the great astronomer sets forth into a world dominated by a mighty church and an authoritarian power: "The cities are narrow and so are the brains," he declares recklessly, and intoxicated with his own insights, Galileo finds himself propelled toward revolution.[2] Not only do his radical discoveries about the movement of the stars free them from the "crystal vault," which received truth insistently claimed fastened them to the sky, but his insights suggest something far more dangerous: that we humans, too, are embarked on a great voyage, that we are also free and without the easy support that dogma provides. Here, Galileo raises the stakes with his activism and risks taking on the establishment in the realm of its own authority—and the powers of church and state strike back fiercely. Like Jenna Lee-Walker, this activist teacher needed to be stopped cold. And he was.

Under the exquisite pressure of the Inquisition, Galileo denounced his discoveries—things he knew to be true—and was welcomed back into the church and the ranks of the faithful, but he was exiled from humanity by his own conforming but dishonest word. In Brecht's play, a disillusioned former student confronts the great scientist in the street: "Many on all sides followed you . . . believing that you stood, not only for a particular view of the movement of the stars, but even more for the liberty of teaching—in all fields. Not then for any particular thoughts, but for the right to think at all. Which is in dispute."

There it is. Activist teachers insist on the liberty of teaching and *the right to think at all*, and they show their students by example why it matters and how it's done. The line between commitment, advocacy, and activism is a wobbly one at best. It's a contested and explosive space, and it's surely in play today—activist teachers uphold the right to talk to whomever you please, the right to read and to wonder, the right to pursue an argument into uncharted spaces, the right to challenge the state or the church or any other orthodoxy in the public square. The right to think at all.

Too often science is taught as something flat and formidable, but science is never an absolute set of certainties. Effective science teaching—activist teaching—frees students from the crystal vault, engages their curiosity and creativity, and encourages them to dive in and sail off on their own voyages of discovery and surprise. Each step in scientific inquiry comes to an incomplete and tentative conclusion that is still, in some important sense, up in the air, leading typically to next questions: What next? What else? Why does it matter?

"Science is a great and worthy mistress," W. E. B. Du Bois wrote, "but there is one greater and that is Humanity which science serves."[3] True, and science is fundamentally subversive—it demands free inquiry, a spirit of skepticism and doubt, a curious disposition of mind, humility, nuance, and a reliance on evidence. Meanings about the world and how it operates are constructed differently in different cultures and the drive for science education should not become license to do violence to the delightful and multiple lenses through which our world can be approached. Science is always queering the common sense by asking the next question, and the next. Science never stands still, and we might ask if science isn't, after all, by its nature political and activist. The answer is yes, both historically and right now.

The accepted science of any particular moment proves to be incomplete and often incorrect. The dogma of Galileo's time, of course, but more recently the pseudoscience of eugenics, promoted in the early twentieth century by the great lights of the Progressive Era. Pursuing their social improvement project, these scientists applied an interpretation of Darwinian theory to suggest that there were provable lower and higher classes and categories of human beings and that, indeed, social policy and law should give "natural selection" an assist, limiting immigration of people from Africa and Asia and curtailing the births of African Americans, Jews, and others they categorized as "idiots" or "morons" or "imbeciles." Eugenics perpetrated discrimination and exploitation in the United States and was adopted by the Nazis in Germany as justification for promoting a "master race" and engineering the Holocaust.

Renowned theoretical physicist Freeman Dyson argues that science is a human activity, not just a set of settled facts. Indeed, science and math are also humanities—they are systems of analysis constructed by humans and changing with every generation. Science is an art form, not a rigid method. He writes:

> Science is not governed by the rules of Western philosophy or Western methodology. Science is an alliance of free spirits in all cultures, rebelling against the local tyranny that each culture imposes on its children. Insofar as I am a scientist, my vision of the universe is not reductionist or anti-reductionist. I have no use for Western-isms of any kind. I feel myself . . . on the "Immense Journey" of the paleontologist Loren Eiseley, a journey that is far longer than the history of nations and philosophies, longer even than the history of our species. . . . I was lucky to be introduced to science at school as a subversive activity of the younger boys. We organized the Science Society as an act of rebellion against compulsory Latin and compulsory football. We should try to introduce our children to science today as a rebellion against poverty and ugliness and militarism and economic injustice.[4]

Good teaching unsettles the questions and invites authentic inquiry. And yes, that has an activist edge. Powerful science and math education does not divorce numerical processes from the social context they live within. Deep learning happens when students work together to solve problems, often inventing the processes or rules necessary to solve those problems.

There is a fundamental incompatibility between the kind of faith in their own infallibility —their hallucinatory megalomania— that too many government leaders and members of the political class seem to harbor, and the practice of scientific inquiry. Politicians tell us that activism and teaching must be separated. In truth, they must be integrated, for they are the same thing.

"Activism" gets a bad rap in our society, and so do the teachers who take it seriously. Any mention of the word conjures vivid images of conflict or chaos, and many perceive that as somehow disconnected from the work of schools. In truth, however, schools in the United States have always served specific public goals that teachers are expected to be instrumental in embracing, enacting, and ensuring. These goals can be broken down into three broad categories: political, social, and economic.

Teachers are asked to induct the young into the polity and the larger democratic order, to prepare them to be actors and leaders in a free society. Teachers are also tasked with cultivating a sense of responsibility and participation in their students, and they are responsible to prepare students for the world of work or a career. Teacher activists can embrace these universal goals in unique ways and can work toward socially just transformational change inside and outside of the classroom. The politics of transformational change require challenging dominant interests and the beliefs and practices that sustain unjust power in everyday life. This change is not bound to or defined by the images of chaotic rabble-rousing demonstrations that the word "activist" may invoke in some. Instead, teacher activists are charged with being politically astute educators. Their work calls them to contribute to equity in outcomes for students, schools, and the wider community in concrete as well as metamorphic ways. An activist orientation develops when educators begin to understand their practices and themselves as responsible and vital participants in relationship to the dynamic society in which they live and work.

Yet the label invites discomfort for teachers who proclaim the title and for those who witness these proclamations. Teachers, and those who come to know and love teachers, often feel more comfortable with the other formal and informal roles teachers take on—mentor, parent, guide on the side, sage on the stage, and counselor. In the current era of standardization, accountability, and corporate-style schooling, the word "activist" often triggers an accelerated heartbeat and an audible sigh. Because of these reactions, teacher activists often find themselves on the defensive with colleagues or supervisors for paying too much attention to happenings outside the classroom, presumably at the expense of what's going on inside it.

Despite the grumblings, teacher activists forge ahead, relying on their understandings of the inextricable nature of inside/outside class occurrences and the interplay of their richness to add real-world context for teaching and authentic learning. Politicians and policy makers may claim that teacher activists proselytize or that teacher activists are too radical, too political. The reality is that there are no politically neutral schools nor any entirely objective and completely detached teachers—there never could be and there never should be. Teaching is a human activity, embedded in social beings and in life itself; teachers who think they are striking a neutral pose are too often unconsciously or implicitly supporting the status quo. Those teachers should name and claim that stance and defend it if they choose. Teachers who question or criticize the way things are in this or that realm should also claim that space and defend their questioning and criticizing.

In 2015 and 2016, New York City public school teachers were pressed by administrators to remain silent about the impact of high-stakes testing on schools, teachers, and students. In the face of the massive, parent-led Opt-Out movement in New York City, administrators told teachers they did not have the right to speak up about the testing regime's value, or lack of value. But parent and teacher activists continued to speak up and act out, and two results are noteworthy: the state shortened the exams, removed time limits, and agreed to suspend the practice of evaluating teachers based on student test scores. Then, the newly elected state education chancellor, Betty Rosa, came out in support of the Opt-Out movement, noting that if she had school-age children, she would refuse to have them tested. Thank you, Chancellor, and thank you, teacher activists!

The election of Donald Trump in 2016 made speaking up even more urgent, as many urban students are immigrants and/or Muslim and have concerns for themselves and their families based on the president's xenophobic and racist statements. Class discussion and activist options make these issues real and solutions actionable.

Teacher activists draw on many frameworks—including multiculturalism, critical theories, theories of care, spirituality and love, multidimensional ethical theory, theories of participatory democracy, antiracism, and anti-oppressive education—to make sense of and reconcile the duality of their lives and work. Education scholars Michael Dantley and Linda Tillman synthesize these theoretical lenses with five specific characteristics that clarify the definition, application, and requirements of teachers as activists: (1) a consciousness of the broader social, cultural, and political contexts of schools; (2) a critique of the marginalizing behaviors and predispositions of schools and their leadership; (3) a commitment to the more genuine enactment of democratic principles in schools; (4) a moral obligation to articulate a counter vision or narrative of hope regarding education; and (5) a determination to move from rhetoric to civil rights action.[5] Teacher activists pursue social justice.

Teacher activists are compelled to engage issues on the basis of a principle that Edward Said argues must be assumed to be universal: "that all human beings are entitled to expect decent standards of behavior concerning freedom and justice from worldly powers or nations, and that deliberate or inadvertent violations of these standards need to be testified and fought against courageously."[6] There are no hard and fast rules to follow in expressing this commitment—in either overt or less recognizable ways. But teacher activists take on a responsibility, according to Said, "to raise embarrassing questions, to confront orthodoxy and dogma (rather than to produce them), to be someone who cannot easily be co-opted by governments or corporations, and whose *raison d'etre* is to represent all those people and issues that are routinely forgotten or swept under the rug." Said argues for someone who is "neither a pacifier nor a consensus-builder, but someone whose whole being is staked on a critical . . . sense of being unwilling to accept easy formulas, or ready-made clichés, or the smooth, ever-so-accommodating confirmations of what the powerful or conventional have to say, and what they do." This unwillingness to accede cannot be simply a passive shrug or a cynical sigh; it involves, as well, publicly staking out a space of refusal. The core of activist teaching and inquiry must be human knowledge and human freedom, both enlightenment and emancipation.

This fulcrum is key for engaged teachers, although it in no way lays out a neat road forward—choose the way of opposition and you do not inherit a set of ready-made slogans or a nifty, easy-fit party line. There are no certainties—and for some this might prove difficult, perhaps even fatal—nor any gods whatsoever who can be called upon to ease specific, personal responsibility, to settle things once and for all.

Activist teachers are out there on their own, with minds and hearts, an ability to empathize, to touch and to feel, to recognize humanity in its many unexpected postures, to construct standards of truth about human suffering that must be upheld despite everything. "Real intellectuals," including teachers, Said writes, "are never more themselves than when, moved by metaphysical passion and disinterested principles of justice and truth, denounce corruption, defend the weak, defy imperfect or oppressive authority." Said is uninterested in allying with the victors and the rulers, whose very stability he sees as a kind of "state of emergency" for the less fortunate; he chooses instead to account for "the experience of subordination itself, as well as the memory of forgotten voices and persons."

Activist teachers maintain a kind of doubleness—something akin to Du Bois's double consciousness, in which African Americans are compelled to see society and the world both as Americans *and* as Black people, this duality being a synthesis and, therefore, greater than either perspective alone. Teachers who embrace activism are both insiders and outsiders, participants in the fullness of social life but simultaneously removed from and slightly askance to any settled associations. They must cultivate, then, a state of steady alertness in order to speak the unwelcome truth—as they understand it—to power.

This does not mean that activist teachers are required to be, in Said's term, whiny "humorless complainers" like Cassandra—the character from Greek mythology who, Said points out, was not only unpleasant in her righteous prophesying but also unheard. It means, rather, that they work at "scouring alternative sources, exhuming buried documents, reviving forgotten (or abandoned) histories and peoples." This, for Said, can be "a lonely condition, yes, but it is always a better one than a gregarious tolerance for the way things are."

We live in a time when the assault on disadvantaged communities is particularly harsh but at the same time gallingly obfuscated. Access to adequate resources and decent facilities, to relevant curricula, to opportunities to reflect on and to think critically about the world is unevenly distributed along predictable lines of class and color. Further, a movement to dismantle public schools under the rubric of "standards and accountability" is in place and gaining momentum. This is the moment when teachers have to choose who to be and how to act.

However teacher activism is understood, in a dynamic, contested, and troubled world—a place as imperfect and out-of-balance as this one—troublemaking can surely be a good thing.

"DISCIPLINE IS THE FIRST PRIORITY FOR EVERY TEACHER, AND IT IS ESPECIALLY ESSENTIAL FOR TEACHERS IN URBAN SCHOOLS WITH LARGE NUMBERS OF BLACK STUDENTS."

President Trump has defined the paramount problem infecting our public schools: "To achieve higher standards, students need discipline. And the failure to teach discipline is where the schools break down."[1]

It's a central responsibility of teachers to reverse this breakdown. In order to achieve higher standards, teachers must become much more serious about insisting that students lead a disciplined life. That responsibility becomes even more urgent in urban schools with large populations of undisciplined youngsters. Most honest and sensible observers agree that the biggest problem in urban schools is a lack of discipline—especially among Black boys. Black boys are much more likely than other students to be suspended or expelled from school, typically for disrespecting teachers, disrupting class, or otherwise misbehaving. Traditional African American culture relied heavily on strict rules and tough and swift discipline—common images included Big Momma or Big Grandpa leading the wayward boy to the woodshed for a good whupping.

However, something has been lost in today's context—perhaps kids having kids, young single mothers and the breakdown of the family; perhaps the negative influences of popular culture and rap music; perhaps the well-known norms suggesting that being well spoken or educated is "uncool"; perhaps the rise of street gangs; or perhaps other factors altogether. Regardless of the cause, it's clear that too many youth—and Black boys in particular—have become unruly, undisciplined, unmotivated, and delinquent. Too many of these youths have not learned to postpone gratification but instead impulsively act on whatever strikes their fancy. As Bill O'Reilly commented:

The decline of discipline in some American high schools—here in New York City, you can be found with drugs in the school, not be suspended. You can threaten a teacher or security guard, not be suspended. You can even get into a physical altercation, and little will happen to you. For example, at the Adlai E. Stevenson High School complex in the Bronx, poor area, student reportedly found with seven bags of marijuana; that means that student is a dealer. He was handed a warning card that said, quote, "Please bring this card home to your parents so you can discuss the matter with them," unquote. I'm sure the dope dealer just ran right home and discussed it with his parents, if he even had parents. Also, the high school did not identify the dealer student to the cops, didn't tell them.[2]

Here's Donald Trump again:

A ghetto public school, Chicago Military Academy-Bronzeville, is experimenting with a new kind of classroom order. Students wear uniforms. If they act up in class they do pushups. The academy is recruiting students for the armed forces. It's an experiment in teaching real discipline to kids who are going to face a struggle. It aims to give them the tools they need to get out into the world and have a chance. Parents and students love it.[3]

No one can learn or grow or achieve in a chaotic, out-of-control environment, and so we need to prioritize discipline, control, and management for those students.

REALITY CHECK

Every new teacher worries about student discipline or classroom management, and why not? Anecdotes of disruptive students and out-of-control classrooms are a staple of the national narrative concerning public schools, and popular movies about teachers amplify the point with tales of besieged instructors struggling against an unruly mob. Even without those terrifying testimonials, new teachers can certainly do the math: a single teacher faces twenty-five, thirty, or even fifty students at a time; if those kids ever banded together and rose up, the teacher would be doomed. That may be too apocalyptic but, surely, getting thirty kids to focus, to get along and go along, is a daunting challenge.

Of course, a productive classroom is a space where youth and adults live together in harmony and balance. But it's a myth that there's a direct path to that end: first, get control; next, deliver the knowledge. The best classrooms have an internal order that can only be achieved when the work of the classroom is accepted by the group as worthwhile and fulfilling in its own right, and when it's more than a bitter pill that must be swallowed in the face of punitive consequences or distant rewards. This issue of classroom order points to the importance of teachers spending time and energy knowing and connecting with their students, as well as examining and refining a curriculum that will offer a compelling invitation to school learning. And rather than seeing "management" as a separate set of tactics or techniques, "learning to live together" becomes a curriculum in its own right, running alongside and in concert with other learning experiences and endeavors. Rather than a thick set of rules to conform to or rebel against, every interaction becomes another teachable moment, another opportunity to refine and experience what associative learning really means.

New teachers are seldom encouraged to resist or find alternatives to their concerns about discipline and management, and these concerns, if they congeal into an unhealthy obsession, reinforce the worst qualities that are already in place in all too many schools, such as contempt for parents, fear of students, the conscious or unconscious lowering of expectations, a mania for control, a culture of conformity and complaint, and an over-reliance on a simpleminded system of behavioral psychology and a regime of punishments and rewards. All of this presupposes that the teacher—and her curriculum—are always right and on point, and that discipline is never internal, and never the result of dialogue or negotiation between teacher and student. Management is rarely constructed as self-discipline.

The ubiquitous little maxims concerning discipline—don't smile for the first several weeks of school, or until Christmas, or for the entire first year; don't let them see you sweat; don't turn your back to them; don't eat lunch in the cafeteria—can be found in teacher-training guides coast to coast, and they are typically acceded to, willingly at times, and grudgingly at other times. Occasionally someone openly resists one or another, but it's not easy because each carries, after all, the odor of common sense. And there's nothing more dogmatic or insistent, more policing and self-promoting, than that kind of common sense. The whole world is chanting that discipline is the first order of business, and if you want to be a real teacher, you need to learn to be tough.

And, still, we hope teachers will resist—the great teachers already do, in large and small ways—and rebel against the primacy of discipline, reject these tired clichés, stand on their own lively feet, and make their way toward the moral heart of teaching at its best.

The aware teacher knows that every student is searching for the answer to a central question: "Who in the world am I?" That question exists, and it perseveres. The wide-awake teacher looks for opportunities to prod the question, to awaken and illuminate and agitate it, to pursue it across a range of boundaries, known as well as unknown. The challenge to the teacher—massive and dynamic—is to extend a sense in each student of both alternative and opportunity, to answer in an expansive, generous way a corollary question: "What in the world are my choices and my chances?" "Sit down and shut up" is not the answer human beings need or deserve.

Teachers need to examine the contexts within which their teaching occurs: social surround, historical flow, cultural web, and economic condition. Though the unexamined teaching life is hardly worth living, the examined life is filled with difficulty; after all, the contexts of our lives include unearned privileges and undeserved suffering, traditional hierarchies of race and class, white supremacy and chauvinism, gender oppression and male superiority, murderous drugs and crushing work, a howling sense of hopelessness for some and the palpable threat of annihilation for others. To be aware of the social and moral universe we inhabit and share, aware, too, of what has yet to be achieved in terms of human possibility, is to be a teacher capable of hope and struggle, outrage and action, a teacher teaching toward enlightenment and liberation, joy and justice.

Education, of course, lives an excruciating paradox precisely because of its association with and location in schools. Education is about opening doors, opening minds, and opening possibilities. School, by contrast, is often principally about sorting and punishing, grading and ranking and certifying. Education is unconditional—it asks nothing in return. School demands obedience and conformity as a precondition to attendance. Education is surprising and unruly and disorderly, while the first and fundamental law of school is too often to simply follow orders. An educator unleashes the unpredictable, while a schoolteacher too often starts with an unhealthy obsession with law-and-order conduct, adult control known as classroom management.

Principal Joe Clark, depicted in the popular film *Lean on Me*, came into the national spotlight in the late 1980s for his no-nonsense approach to discipline and management at Eastside High, a predominantly Black and Hispanic school plagued by drugs and violence. Clark reinforced a powerful image: a sturdy Black man particularly suited as a disciplinarian for out-of-control city kids. Clark could be physical with the students, and he could offer himself as a role model for those tough youth. You might remember his familiar bullhorn and Louisville Slugger baseball bat, which he toted as he patrolled the halls of Eastside High. Clark maintained an environment of strict discipline at the school, regularly expelling students who were disruptive or truant and firing teachers who disagreed with his policies. Clark's approach to discipline and control won him national prominence, including praise from Ronald Reagan, who held up Joe Clark as an example of the tough leadership necessary to manage inner-city schools in crisis.

But let's look at the assumptions that lie behind the urge to cast African American men in the role of disciplinarian. In the first place, we must recognize that schools in the United States are complicit in developing an apartheid education system and culture by failing to recruit, retain, and expand the number of teachers of color.

Students need to see teachers who look like them, teachers who have similar life experiences and cultural references. Strong relationships between teachers of color and students of color not only support a positive learning environment, but they also invite new kinds of inquiries, new directions in the curriculum, that can serve their communities better than the more traditional body of school knowledge.

But too often students of color who are thinking about teaching as a career already know that it's devalued. They know they won't earn either a lot of money or a fair share of respect, and they've been told by family and friends that they could do much, much better. And yet those who come to teaching typically say they want to make a difference in children's lives or that they want to give back to the community. They bring a hope that they will do great things in spite of a system they know to be corrupt and dysfunctional. But the predatory structure pressures them to accept its self-serving propaganda about test scores, achievement gaps, accountability, and personal responsibility.

The Joe Clark story builds on racial myths, inspiring reformers today to promote strong Black men to project power and vigor
to Black youth, as well as to bring some law and order into those
schools. The notion that Black men make excellent disciplinarians in schools is made for TV—or more accurately, made *by* TV.
Joe Clark is symbol and prototype, but the image of a strong Black
male bringing down the hammer (or baseball bat) on unruly juvenile delinquents is deeply embedded in popular culture and runs
deep in the American psyche. Think of widely circulated social
media clips of Black fathers and father figures physically punishing their presumably naughty Black children. Think of popular sit-
coms like *Good Times* and *The Bernie Mac Show* and reality-TV series
such as *Save My Son* and *Blackboard Wars*—each with a central buck-
stopping Black papa. In many people's minds, the Black male pa-
triarch who exercises disciplinary authority over Black children
represents the ideal of social control. It is also seen as too often
missing in the lives of young Black boys.

Let us backtrack and start again on more solid ground: stereotyping is stupid. It colors and shades our perceptions in ways that
reduce and narrow our thinking, limit and bind the reach of our
vast possibilities. But the socially constructed image of Black men
as disciplinarians is particularly damaging when used as a simplis-
tic frame to understand the complex task of educating Black children, especially young men.

Beyond observation and intuition, much scholarship provides
concrete evidence about the magnitude of the plight facing Black
male students in our public schools. At all levels of the K–12 school
trajectory—elementary, middle, and high—Black young men lag
behind their peers academically. On every indicator associated
with progress and achievement—enrollment in gifted programs,
Advanced Placement classes, and other enriched courses—Black
males are vastly underrepresented. On the other hand, in every
category associated with failure and distress—discipline refer-
rals, grade retention, expulsions and suspensions, absences, and

dropout rates—Black males are overrepresented. They have the lowest graduation rates in most states, and nearly half of all Black adolescent males in the United States quit high school before earning a diploma. Black young men are underachieving, the myth assumes, not because of culturally irrelevant curricula or unresponsive teaching or unhealthy school milieu or underfunding and under-resourced spaces or any other well-documented, structural reason, but because they do not have Black male authority figures on their asses, pushing them to work and succeed.

Educational researcher Ed Brockenbrough points out that Black male teachers are immediately spotted and

> thrust into the hallway either as someone who needs to resolve another teacher's "problems" or as the dean for the floor. They're the ones asked to find out who pulled the fire bell, who called the other teacher a sexist, or who's getting inducted into which gang. They're the ones who have to break up the fights, tell the kid to pick his pants up, and address the use of the n-word. As they're asked to do these things for student discipline, they're pulled further from the academic aspects of their work, and from developing relationships with young males as non-judgmental role models. Plus, too many Black children see school as a place where they're supposed to get reprimanded and by putting black educators as main executioner, we're essentially fortifying centuries-old traditions of promoting blacks as overseer in the proverbial plantation.[4]

Pigeonholing Black male educators does them—and students—no favors.

Chris Emdin, author of *For White Folks Who Teach in the Hood. . . . and the Rest of Y'all Too*, adds,

> Black male teachers are not just expected to teach and be role models; they are also tasked with the work of disciplinarians. The stereotype is that they are best at dispensing "tough love"

to difficult students. Black male educators I work with have described their primary job as keeping black students passive and quiet, and suspending them when they commit infractions. In this model, they are robbed of the opportunity to teach, while black male students are robbed of opportunities to learn.[5]

Monique W. Morris, the cofounder of the National Black Women's Justice Institute, extends the challenge and points out in her book *Pushout: The Criminalization of Black Girls in Schools* the ways that Black young women are oppressed by this same set of assumptions. Schools, she argues, are "structures of dominance that can either reinforce negative outcomes and ghettoize opportunity or actively disrupt conditions that render black girls vulnerable to criminalization." Morris goes on, "I believe that the investment in black boys, and other boys of color, is necessary. However, that investment should never be to the exclusion of black girls. Blanket policies and practices that have been constructed based upon the experiences of boys and young men must be reevaluated."[6] The national Women's Equity Project points out that Black girls and young women face their own set of challenges, from increased sexual harassment to teacher hostility to discipline.[7] Nobody familiar with the world of teaching and learning will be shocked to find out that young people are active thinkers, agents of their own hopes and dreams, movers and shakers of the world, and that in each of them is the capacity to make sense of their surroundings, to claim expertise on their own lives. When Black male educators are largely absent from their learning environments or present but pegged as fixers not pedagogues, young people recognize what's up.

Often, the disciplining of students seen as nonconforming, who are also often students of color, is coded with medicalized terms and addressed with pharmaceutical solutions. Schools' single-minded focus on discrete skills, the elimination of arts and sports, and the increasing disregard for the real rhythms of children's growth and development contribute to a classroom culture that punishes students who won't focus passively for hours. Consequently, schools in many districts have become legalized drug dispensaries, with the well-known over-prescription of Ritalin for attention-deficit/hyperactivity disorder (ADHD), for example. A newly invented category of mental problems known as "conduct disorders" is squeezing through the schoolhouse door right now.

The definitive handbook for psychiatrists and counselors and all mental health workers, the *Diagnostic and Statistical Manual of Mental Disorders* (fifth edition), includes an affliction it calls "oppositional defiant disorder," which is described as "a pattern of angry/irritable mood, argumentative/defiant behavior."[8] A child with ODD, according to the *DSM*, "often argues with . . . adults," "actively defies or refuses to comply with requests . . . or with rules," and is "touchy or easily annoyed." The quick and easy way to treat "ODD" is—you guessed it—with powerful antipsychotic meds.[9] As these things always go, "ODD" was diagnosed in the lower single digits when it was first "discovered," but by 2009, it had accelerated into the double digits—up to 16 percent of school-age children have it, according to the American Academy of Child and Adolescent Psychiatry.[10] Predictably, "ODD" and other "conduct disorders" are primarily illnesses of the descendants of formerly enslaved people and children from lower socioeconomic classes.[11]

Jerome Kagan of Harvard University argues that, in fact, ADHD is a medicalization of normal youth behaviors that were previously regarded as part of the maturing process.[12] The longer and longer hours that young children are forced to sit still in classrooms have, predictably, expanded the diagnoses of ADHD, as more children are deprived of the right to move their bodies in play and exercise during the course of the school day.[13]

Research professor Norm Diamond, tongue firmly in cheek, suggests the existence of a far more dangerous and prevalent ailment gripping the country: "CAD: Compliance Acquiescent Disorder."[14] Symptoms of CAD include thoughtlessly deferring to authority, reflexively obeying rules, blankly taking in and believing the commercial media, hesitating to argue back, and staying calm and restrained when outrage is warranted. But this scholarly satirist has deep, sober, and serious concerns: Diamond believes that people who are incapable of outrage and resistance in the face of terrible injustices, dehumanization, and unnecessary suffering are a great menace to humanity. Critically examining and even breaking some little rules might be the anarchist calisthenics necessary to prepare us for breaking big rules when history calls.

In his memoir *The Beautiful Struggle*, Ta-Nehisi Coates asserts,

> No matter what the professional talkers tell you, I never met a black boy who wanted to fail. . . . Fuck what you have heard or what you have seen in your son. . . . He may lie about homework and laugh when the teacher calls home. He may curse his teacher, propose arson for the whole public system. But inside is the same sense that was in me. None of us ever want to fail. None of us want to be unworthy, to not measure up.[15]

Many reformers and some educators claim to have evidence to the contrary, but while there are surely anecdotes and incidents that support those claims, those contentions tend to skate glibly on the surface of things and fail to go deep enough in search of root causes. Some teachers reject the idea that they are at least in part agents of the state, bit players in a white colonial space, while others argue that teaching can never be even partially useful—let alone reach toward transcendence—until teachers fully face the friction and gaping contradictions inherent in their teacher-roles, and are willing to explore system-disruption and radical reconstruction. In this view remediating the students is a ridiculous misdirection.

"I was a curious boy," Coates writes in *Between the World and Me*, "but the schools were not concerned with curiosity. They were concerned with compliance."[16] That perfectly describes the obsessions that characterize American classrooms today, especially urban classrooms and schools populated by the poor, recent immigrants from impoverished countries, First Nations peoples, and the descendants of formerly enslaved people. The overarching goal is obedience and conformity; the watchword, control. These schools are characterized by passivity and fatalism, and infused with anti-intellectualism, dishonesty, and irrelevance. They turn on the little technologies of constraint; the elaborate schemes for managing the fearsome, potentially unruly mob; the knotted system of rules; the exhaustive machinery of schedules and clocks and surveillance. The corporate reformers offer no relief and simply create charter or voucher schools that enact this whole agenda on steroids. They are not concerned with curiosity or imagination, initiative or courage, because their purpose is elsewhere: everyone more or less submissively accepting their proper place in the hierarchy of winners and losers.

Coates claims that "the streets and the schools [were] arms of the same beast. One enjoyed the official power of the state [but] fear and violence were the weaponry of both."[17] The system is built on theft and lies and the plundering of Black bodies, Coates says, and it's a predatory system, a racist system: "If the streets shackled my left leg, the schools shackled my right." The shackles were fear and violence, and also lies and denial.

Urban schools chug along on the rails of indoctrination and propaganda: everywhere you look and in every direction lies the hype of the curriculum and the disingenuous spin about young Black people. Students are routinely subjected to an alphabet soup of sticky, inaccurate labels, mistrusted and controlled, and defined as lacking the essential qualities that make one fully human. On a daily basis and as part of the normal routine, schools engage in the toxic habit of labeling students by their presumed deficits and officially endorse failure—especially for children of the least powerful—in the name of responsibility and objectivity and helping.

The language of singling out and repressing "those students," the problem students, is freighted with coded meanings, and we all know that the narrative about school problems suggests that these resistant students, these recalcitrant students, are the biggest challenge. The truth is that African American and other marginalized students have been fighting for decent and relevant education from the beginning of this country's founding. During slavery, during Jim Crow, during the civil rights era, and today, their families have fought for access and the right to a meaningful education. And during all these periods, the charge, the slander, made against these youth was that they were lazy, distracted, out of control, or unable to learn.

The truth is that we do not need more Black men in schools as bouncers or unyielding enforcers of urban discipline. More Black men are needed in schools to make the education profession and the school workers a force on the side of the communities. More Black men are needed so that non-Black students and adults alike can see them in ways that run counter to the manufactured popular perceptions. More Black men are needed to work against the school-to-prison pipeline and to offer what we know works in teaching—teaching with love, toward justice, and with joy—for all students. More Black men are needed so that Black boys envision an older and hopeful version of themselves.

The brilliant Chicago poet Quraysh Ali Lansana gives us spirit words to help all of us keep clear and moving forward:

MALE BONDING

for Adrian, J., Christopher, Matthew, Major & Randall

i want my sons to know
men who smile

i want my sons to know men
who own their imperfections

i want my sons to know
men who listen

i want my sons to know
men who hear hearts, see words

i want my sons to know men
who honor women

i want my sons to know
men who appreciate the arts

i want my sons to know
men who adore their mamas

i want my sons to know men
who aren't afraid of tears

i want my sons to know
men who respect their fathers

i want my sons to know men
who use fists in self-defense only

i want my sons to know
men who value and dignify men

men who work hard, can't
spell quit, understand no

i want my sons to know
men who apologize

i want my sons to know men
who have relations with The Divine

men who question everything
men who know humility

i want my sons to know
men who read books

i want my sons to know men
who laugh at themselves

i want my sons to know
men who see possibility[18]

The strategies to sit on, control, and silence young African American students only expose the authoritarians' desperate fear of a Black uprising. And what we've highlighted here can be transposed to other colonized populations, other marginalized youth—from Native American to Latinx to Asian and Pacific Islander—and to other outsiders, working-class youth to women to queer and gender-nonconforming rebels. And the same strategies, from direct violence to neocolonial structures with indigenous overseers, have gone back to the beginning of class society. The number-one lesson of schooling for them is passivity, acceptance, and compliance. Teachers know we can be better than this. We can choose to take the side of the child.

"Teachers Need to Set High Standards and Drive Kids Hard."

US students have slipped precipitously in international rankings of achievement in recent years. While other countries have taken the demands of the modern era seriously, US policy and practice have allowed weak and watery standards to undermine our position. Too many American teachers are informed and guided by a fuzzy nostalgia for a time when all a teacher needed to be was a sweet lady who read books to kids. That day is gone. We need an educational revolution—a cultural revolution, a revolution in values and expectations, a revolution in priorities. We need to sweep out the feeble and unfocused teachers in favor of muscular educators to enact the necessary strict and rigorous practices employed by successful countries like Singapore and South Korea.

This means implementing sensible reforms like an extended school day, Saturday school for all students, a year-round school year, and a serious focus on productive study, including more demanding homework schedules to prevent students from drifting toward TV or video games. Most important, teachers have to grasp the central place of competition as an incentive to learn and as the engine of progress and prosperity.

REALITY CHECK

In reality, schools and teachers are driving students dangerously hard. Modern American schools, in the words of *Race to Nowhere* director Vicki Abeles, are "actually making [kids] sick."[1] She bases her assessment on several research studies that have found astronomical (and increasing) levels of both depression

and anxiety among schoolchildren of all ages and across the socioeconomic spectrum.

It makes some sad sense: seven or more hours of school five
days a week; hours of homework every night; athletics or extracurricular activities after school if you're lucky enough to attend
a school with the resources to provide them; weekends devoted to
long-term class assignments, projects, or research papers; and
constant reminders that their futures are going to be bleak unless
they beat the competition and get ahead of the pack in this dog-
eat-dog world. Indeed, children in first and second grades get the
message that they are in competition and that their performance
will determine if they end up homeless or wealthy. Early on, kids
are reminded that they're never really ever off the clock.

All of this has consequences. The Centers for Disease Control
and Prevention reported that the vast majority of teenagers get a
minimum of two hours less sleep than the amount recommended
by doctors, and that same study revealed that the more homework
students did, the less sleep they got.[2] The American Psychological Association says that close to one in three adolescents report
that stress is making them sad or depressed, and that school is
their primary stressor.[3] Meanwhile, there's a steady rise in reported cases of ulcers among young children, and an astonishing
94 percent of college counseling directors report an alarming rise
in students with severe psychological problems.[4] It's well known
that long-term stress leads to higher risks of mental illness, heart
disease, and cancer.[5]

These shocking statistics raise a critical question: in our collective push to improve education for children, are we barking up the
wrong contradiction? Are test scores really the Holy Grail? How do
children learn and how do schools potentially help them grow into
healthy, happy, and productive people? And, more fundamentally,
what is the purpose of public education in a free society?

It's worth noting that two countries that are often cited by
the market reformers as models worth emulating—China and

Singapore—are authoritarian countries ruled by despots. Two others, Japan and South Korea, are renowned throughout the world for astronomical teenage suicide rates—Vicki Abeles's argument made tragically clear. And, it turns out, education officials in these places worry that they are turning out compliant technicians but not autonomous citizens who can think creatively. These are not systems to mimic; each is, rather, in its own way a cautionary tale.

And "rigorous" may not be the banner that we most want to march under; it seems to have slipped uncritically (and unexamined) into our conversation about schools and children. We may imagine that "rigorous" innocently implies something like "serious," but that assumption is incorrect, for it misses the hidden and more odious significance of "rigorous": "strict and unbending," "harsh and demanding," "rigid and stiff." Think: rigor mortis.

Authoritarian classrooms tell students in a thousand implicit (and at least one explicit way) to sit down and be quiet. Turn your attention to the front of the room, because that's where the knowledge is. Be obedient and competitive. Perhaps a particularly compliant teacher might want to take that a step further, posting charts of comparative international test scores with the motivational slogan "Work harder to beat the third graders of China and India!" These schools turn on technologies for control and normalization, including public posting of scores, classroom chants about compliance, and control of bodily functions through bathroom permission.

School people everywhere want their students to study hard, learn the curriculum, stay away from harmful drugs and alcohol, complete their homework, and so on. Schools serve the societies in which they're embedded—authoritarian schools serve authoritarian systems, apartheid schools serve apartheid societies, and so on. In fact, none of these features distinguishes schools in fascist Germany or medieval Saudi Arabia or apartheid South Africa from schools in a democracy, and indeed many of those other school systems produced great artists, athletes, scientists, and generals.

Surely many teachers in those other societies worked hard, struggled with management and discipline issues, and brought energy, commitment, and concern for the young with them into their classrooms. But those systems lacked an essentially democratic culture, and so they also produced obedience and conformity, moral blindness and easy agreement, obtuse patriotic nationalism, and a willingness to follow orders right into the furnaces. And most—certainly not all—teachers went along.

In a democracy, we want our students to be able to think for themselves and to make judgments based on evidence and argument. We want them to learn to ask essential questions that are—like the students themselves—always in motion, dynamic, and never twice the same. Our goal should not be to train students to think alike, to draw strictly within the lines, to focus exclusively on acing the standardized tests. We must instead have as a central goal the development of free people who can question, explore, discuss, and discover—those should be held as the highest standards.

To be a good teacher in and toward democracy, to actively resist the pressure to set "high" standards that may have nothing to do with the aspirations and possibilities of your class, to refuse to "drive the kids hard" when the stress is clearly counterproductive, means to have endless, regenerating faith in people and to believe in the possibility that people can create and change things. The fundamental message of the teacher, after all, is this: you can change your life. Whoever you are, wherever you've been, whatever you've done, the teacher invites you to a second chance, another round, perhaps a better outcome or a different conclusion. The teacher posits possibility, openness, and alternative, not "strict," standards; the teacher points to what could be, but is not yet. The teacher beckons you to change your path, and so she has one basic rule, which is *to reach*.

As students and teachers begin to see themselves as linked to one another, as tied to history and capable of collective action, the fundamental message of teaching becomes broader, more generous: we must change ourselves as we come together to change the world. Great teaching invites transformations, not conformity.

The great Chilean poet Pablo Neruda wrote a poem to his fellow writers called "The Poet's Obligation," in which he instructed them in their core responsibility. You must, he said, become aware of your sisters and brothers who are trapped in subjugation and meaninglessness, imprisoned in ignorance and despair. You must move in and out of windows carrying a vision of the vast oceans just beyond the bars of the prison—a message of hope and possibility. Neruda ends with this: it is through me that freedom and the sea will call in answer to the shrouded heart. This could be the credo for conscious and effective classroom teachers: your classroom can still become an oasis of freedom and a beacon pointing toward a better world. Make it happen in this corner of this space, right here, right now.

"TEACHERS ARE POORLY SERVED BY THE UNIVERSALLY DREADFUL TEACHER-EDUCATION PROGRAMS CURRENTLY AVAILABLE."

The journalist Fareed Zakaria notes, "Half of America's teachers graduated in the bottom third of their college class," in sharp contrast to countries that have more successful schools, such as Finland, South Korea, and Singapore, places that consistently draw 100 percent of their teachers from the top third of graduates.[1] Finnish students are dependably at or near the top in international examinations, which makes sense since their teacher corps is drawn from the best and the brightest.

Nancy Gibbs, editor of *Time* magazine, concludes that this discrepancy explains why "our kids' performance falls below that of students in Estonia and why one-third of those who make it to college in the US need remedial education."[2] The well-qualified are denied access to the schools, and teacher-education programs enlist the halt and the lame. As a result—and is it any wonder?—our students are failing miserably compared to students in the rest of the world.

Traditional teacher-education programs are a joke, an unrigorous, cobbled-together amalgam of watered-down classes in psychology and philosophy and teaching methods, followed by "student teaching," a lazy affair consisting of superficial classroom activities supervised by veteran losers who do little more than try to induct new teachers into the cynical culture of teachers' unions, school failure, and complaint. Researchers Jason Richwine and Andrew Biggs say, "Given the relative lack of rigor of education

courses, many teachers have not faced as demanding a college curriculum as other graduates."[3] And Joel Klein, former New York City
Schools chancellor, claimed that poor training is part of the reason
most graduates of traditional teacher-education programs don't
think that the experience was worthwhile nor the teaching creden-
tial of much value.[4]

REALITY CHECK

When the corporate reformers came into our schools—testing and
measuring, judging and sorting students, reducing the concept
of an educated person to a single anemic metric on a high-stakes
standardized test, all the while compounding the inequalities that
have always plagued US public schools—conscientious teachers
resisted. But teachers were also in the reformers' sights, and the
corporate reform group worked to reduce the reality of teaching
actual children—complex, multidimensional, and challenging—to
a simple matter of delivering rote lessons in test preparation to
passive and obedient kids.

As Kevin Kumashiro, former dean of the School of Education
at the University of San Francisco, points out, "Under current
reforms, the more students struggle, the less their schools are
allowed to teach, and the less they are made to look like flourish-
ing school systems in this country and to other nations."[5] Behind
each of these moves lurked a deeper, ideologically driven goal: the
replacement of the public education system with a private educational business. This is a recipe for inequality inflamed and would
inscribe even more emphatically the reality of a high-quality education for the privileged and under-resourced schools focused on
discipline for poor students and students of color.

Education, no longer a common good nor a universal human
right, would be fully transformed into a product to be traded in the
marketplace like any other commodity, a hammer and a box of nails,
say. The winners would be sorted out and separated from the losers, and significant profits would be made. For teacher-education

programs, the reforms in the pipeline all pointed toward a resurgence of the privilege of white and male power.

The corporate reform crowd—the marketeers, the banksters, the hedge fund billionaires, and their allies among the political class—have worked to steer the reform efforts and the privatization of public education for three decades. The corporate education agenda sits on a three-legged stool: test scores as a proxy for learning; teaching as little more than clerking; education as a commodity like any other.

One current initiative from the federal government and the corporate sector is called the College Scorecard, a metric that ranks colleges based on post-graduation earnings of students. Surprise: Harvard graduates earn more than Howard graduates! This is social science in the service of the self-evident and the status quo.

The *New York Times* recently criticized university-based teacher-education programs in an editorial ironically titled "Help Teachers Before They Get to Class."[6] Starting with an obligatory bow to the effective Finnish school system, the editorial hits the central tenets of the corporate reform agenda for schools, including the assertion that US schools of education should, like those of the Finns, raise admissions standards. This is an astoundingly narrow conclusion from the broad evidence of what makes Finnish schools work. In the first place, teachers in Finland receive much higher salaries and benefits than their counterparts in the United States, one that places them firmly in an economically secure position. Many US teachers can't afford basic housing and living costs on their teaching salaries; a perhaps not unsurprising number moonlight as Uber drivers, bartenders, and clerks. Moreover, the respect and esteem with which teachers are held in Finland is a full 180 degrees from the national teacher-bashing narrative promoted by politicians and conservative pundits in the United States. Finally, Finland does not have nearly the income disparity and the massive poverty that plagues the United States and which stands behind so much school failure in this country.

The result of these conditions is that applications to teacher education programs in the United States are down 53 percent from ten years ago. And many teachers are discouraged by what they find in the profession, from low pay to constricting regulations and intensive, sometimes obsessive high-stakes standardized testing. By five years in, fully 50 percent of teacher-education graduates leave the profession.[7] If this kind of hemorrhaging appeared in the medical or legal professions, it would be declared a national crisis. In this context, for the *Times* to carp about low admissions standards would be laughable, if it weren't so wrong-headed.

The *Times* charges teacher education with another sin: preparing teachers for the humanities when there is a much greater shortage in math and science. This is either a cynical charge or an incredibly blinkered observation. Can you imagine teacher-education programs not wanting to prepare math and science teachers? Again, the problem is that people with math and science degrees, especially advanced degrees, with the concomitant student debt, are drawn to much more lucrative professions.

The forces of corporate education reform and their media followers who claim to believe so fervently in the market as the way to heal all ills refuse to see the ways that economic incentives and disincentives are driving this crisis. We have a teacher shortage across the country—San Francisco alone this year was looking for over four hundred teachers[8]—and the *Times* is fiddling at the edges.

The corporate reformers suggest that teaching teachers involves nothing more than the transmission of a narrow band of white middle-class attitudes and information into passive students whose mastery will be evaluated through standardized tests. Everything in this formula stands on faulty assumptions, including the erroneous idea that high-stakes standardized tests can measure effectiveness in the classroom or that a teacher's work can be understood as the easy enactment of lesson plans removed from social or cultural context.

When it's all boiled down, the vision the reformers put forward is that teachers should be narrowly training students. And when we say schools are failing to teach African American, Latinx, immigrant, and other marginalized students, we must also interrogate the content and the "knowledge" we are supposed to be teaching. We can argue that it is not really education if the history is overwhelmingly European-centered history, if the literature is created by primarily white male authors. We need to examine and refocus what we call valid or important knowledge. This question goes beyond content too. It includes the kinds of discourse used in debate, the approach to science, the exploration of mathematical sense. Simply put, the finite amount of white middle-class knowledge should not be the gold standard for what is important. And the problem for oppressed communities is compounded when such knowledge is simply imparted by downloading information that will then be evaluated through standardized tests.

We recall a standardized test for tenth graders that asked, "What were the reasons for US expansion in the Pacific after World War II?" The possible answers were a) to consolidate the defeat of Japanese expansionism, b) to counter the spread of communism, c) to expand market opportunities, and d) to spread Western values. What could a student possibly do when confronted with this question but try desperately to guess the perspective and point of view in the mind of the test writer? How would a Hawaiian youth read it? Someone from East Timor? A Vietnamese immigrant? The question and its assumptions drip with white Western positionality. And there was no space to write "all of the above" or "none of the above."

Everything in the corporate reform approach to education stands on faulty assumptions, such as the following:

1. The task of public education is to help America defeat other countries in economic and military competition.
2. Strong math and science skills will make the United States win this competition.

3. Poor students need to be trained to obey rules and regulations unquestioningly.
4. Education alone will end poverty.
5. Success for Black and Brown people is measured in how much their knowledge and performance approaches white knowledge and performance.
6. We know what skills and capacities will be needed fifty years from now.
7. Standardized tests measure these skills and capacities.
8. Competition, between students, teachers, schools, states, and countries, is the best way to advance social goals.

The list goes on and on.

Corporate reformers advocate basing teacher education on a utilitarian "competency" scheme rather than requiring students to complete a full university education. In this context, competency can be demonstrated through a series of online tests that allow education students to bypass or skip certain classes. It is an approach that foregrounds a mechanistic training while it eliminates the study of history or philosophy, an understanding of the psychology of learning, or the importance of raising the fundamental curriculum questions: What knowledge and experience is of most value, and how can students gain full and equitable access to that valuable knowledge and experience?

Many of the other practices promoted by corporate reformers are entirely upside down: distance learning, including virtual avatars and virtual classrooms for student-teaching experiences, is not an adequate facsimile of classroom life; competition between students, teachers, schools, states, and countries is not the best way to advance intellectual and social goals; poor students will not be well served in an environment that demands their passivity and compliance; education alone will not end poverty. Corporate reformers display no grasp of teaching and learning, nor have the thinnest understanding of the complexity of teaching teachers, but they hurriedly gloss over their ignorance and cover up their glaring blind spots with mandates and regulations, rankings and bullying, in order to have their way in spite of evidence to the contrary.

Teacher education should at minimum tell teacher candidates the truth: poverty is the greatest predictor of school failure, and school integration dramatically improves school performance for everyone. In the United States, 20 percent of children are poor, making it a dismal thirty-first out of the thirty-five top capitalist countries.[9] The percentage of poor children in the United States is larger than the percentage in Russia, and three times that of the Netherlands and Norway. A simple solution is at hand: eliminate the child tax credit ($58 billion) and the child deduction ($40 billion) entirely, policies that have failed to adequately reach the poor, and provide instead a monthly check of $250 to every child in the country. Child allowances in other countries have been remarkably successful at reducing child poverty, as well as simple to administer. In the United States, child allowances could dramatically reduce child poverty in a short time. This and other options could be addressed and debated, for they actually target poverty. But in the United States, we are stuck in this never-never land of presumed cause and effect between a dumbed-down education and poverty alleviation.

School desegregation began in earnest in the United States in 1971, and at the time, the so-called "racial achievement gap"—the difference between the average reading scores on standardized achievement tests broken out by racial groups—was around forty points. This was an effort driven not by a desire by people of color to simply sit next to white students; desegregation has always been about educational resources and gaining access to them. In 1988, at the peak of school integration efforts, the gap was eighteen points. In other words, after 352 years of enslavement, Jim Crow, redlining, and racial separation, the gap was cut by more than half in seventeen years. With the abandonment of integration efforts across the nation and a concerted retreat from racial justice in every form, the gap has been galloping upward ever since.[10]

And society has moved backward ever since, resulting in what journalist and music/culture critic Jeff Chang calls "the paradox of the post-racial moment"—the widely distributed images of a society moving toward integration while resegregation is the reality on every social index.[11] The gap has widened ever since, caused by a failure of political will and a result of social choice, not inferiority, real or imagined. Integration has barely been tried, but it's clear that where it's been policy, it's worked. This is a narrative about policy not magic.[12]

To be effective or fair, the content of teacher education must include practices that hold out the possibility of enlightenment and liberation, progress and even transformation: a curriculum of inquiry and questioning; attention to community goals and needs; the development of citizens educated to exercise their agency and their critical minds in a democracy; respect for diverse cultures, language practices, and historical interests within the United States; the needs and ways of seeing the world of differently abled kids; nurturing creativity, curiosity, and joy in school. The arts of liberty—curiosity, imagination, courage, initiative—must be foregrounded, and the woes of oppression—obedience and conformity—banished from the classroom.

The mandates for a campaign to undermine teacher education come from corporate think tanks as well as the federal Department of Education (DOE). They have decided that university-based teacher-education programs are too clunky and broad. Who needs courses on social foundations of education? Why bother with learning theory? What good is a diversity or an ethics course?

One telling piece of evidence is the new DOE teacher-preparation regulations under the National Education Act.[13] The National Education Policy Center early on analyzed the failures of the department's regulations, pointing out that the DOE blames individual teachers rather than systemic causes for the "achievement gap."[14] Narrow training is what the government relentlessly pro-motes—simple input of techniques with measurable outcomes in performance.

This brings value-added measurement (VAM) back with a ven-geance. Where VAM has been found to be inaccurate and ineffec-tive in evaluating teachers, as we discussed in relation to Myth 3, now VAM will be blindly pushed up the chain to draw conclusions about the teacher-education programs new teachers attended. The promoters of VAM purport to evaluate the effectiveness of teacher-education programs by tracking the graduates of these programs and then correlating "effectiveness" with student test scores years later. The pseudoscience of such a project, the multiple points where the data will be impossible to really evaluate, the incentive for teachers to cheat, to group the "successful" students under their tutelage while pushing aside those with special needs, is obvious.

Working in concert with the Department of Education cam-paign is the self-appointed National Council on Teacher Quality (NCTQ), an outfit that has partnered with *US News & World Report* to rank all teacher-education programs.[15] As with the publication's ranking of colleges, such list making not only reduces complex factors to silly competition but also allows corporate interests to highlight the qualities they want for education without any input from parents, communities, educators, or elected political bod-ies. The *New York Times* editorial writers repeated the NCTQ "find-ing" that only 10 percent of teacher-education programs are rated as "adequate."[16] Those findings mask a noteworthy fact: the vast majority of teacher-education programs, including many of those at the most respected universities in the nation, like Harvard and Stanford Universities, refused to participate in the survey and thus were rated "inadequate."

Backing up these attacks are the standards defined by the Council for the Accreditation of Educator Preparation (CAEP) and the Education Teacher Performance Assessment (edTPA), the lat-ter developed at Stanford's Center for Assessment, Learning, and

Equity. And perhaps the biggest gatekeeper, the one that relentlessly keeps teachers of color out of classrooms, are the subject-area standardized tests (CSET in California) that must be passed before one even begins a teacher-education program. These have all been analyzed by educators and found fundamentally flawed, if not fraudulent.[17] These gatekeepers function, at the graduate school level, just like the standardized tests in K–12 education. Presenting culturally biased discourse styles and approaches to knowledge, privileging the cultural capital of white middle-class candidates, the assessments turn away thousands of passionate and committed future teachers—especially candidates from working-class and Black and Brown communities.

In the end, we can be sure, the data will not support the proposition that narrow training programs produce better results, even by their own pathetic measures. But by then it will be too late, as thousands of teacher-education programs will have been shut down or harnessed to the corporate reform agenda. The effect of these efforts certainly is not to make teacher-education programs serve the needs of public school students or their communities. Instead, they serve to make the teaching corps even more remote from, alienated from, and ineffective within their communities.

Teacher education has ample—dare we say infinite—room to improve. Anyone who understands the complexity and challenge of teaching knows that we should have an extended induction process, much as we do in the study of medicine. Teacher education should be free of charge, for we need people in this crucial field and should not saddle them with debt as they head out to draw moderate salaries. Teacher candidates should have extensive education in the foundations and context, in theory and practice. They need a multiple-year internship period with coaching by peers and experienced practitioners. New teachers need to be more than narrow skill trainers and sorters of students. They need the experience to become critical educators, community leaders who advance social justice and critical thinking with their students.

But the corporate reformers and government overseers don't actually plan to fund or support more thorough teacher-education programs. If anything, their broadsides against university teacher preparation pave the way for quick and narrow programs (and accelerating failure) such as Teach for America and district-sponsored credentialing programs.

We never see from these powerful critics any proposals for teacher education to be actually improved. In a democratic society, policy makers should be supporting high-quality, extensive university preparation programs and sustainable salaries rather than fast-track schemes.

What is to be done? Certainly, the framing of the whole debate must change. And the way to start is to listen to the actual people doing the work—the teachers in the classroom, the students and community members, the teacher candidates, and the teacher educators. Why the people who are a million miles from the classroom have the loudest megaphone is a particularly American way of doing things.

"Too Many Bad Teachers Have Created a Public School System That Is Utterly Broken, and the Only Solution Is to Wipe the Slate Clean and Start Over."

In an interview with broadcast journalist Roland Martin in 2010, Secretary of Education Arne Duncan famously commented on the state of public education in New Orleans. "I spent a lot of time in New Orleans, and this is a tough thing to say, but let me be really honest. I think the best thing that happened to the education system in New Orleans was Hurricane Katrina," he said, referring to the devastating 2005 storm.[1] "That education system was a disaster, and it took Hurricane Katrina to wake up the community to say that 'we have to do better.'" Duncan continued to say that New Orleans still had a "long way to go," but that the city "was not serious about its education. Those children were being desperately underserved prior, and the amount of progress and the amount of reform we've seen in a short amount of time has been absolutely amazing." Duncan's advocacy and leadership over many years has pivoted on closing "failing schools," and he takes personal credit for closing sixty public schools (and opening several charters) during his tenure as head of the Chicago Public Schools, standing strong in the face of ongoing parental and community protest. Expressing sympathy, he nonetheless explained that in the long run closing "underutilized" and "underperforming" schools would benefit kids. There may be some value to community schools, he noted, but district-run schools have failed low-income families for generations, and the pro–status quo position limits choice and preserves schools-by-assignment—low-income families assigned to a failing or dysfunctional school have no options. We clearly need more options, new models and new schools, new teachers and new staffs. It's time for a restart—out with the old!

REALITY CHECK

Arne Duncan is not alone. Closing schools, firing staffs, *starting over* have been key components of the mainstream market school-reform ideology and agenda for decades, and secretaries of education from both political parties have, with few exceptions, followed suit: Duncan, surely, but beginning with Jimmy Carter's education secretary, Shirley Hufstedler, and then on to Terrel Bell, William Bennett, and Lamar Alexander, followed by Richard Riley, Rod Paige, Margaret Spellings, John King Jr., and finally Betsy DeVos, who imagines turning education into the "gig" economy, making the incredibly naïve comparison between schools and Uber ride-sharing. In her first policy address as education secretary, she remarked, "Just as the traditional taxi system revolted against ride sharing, so, too, does the education establishment feel threatened by the rise of school choice. In both cases, the entrenched status quo has resisted models that empower individuals."[2]

They all peddle a version of dismantlement, a powerful ideology of mistrust of anything called "public," accompanied by a blind faith in the private marketplace. And so we witness public money transferred to private profit as the putative leaders of public education advocate tearing down the institution they are pledged to protect and build up—in the name of school reform and improvement.

In 2013, after Duncan had been in Washington for several years, the Chicago Public Schools issued a list of 129 schools being considered for closure, and eventually Mayor Rahm Emanuel closed 54 of them in one fell swoop—the largest mass closure of schools in the country's history. Michigan governor Rick Snyder appointed an emergency manager to run the Detroit Public Schools in the same year, and that manager intensified a strong austerity program already underway by laying off more teachers, administrators, and support staff, and by closing or consolidating more schools. And the current secretary of education, Betsy DeVos, is explicitly opposed to public schools on principle. Through vouchers, charters, and direct closures, her Department of Education will indeed set out to dismantle the public school system and reshape and rebrand the entire enterprise. Although voucher schemes have historically resulted in disasters for children, the DeVos regime promises to intensify and double-down on past failures.[3] A bill in the US House of Representatives, HB 610, begins the defunding of public schools and attempts to impose vouchers for children in K–12 schools. It abolishes the Nutritional Act of 2012 (No Hungry Kids Act), which provides nutritional standards in school breakfast and lunch, and it erases accommodation language for children with disabilities.

In *The Shock Doctrine: The Rise of Disaster Capitalism*, journalist Naomi Klein illustrated the ways in which powerful predators work feverishly to turn every crisis into an opportunity.[4] Capitalists are quick to jump in, shoving aside law and regulation, expanding private power, and developing new areas for accumulating profit. There's no need to wonder whether tearing down the New Orleans school system and starting over with all charter schools will work; Louisiana and federal officials embraced the storm and followed the disaster capitalism playbook post-Katrina.

Secretary Arne Duncan's intent and his practice were fully aligned with the privatization agenda, as he himself said repeatedly, and he routinely deployed the language of business as he spoke of "outsourcing," "downsizing," "spinning off unproductive units," and closing the least successful of the nation's "portfolio." Who knew public schools were a portfolio?

Mayor Rahm Emanuel's fifty-four shuttered Chicago schools were located in low-income Black and Latinx areas of the city. To protest Emanuel's action, upwards of seven thousand parents, students, and teachers took to the streets in an angry three-day protest, but never mind. The elite always thinks it knows what will be good for the great unwashed, and so protests and community meetings and mass actions were—as always—dismissed as the work of professional whiners or the ignorant masses who can't even understand their own best interests.

Corporate reformers (like Duncan, Emanuel, DeVos, and many charter operators) hold to an ideology that tells them that the "achievement gap" between poor, African American students and their more privileged white counterparts is not caused by poverty and its effects, as well as the very knowledge that is privileged and measured, but by undisciplined kids and bad teaching. They insist that the "gap" can be overcome with higher expectations and more rigorous teaching methods using a uniform and scripted curriculum geared toward success on high-stakes standardized tests. Many charter schools proudly display time-management charts and elaborate behavioral systems and routines that all children must follow. There are few opportunities for play, for relaxation, for sports or games or the arts. It's "drill-and-kill" morning till night, weekends and holidays too, with a special focus on math and reading because what's tested is what's taught.

Time and discipline in these schools are joined at the hip: kids learn that every minute not "on task" is time wasted, and that fooling around will shatter the order needed to learn. Strict compliance with authority is basic to learning, they're told, and they must conform in order to learn. Learning is a passive, not an active, enterprise—all about taking in rather than thinking and participating, speaking and discussing, sharing and taking initiative.

The obsession with rules in many of these schools is frenzied: keeping your hands folded on your desk, leaning forward and looking constantly at the teacher, having your feet firmly planted on each side of the center of the desk become a focus of discipline and behavioral training. This is part of a theory too: every little rule must be followed in order to avoid a cascading effect of broken rules with negative consequences for the whole classroom and school leading to absolute bedlam. Punishments vary, but they are typically meted out without any recourse or appeal, and they are deployed liberally; sanctions can include exclusion and public shaming, like sitting on a lower bench than the others, wearing clothes that designate the wearer a miscreant, or displaying a record of misdeeds on one's shirt.

But let's focus on results. For example, is former secretary Duncan correct that "the progress that they've made [in New Orleans] . . . since the hurricane is unbelievable?" Are Chicago's or Detroit's schools reaping the positive benefits promised by the political class and their corporate reformer cronies when they closed public schools, implemented "sound business practices," and pushed "refresh"?

If Duncan was talking about the "amount of reform" as improved student achievement on standardized tests, then, no, NOLA has not made measurable progress.

If, on the other hand, he was referring to the "amount" of disruption, upheaval, teacher turnover, and general churning of the system, then yes, NOLA has experienced a huge amount of reform. But toward what end? Corporate reformers tout the New Orleans model mainly because it has been a scorched-earth policy. There have been massive school closings, and an entire public school system has been handed over to private managers. The last few public schools in New Orleans were recently converted to charters, making NOLA the first US city to go all charter.[5] Classes are now steered by an influx of large numbers of young teachers without certification, a zero-tolerance policy, and a relentless focus on test scores. It's called big change and real reform, but outside the echo chamber of self-congratulation, there's little to celebrate. Test scores—the gold standard of the corporate reformers—have not improved dramatically, as we explain below.

African Americans had struggled mightily to have reasonable control and authority of a school system that had been miseducating their children for more than a century. After Katrina, the state quickly took over that district without consultation with, or regard for, the community or for the elected African American leadership. It was experienced by many as a colonial invasion, and there has been increasing racial tension since. Suddenly, 20 percent fewer teachers were certified, 20 percent fewer teachers had at least ten years of experience, and teacher turnover was widespread—50 percent or more a year.[6] Out of the chaos, 7,500 teachers were dismissed and a huge number of young, white, and short-term teachers took over. The majority of NOLA's African American teachers, long a backbone of local communities, were fired. Black teachers became a much smaller share of the teaching corps, from 71 percent to 49 percent, and the percentage of teachers with local roots has declined since the reforms were put in place.

In spite of valiant efforts by charter advocates to cook the books, people on the ground tell a different story. Black community activist and former principal Raynard Sanders points out that the New Orleans schools were grossly underfunded by the state and badly underperforming before the storm. After the storm, private investors poured in billions of dollars to set up charter schools. Yet the tiered system that resulted has only reproduced the high achievement of a small sector of the students (the same students who were served by "admission only" public schools before Katrina), and the mass of the students are generally achieving at lower levels under the new system.[7] Privately run charters have operated with little oversight, and many have attempted to increase their test-score profile by keeping out students with special education needs or expelling those who are not compliant. Indeed, expulsions in NOLA charter schools are at ten times the national average.[8]

Serious researchers looking at New Orleans acknowledge that it's problematic to compare the public schools before and after 2005. For example, standardized test scores, always inadequate, are the only measure being used to compare students pre- and post-Katrina. The population hardest hit by Katrina was poor and African

American, and they've faced the greatest obstacles trying to return to the city—a hundred thousand are still missing—so that the school population being tested today has a higher socioeconomic profile than the population being tested before the storm. Test-based accountability distortions mean that many of the new charter schools flooding the city have a single-minded focus on test prep. Also, there are now harsher policies in effect concerning student discipline, so large numbers of students are being excluded through suspensions and expulsions. Further, massive amounts of private money have poured into the new charter school system set up after Katrina, and the construction of new facilities has accelerated.

A recent report on the LEAP (international test) results by Charles Hatfield demonstrates that, despite the billions of dollars poured in, student performance has not improved.[9] Does this mean that learning cannot happen, that "these kids" can't be taught? Not at all. It does mean that the drill-and-kill approach, the top-down repressive approach, brings about no authentic improvement. Deep learning, community-responsive schools, relevant and meaningful curricula, can make a difference, not only in improving measurable outcomes but also in making the classroom lives of these thousands of children less miserable.

After Hurricane Katrina, FEMA put in $1.8 billion for the actual rebuilding of schools; the US Department of Education awarded approximately $1 billion in grants and recovery money to charter schools and pro-charter groups to improve public education in New Orleans; and private foundations ponied up over $80 million over a three-year period.[10]

If the nearly $3 billion squandered after Katrina had been directed toward developing these kinds of public schools, imagine the engaged intellectuals these communities might have produced. As we've seen, even with all this investment and disruption, test scores in New Orleans are up only incrementally.

And this is true nationally as well—in study after study, charter schools do not outperform traditional public schools in the same geographic area serving children of similar backgrounds. In fact, only 17 percent of students who moved from a traditional public school to a charter school improved according to standardized test scores, almost half remained the same, and 34 percent lost ground, according to a nationwide study in 2009.[11] In the 2009–2010 school year, only 26.3 percent of Illinois charter schools made adequate yearly progress under No Child Left Behind, and that percentage decreased to 13.6 percent in 2010–2011. In Chicago, there was no statistically significant difference between charter and traditional public high schools in a comparison of 2006–2008 ACT composite scores.[12]

And all of this is against a background—as in NOLA—of a stacked deck in favor of charter schools, which are all removed from democratic decision-making processes and remain largely unaccountable to the public. For example, charter schools do not have representative enrollments of special education students or of English-language learners (ELL). In Chicago, to take one example, the overall enrollment of ELL students is 15.8 percent, but the enrollment of ELL students in charter schools is 8.4 percent. Charter schools typically select their students by an application process—including test scores and possibly a lottery—but they do not have to accept students from the neighborhood in which they're located. They are able to boost their data and claim magical improvement by keeping out "problem" children and counseling out those who are difficult to teach, whether because of family circumstances or learning challenges.

Charter schools are far more segregated than public schools in every state, and African American charter school students are twice as likely to attend racially isolated schools than any other group. Charter schools have fewer students eligible for free and reduced lunch programs and are generally less accessible to children from low-income families. In North Carolina, for example, charter schools are legally exempt from providing transportation and meals. And charter schools are funded with public money but are privately operated, sometimes by for-profit entities.

There are folks in charter schools doing wonderful work to be sure, and some charters are, not surprisingly, good schools. But overall, for all the infusion of large bags of cash and for all the collateral expense such as the closing of neighborhood schools, for all the side-stepping of teachers' unions, for all the extravagant claims about improved results, for all the swirl and churn and disruption, closing community schools and opening charter schools as a road to improvement has fraud written all over it.

Big urban districts facing large budget deficits sometimes look to school closings as a quick fix, but it rarely works out in practice as well as it does on paper. There are a number of upfront and hidden costs in closing schools. In Washington, DC, for example, an audit determined that closures designed to save the district $30 million, as projected by former schools chancellor Michelle Rhee, actually cost the city $40 million, after factoring in the expense of demolishing buildings, removing furnishings, and transporting students. Add to this another $5 million in federal and state grants lost as students left the system, some dropping out, others enrolling in the charter schools being built in tandem with the closings.[13]

Research on school closings in six cities in 2011 determined that school closings did not save the districts as much money as was projected or planned.[14] In Chicago and elsewhere, districts have had difficulty selling or leasing these properties, and closure-related costs—site maintenance or demolition, repurposing, relocating social services, support for both displaced students and the schools that must receive them—have cut deeply into savings. Furthermore, savings can be wiped out by the costs associated with opening new privately managed charter schools. In Chicago, hundreds of millions have been budgeted for the Office of New Schools, the bureau devoted to developing new charter and contract schools.

Rationales for closing community schools vary, but two reasons are often cited: underutilization and underperformance. Underutilization is linked to cost and budget, underperformance to student test scores, period. Before the mass closings, the Chicago

Board of Education determined that thirty children in a classroom was the ideal—or most efficient—class size for kindergarten
through eighth grade, and therefore classrooms with fewer than
thirty students are deemed underutilized. As educators and citizens, we reject the idea that thirty students in a class is a proper
standard—educators agree, for example, that special education
students *need* and *deserve* smaller, more intimate learning spaces—
and we note that if these standards were applied universally, the
classrooms attended by the children of the privileged, those in the
University of Chicago Laboratory Schools, for example, would all
be closed. But these standards are not applied uniformly or universally, and when applied only to Chicago Public Schools, a huge
percentage of neighborhood schools might be considered "underutilized" and may, in fact, be more in line with what the privileged get as a matter of course.

The most comprehensive research on the impact of class size
finds that students randomly assigned to smaller classes (average
fifteen) outperformed students assigned to larger classes (average
twenty-two) on standardized tests by the equivalent of three additional months of schooling. The difference of just seven students
had a significant impact on standardized measures of achievement. Researchers also found that African American students,
lower-income students, and students from urban areas benefitted
the most from smaller class sizes.[15]

Underperformance is the other rationale for closing schools,
but here again, the evidence does not justify the practice. In Chicago, an average charter school performs 10 percentile points below a comparable traditional community school on reading test
scores; charters consistently underperform by 12 percentile points
on reading and 2 percentile points on math relative to comparable
public magnet schools. A 2009 study by the University of Chicago Consortium on Chicago School Research (CCSR) found that
82 percent of students from eighteen elementary schools closed
in Chicago moved from one underperforming school to another

underperforming school, including schools already on probation.[16] According to the study, "One year after students left their closed schools, their achievement in reading and math was not significantly different from what we would have expected had their schools not been closed."

Overall, there were no significant positive or negative effects on academic achievement resulting from the closures when students transferred to comparable schools. In several studies, researchers found that students who transitioned into new schools following closures scored lower on tests one year later; they were at an increased risk of dropping out, as well as an increased risk of not graduating. Interview data suggests closure was viewed negatively by transitioning students, imposing a stigma on them as they entered new schools. Furthermore, school closings and consolidations often lead to increased class sizes and overcrowding in receiving schools. The pace of instruction slows and the focus is diluted, so scores for students—both those who move and those who stay—tend to be lower in schools with high student mobility rates.[17]

In reality, when schools are closed and facilities shut down, school staff displaced, and children sent to other schools, communities lose vital resources. School closures have led to severe negative experiences for displaced students in many cities, including an astronomically higher likelihood of dropping out, increased school violence, and disrupted peer- and adult-student relationships.

There's a broad consensus that schools for the children of the poor—and more precisely classrooms and schools attended by First Nations peoples, recent immigrants from impoverished countries, and the descendants of formerly enslaved people— have failed to educate the students they are responsible to, the kids in their care. There is, however, no consensus whatsoever that these schools can or should be fixed. Instead there's a noisy sentiment in the halls of power, resisted by parents, students, and teachers, that they should be bulldozed—metaphorically to start and literally to finish.

One of the fatal flaws at the heart of corporate school reform is that while proponents advocate closing failing schools, when it comes to replacements, they have nothing to offer. But there is nothing natural about the spectacular failure of schools for the poor—and there are illuminating alternatives to both the unsuccessful status quo and the wrecking ball looming over public education. The Central Park East schools in Spanish Harlem, founded by Deborah Meier, for example, have demonstrated that schools for poor urban youngsters can work when they are organized as small schools with an intimate link to communities and when every child is known well by a caring adult who is herself working in a cohort of mutual responsibility and support. Here the faculty focuses on a student-centered curriculum and a rigorously engaged pedagogy. Students graduating from CPE present a full sixteen "performances of knowledge," which are reviewed by a board that includes teachers, parents, fellow students, community members, and outside experts. These performances range from the critique of a public piece of art to a science experiment to a physical challenge. The CPE model is thorough and deep—and would require the commitment of resources to replicate. But instead we watch as billions of dollars are going into private profit ledgers as one unproven top-down fix after another is proffered as the ultimate solution.

The corporate reformers are not daring or bold or experimental, and in fact they mostly mimic what was catastrophic in the *status quo ante.* Corporate reformers mostly double-down on the worst features that already characterize failing schools—measuring success by limited metrics, including high-stakes test scores; the obsession with obedience and conformity as the cultural centerpiece of every school; the rewarding of passivity in curriculum and school culture; the elimination of a broad curriculum, including the arts and sports.

These supposedly new and soon-to-be excellent schools turn on the same old technologies of constraint, the elaborate schemes for managing the "fearsome," potentially unruly mob, the knotted system of rules, the exhaustive machinery of schedules and clocks and surveillance, the laborious programs of regulating, disciplining, correcting, assessing and judging, testing and grading. The new schools aren't so new after all, they offer no relief and instead recreate a worse version of the whole mess but now under the shiny label of "charters" or "alternative schools." These charters are not concerned with curiosity or imagination, initiative or courage, because their purpose lies elsewhere: everyone under control, everyone more or less submissively accepting their proper place in the hierarchy of winners and losers. They do not nourish or unleash the agency of students because the order of the day is compliance. And, of course, none of this is worthy of the soul of democracy, none of it an expression of a living and breathing democratic culture.

It's true that all parents and all students deserve educational choices—all parents and students, with all kinds of choices. But when the corporate reformers wipe the slate clean, they offer only anemic replicas of what already existed for the children of the poor—and this is choice in form only, not in content, and so it is, after all is said and done, no choice at all. It's fraudulent choice, like choosing between an apartment with no furnace and one with no doors or windows. No corporate reformers are saying, "We will wipe the slate clean in order to build a University of Chicago Laboratory School, or a New Trier High School, or a Sidwell Friends, or a Phillips Andover right here next door to this failing school, and you can choose." No one says that. Real reformers who want to develop a system of authentic choices, by contrast, advocate for generous and fair funding for all public schools and, as happened in Spanish Harlem years ago, the creation of robust and vital alternatives driven by the experience and wisdom of parents, teachers, and communities within existing or renovated spaces.

"TEACHERS ARE UNABLE TO DEAL ADEQUATELY WITH THE DISCIPLINARY CHALLENGES POSED BY TODAY'S YOUTH, AND WE NEED MORE POLICE IN OUR PUBLIC SCHOOL BUILDINGS TO DO THE JOB AND MAINTAIN LAW AND ORDER."

Public schools are plagued by gangs and fighting, assault and battery, drug dealing, and other criminal behavior, including, in extreme instances, actual shoot-outs between students. All of these hard realities demand an active and alert police presence to maintain safety, order, and discipline.

Schools must be safe havens for all kids, as well as for all school personnel. The good kids who want to learn and feel secure must be shielded from the actions of a minority of bad kids who get no discipline at home and have no respect for their classmates, the teacher, or learning itself. Suspending kids for bad behavior and sending them home may have made sense decades ago, but it's no longer an adequate control: too often parents don't believe in strong management and probably aren't home anyway because the mother may be working two jobs, and in many cases the father isn't home because he has left or is in prison.

Furthermore, teachers can't handle the evident and imminent threats of the modern world. The incident at Sandy Hook Elementary School in Newtown, Connecticut, in 2012—the senseless murders of twenty first graders and six educators—is a cruel reminder that our most vulnerable population must be protected from unpredictable violent forces. Armed police officers at Sandy Hook could have prevented that horrific massacre.

Public schools are paid for with tax dollars. The community has a right to expect that their tax money is supporting a secure space for student learning, and students who want to learn have a right to expect a safe school and a calm classroom environment. When a disruptive student refuses to obey the rules necessary to establish a good learning environment, that student must be disciplined. If a student is told to leave class, for example, because of a disturbance, that student must comply; when a student defies the teacher's legitimate authority, that teacher—acting legally *in loco parentis*—must have the ability to summon back-up.

Currently, there are more than 43,000 school-employed police—often officially referred to as "school resource officers" (SROs)—and an additional 39,000 "security guards" in the nation's 84,000 public schools, according to the National Center for Education Statistics.[1] Their presence in public schools is indispensable to the mission of preserving order, allowing teachers to do their jobs, and strengthening trust between young community members and the police. We need even more.

REALITY CHECK

A cellphone video taken in 2015 inside a classroom at Spring Valley High School in South Carolina captured images of a white sheriff's deputy removing a Black female student from her class. The school resource officer (SRO), a law enforcement officer, had been contacted by a teacher who'd asked for assistance in removing a student who had violated school rules by using her cellphone and refusing to leave class. The SRO grabbed the student around the head, flipped her desk over, slammed her to the floor, and dragged her out of the classroom. The graphic and disturbing video raced across social media, merging with the national focus on police force and violence deployed against youth of color, and prompted a federal civil rights investigation as well as the officer's dismissal.

Other high (or low) lights from 2015: In Kentucky, a video caught a sheriff's deputy handcuffing disabled children who'd failed to follow his instructions; the American Civil Liberties Union filed suit. In North Carolina, a water-balloon fight—initiated as a high school senior-day prank—resulted in the arrest of eight students; two dozen police officers were dispatched to the campus "to restore order." In Florida, an SRO pushed a thirteen-year-old student to the ground and violently twisted his arm; the officer was arrested and charged with child abuse. In Birmingham, Alabama, a federal judge ruled that SROs used excessive and unconstitutional force by routinely pepper-spraying students—including a pregnant student whose transgression was crying in a hallway—for small disciplinary offenses. Not surprisingly, most of the students experiencing physical violence are Black or Brown.²

The beat goes on and on and on: In Virginia, a four-year-old having a temper tantrum in his pre-K classroom was handcuffed by an SRO and driven to the sheriff's office. In Texas, a fourteen-year-old named Ahmed Mohamed, who had built a homemade clock from scratch and proudly brought it to school to show friends and teachers, was detained on suspicion of making a bomb (or perhaps only of making a bomb scare) and eventually arrested and taken to a juvenile detention center.³ He was later cleared of any crime or criminal intent, and his family sued the school district. Federal money had already been invested in putting police and police equipment into schools weeks after the Sandy Hook school shooting, but President Obama called for an investment of an additional $150 million to put a thousand police officers in schools.

There were 26,000 violent incidents reported in 13 percent of US schools in 2013–2014.⁴ And a telling bit of information: more than 64,000 students were arrested at school in 2011–2012—the most recent federal data available—and while Black students accounted for just 16 percent of the overall student population, 30 percent of those arrested were Black. The data on school-based arrests are incomplete because the federal government has only recently begun to require schools to follow uniform reporting protocols. But the trend holds up in states with more meticulous data sets; in Florida, for example, Black students accounted for 53 percent of school-based arrests in 2013–2014 while they constituted only 23 percent of the population.

So it seems the police are not confronting armed intruders but students. Why are Black students more likely to be arrested in schools than their white counterparts? Are Black students more prone than whites to breaking the law during school hours or to committing egregious acts against their fellow students? Or is the behavior of Black teenagers viewed by school authorities through a lens of pathology and criminality?

It may not be possible to get answers by conducting a perfect experiment complete with isolated variables and control groups, but there are useful indicators all around. A dramatic and much-discussed incident, for example, occurred in Decatur, Illinois, in 1999. Some young African American men got into a shoving match in the stands of a football game; it, too, was caught on video and the fight was not pretty. On the other hand, no one was hurt, and it was over in a matter of seconds. But the video had an outsized impact. As the incident played over and over in the media, it was consistently described as a "melee," a "brawl," and a "gang fight." Several students were expelled from school, criminally charged and arrested.

The Reverend Jesse Jackson became deeply involved in defending the young people in Decatur and argued that school officials slapped a blanket punishment on a large group of teenagers whose involvement in the pushing and shoving incident varied as widely as their other school experiences. He also noted that a "prank" in a white suburb where a large group of teenagers acted dopey—hazing and humiliating girls as someone's notion of a cool initiation into their senior year and landing several in the hospital—resulted in sanctions, but every student was offered a pathway beyond that sad, sorry event. A year later, each was in college and pursuing a brighter future; a year after the Decatur incident, those students were still out of school, mostly unemployed, and still paying dearly for their transgression. Words are revealing here—the use of "brawl" and "gang fight" in one case, the use of "prank" in another. Language has been under particular scrutiny in this Black Lives Matter moment.

These incidents—anecdotal but emblematic—highlight difficulties inherent in any situation where policing meets teaching or education intersects with criminal justice. Police officers most often meet a person at life's low point—a cop's presence is either the messenger or the proof of bad news—while teachers work with students on a higher and more hopeful plane. The emblems and tools of the trade are also distinct: books, words, and conversation for one; Kevlar vests, handcuffs, and guns for the other.

When police enter school environments and begin to mingle, disciplining students—often for behavior as innocent as a childish stunt or as mundane as a temper tantrum—schools can easily "become annexed" by law enforcement and elide the realm and influence of teachers. In 2013, 882 students were arrested in New York City public schools and 1,666 children were issued tickets—their "crimes" ranged from tagging graffiti to possession of marijuana. Interactions that might normally have been "teachable moments" were transformed into moments of fear, humiliation, and resentment by students interacting with those who have nothing to do with education.[5]

School people, community folks, students, parents, and civil rights advocates tend to think that SROs should *not* be involved in student discipline, and yet, in our experience, security personnel are quite routinely involved in discipline matters. This has led to the criminalization of typical teenage behavior, as well as the discriminatory enforcement of ill-defined rules and laws. And teachers have begun to worry about the excessive use of physical force against children in school spaces where they should be able to feel safe. Those encounters mean that the first experiences many Black and Brown students have with the police is in a school building—it's where many learn to fear police, and it's where some enter the criminal justice system, feeding the school-to-prison pipeline.

When Tamir Rice, a twelve-year-old out playing in a city park, was set upon and immediately shot dead by Cleveland police, he was described as "menacing" and "in an adult body." When Mike Brown, eighteen years old, was shot and killed by a policeman in Ferguson, Missouri, the officer said that Brown appeared unstoppable, like "Hulk Hogan." When Sandra Bland, a twenty-eight-year-old Black woman was stopped for "failing to signal when changing lanes," roughed up, threatened, and later found dead in a county jail cell, the trooper who initiated the confrontation described her as "defiant" and "resistant." And when Eric Garner was confronted in New York City for participating in the informal economy by selling "loosies," he, too, was described as "defiant" as he was put into an illegal choke hold, piled on by police officers, and recorded desperately pleading, "I can't breathe, I can't breathe," until he lost consciousness and died.

What is it about the word "defiance," or the word applied selectively: *defiant* young people, or *defiant* Black teens? According to school and police authorities, the young woman attacked in her classroom at Spring Valley High School was responsible for initiating the episode with her "defiance." The deputy sheriff was fired after the video of his assault went viral, but the misdemeanor charge against the student was pursued because she had not been compliant enough.

At a time of corporate-style reform, high-stakes testing gone wild, and unprecedented levels of regimentation, order and predictability stand as proxies for teaching and learning. Furthermore, rigid routine and detachment from the messiness of real teaching and learning seem like predictable ways to keep your job (and sanity), as teachers are pushed to create quiet classrooms and obedient students at the expense of thoughtful and actively engaged students.

Some communities are calling for explicitly limiting SROs' activities in schools—we ourselves think that if police are to be placed in the schools, they should be required to teach something valuable like knitting or handicrafts—while others are calling for the abolition of the police altogether. In May 2016, after a long organizing campaign and a mass community mobilization, the Los Angeles Unified School District (LAUSD) and the School Police Department (SPD)—a force of five hundred officers and staff—became the first government agencies to return all military grade weapons to the Department of Defense granted through the "Excess Military Equipment Program," or the 1033 program, which has been arming police departments all over the United States.

After withdrawing from the program altogether and providing a complete inventory of every weapon received and returned, LAUSD and SPD issued a public apology to the Black and Latinx students and communities whose lives were threatened by the program. In particular, they returned one tank, one mine-resistant ambush-protected (MRAP) vehicle, three grenade launchers, and sixty-one M-16 rifles.

In addition to the weapons accrued by the SPD, the DOD 1033 program had awarded the Los Angeles Police Department with more than 1,600 M-16 assault rifles, a military truck, a military cargo plane, and a helicopter, and the LA Sheriff had assembled more than a thousand M-16 assault rifles, two tanks, and sixty-two mine detectors. But organizers had started their work with schools because they were already engaged in campaigns to disrupt the school-to-prison pipeline. For instance, organizers from the Labor/Community Strategy Center had overturned a Daytime Curfew Law, which had resulted in thirty-eight thousand tickets being issued to Black and Latinx students for "truancy." And to eliminate the offense of "willful defiance"—which they had argued was a thinly veiled code to allow disciplinary actions against Black boys—they had also passed a "School Climate Bill of Rights."

These activists argued that the expansion and militarization of urban policing was designed from the start to lock up Black and Latinx youth for jaywalking, marijuana and alcohol possession, "resisting arrest," "parole violation," disorderly conduct, and loitering—virtual reenactments of the Black codes that followed the abolition of slavery. They argued that police expansion and increased armed force against unarmed communities was a form of colonial control and the antithesis of the interventions needed to support communities—housing, jobs, mental health clinics, health care, vibrant schools, and a dramatic reduction in police. Many communities are now mobilizing to move the police out of the public schools—and to demand that they keep their hands, batons, and cuffs off our children.

SROs are not equipped or trained to do this kind of work.

Teachers, at their best, are expert at this kind of social and emotional interaction. The fundamental problem plays out in myriad ways depending on concentric circles of context—history and culture, class and race, gender, economic condition and sense of agency—but it boils down to this: good teaching is personal, and it's built carefully, over time, on a base of care, mutual regard, trust, and dialogue, while policing is impersonal and objective, a fast-moving monologue. Both exercise authority, of course, but the teacher's authority at its best is earned through day-to-day practice, while the police officer's is recognized as an external fact.

Whatever else is taught or learned, "learning to live together" is the subtitle of an essential curriculum, sometimes hidden but occasionally intentional. "Learning to live together" might involve instruction in respect, for example, and fellow-feeling, not as a lecture typically but as a response to actual events in the day-to-day interactions of classroom life. Learning to live together cannot be reduced to the arid concept of "classroom management"—the management model assumes applying a set of techniques to control people in order to hurriedly get to the real lessons, but learning to live together *is* the lesson.

We might practice listening to one another, or speaking forcefully and persuasively, or on occasion taking care of one another. When someone dominates the space, we might consciously help that person offer a bit of space to others; when someone holds back consistently, we might search out a suitable stage and spotlight. When someone is angry we might help find an appropriate expression and outlet; when someone is struggling to understand, we might offer coaching and support. Whatever the instance or the circumstance, and for better or for worse, these early experiences of community and connection offer templates, frameworks, and lessons for life.

And learning to live together—in a family, a classroom, or a larger community—always involves contradiction and conflict, as it is a normal, natural part of community life. To habitually send someone to the office disrupts the field of learning; calling the cops blows the field to bits. These are places where the wise teacher or parent finds the richest and most fertile ground for teaching life's deepest and most abiding lessons.

In classrooms across the country, teachers are learning to implement restorative justice practices, allowing the community to come together, identify problems and wrongs that have been committed, and devise ways to make the community whole again. Further, these classrooms begin to explore possibilities of transformative or liberatory justice—a practice of justice that does not isolate a student transgression as a "crime" but instead explores the social context, the reasons such a violation occurred in the first place. This is the longer, harder work of making community work and getting to the bottom of social ruptures.

Black educator Jawanzaa Kunjufu argues, "You cannot teach a child you do not love. You cannot teach a child you do not respect. You cannot teach a child you do not understand."[6] These are critical elements necessary for the creation of safe and productive learning environments. And this kind of intimacy means giving a damn, and worrying about what happens to people in their everyday lives, not bringing in armed and uniformed men to control and intimidate our kids.

"TEACHERS NEED TO STICK WITH TEACHING THE GREAT LESSONS OF WESTERN CIVILIZATION IN ORDER TO CIVILIZE YOUTH AND MOLD THEM INTO THE GOOD CITIZENS OF THE FUTURE."

Our educational landscape has been fragmented by the competing claims to appropriate content, introducing a mishmash of different prejudices in history classes and random book selections in English. New teachers raised on a steady diet of "political correctness" in their college years now question everything about our values and traditions. In the process all the achievements of Western civilization and the United States are pushed to the background and questioned. While this is supposed to be in the interest of immigrants and minorities, such an approach actually makes it more difficult for these others to gain access to America's dazzling cultural wealth, and it positions them as eternal outsiders. Cultural values, ethical norms, the obligations of citizenship—these are all thrown out the window in the hands of the multicultural crowd and todays educational relativists.

E. D. Hirsch expressed these insights powerfully in his most influential book, *Cultural Literacy: What Every American Needs to Know.*

> Shared literate information is deliberately sustained by national systems of education in many countries because they recognize the importance of giving their children a common basis for communication. . . . [Multicultural education] should not be allowed

to supplant or interfere with our schools' responsibility to insure our children's mastery of American literate culture. . . . Once we become aware of the connection between literacy and cultural literacy, we have a duty to those who lack cultural literacy to determine and disclose its content.[1]

Hirsch understands that something critical that gets easily lost in the cacophony and chaos promulgated by advocates of multicultural education: our children need to partake in the common cultural traditions that have made our civilization the best in all of history, and they must have full exposure to our shared intellectual foundations in order to thrive in the modern world.

William Bennett, secretary of education under Ronald Reagan and former head of the National Endowment for the Humanities, provides a further argument for curing the pathology of youthfulness and civilizing the young in *The Book of Virtues*, his timeless collection of stories that he describes as a "'how-to' book for moral literacy."[2] Bennett aims to help children get on the right track, and to assist their parents in raising right-thinking kids, by offering fundamental lessons in ethics based on traditional tales that can "help anchor our children in their culture, its history and traditions." Bennett offers a useful *McGuffey's Reader* of do's and don'ts from the best works in literature around core principles that children desperately need now: self-discipline, compassion, responsibility, friendship, work, courage, perseverance, honesty, loyalty, and faith.

Bennett's perspective on work, to take just one example, is extremely useful for today's youth, and he packs ninety-four pages with Bible verses and other classics from the Western canon: Theodore Roosevelt weighs in with "In Praise of the Strenuous Life"; Booker T. Washington, a "soul who is willing to work and work and work to earn an education," describes his climb in "Up from Slavery;" Shakespeare provides this from "Henry V": "So work the honeybees;/Creatures that, by a rule in nature, teach/The act of order to a peopled kingdom."

David Coleman, the architect of the Common Core State Standards and head of the College Board, has adapted these insights in order to promote critical policy initiatives for our times. While American culture includes many voices, it is crucial that we settle on the "core knowledge" that is our common inheritance. Teachers need to be brought back to the basics through systems of accountability. Otherwise each teacher will do whatever the hell he or she feels like doing, which badly serves their students.

REALITY CHECK

Schools are institutions where we contend daily with basic questions concerning who we are and what kind of society we want to become. Public schools are where we work out and debate the meaning of democracy and the content of our core values. In our wildly diverse and incredibly vast country, teachers work in every village and town or community and neighborhood with children of great wealth and advantage as well as children of poverty and oppression, children of privilege and children of formerly enslaved people, First Nations people, and immigrants from poor countries who arrive with little more than the clothes on their backs. Teachers see it all, and teachers are in a position to recognize the richness of our diversity. Refusing to freeze culture or knowledge in packaged and unassailable towers, teachers can embrace a more dynamic diversity and a richer complexity, dive into the whirlwind and improvise, explore, and change day by day, year by year. This leap into the unfinished and the unknown makes schools one of the most vital and effective places to teach and model democratic life.

The fact that our cultural stories are in flux, incomplete and insufficient, in motion and always in need of further conversation, is one of the strengths of the United States. The white Europeans who dominated the continent from the first colonial incursions are soon to be a minority. There is an anxiety, a fear, that drives the elites—they insist on maintaining control of the national narrative as well as the institutions of power. While the old "culture wars" over the canon—what to read—was a bit overheated, there is nothing educational about an elitist approach to education.

European educators have been enamored of their own story for so long that it takes on the trappings of common sense. World history becomes the history of Western empires; literature is regarded as the trajectory of Western writing. They reduce the story of European culture, and even the body of knowledge that is science and mathematics, to settled facts, flat assertions of the way it is. Isaac Newton, in this telling, invented physics and here are the important formulas. The creativity, problem solving, and engagement that characterizes the best of studies is banished from the K–12 classroom, where boring recitation of apparently settled facts are described as "building blocks" for later learning.

With a democratic education, the world is not something one simply knows but rather is something to be explored, interrogated, interpreted, and regularly reconstructed.

E. D. Hirsch followed *Cultural Literacy* with a series of books in the 1980s and 1990s on the theme of "what every child needs to know." The conservative establishment championed the books because they promoted the idea that there was a superior and unitary elite culture, and the books were distributed widely through a generously funded national campaign. Hirsch explicitly opposed teaching that attempted to involve students in posing questions, exploring and experimenting, or drawing on their own experiences as a source of curriculum development. Hirsch's efforts were part of a larger offensive against the spread of multiculturalism carried out by a group of right-wing culture warriors: Lynn Cheney, Abigail and Stephan Thernstrom, Chester Finn, Sol Stern, and William Bennett.

Bennett's *The Book of Virtues* purports to separate the "complexities and controversies" of a moral life from the "basics" and distinguishes *lessons in ethics*, which he favors, from *moral activity*, which he advises suspending until maturity. It's important that youngsters remain passive recipients rather than active co-constructors of values: "these stories help anchor our children in their culture, its history and traditions."

Leaving aside what he chooses to tune out or delete—solidarity, say, or thoughtfulness, integrity, passion, generosity, curiosity, humor, social commitment—Bennett's proclaimed virtues reflect a specific ideological posture. His collection on work, for example (noted above), includes "Wynken, Blynken, and Nod," "The Little Red Hen," "The Three Little Pigs," "The Shoemaker and the Elves," and "How the Camel Got His Hump." It's heavy on ants and bees but lacking anyone who might interrogate work from all sides—there's no Karl Marx here, of course, but neither do we find Herman Melville, B. Traven, Tillie Olson, or Charles Dickens. There's no Studs Terkel, either, someone who would have eschewed the righteous preaching and probed the complexities and contradictions of work; the violence it can contain, for example, the ways in which human effort can lead to the transformation of people and their world, or the ways in which labor can be sometimes liberating, sometimes enslaving. Instead, we are instructed on the natural state of things: kings rule, soldiers fight valiantly, masons stack the bricks, and porters carry the heavy loads—everyone in his or her place, and a place for everyone—lots of bees and ants, working away.

Perhaps the example of French education and how they relate to youth from their former colonies will shine some light on the US dilemma of race—because French education authorities suffer from the same blind spots. We know an Algerian student who went through her whole high school career in a French speaking school in the Congo, and during the entire four years, she never read a single book or essay by an African author. It was all classic Greece and Rome, the Enlightenment, the Renaissance, and the like. This curriculum reveals a profound arrogance and lack of curiosity that infects colonial educators who reside in the richest continent in the world and still manage to ignore everything around them.

Laurent Cantet's film *The Class* (based on François Bégaudeau's autobiographical novel, *Entre les Murs*), explores the author's teaching experiences in Paris. Cantet takes us into the classroom and those routine moments that define the line between engagement and outright rebellion, and he illuminates the deep rift between the mission and self-image of the traditional school and the world the students are coming from. This is not the France of the 1950s, white and authoritarian and homogeneously Catholic. This is postcolonial France, with a student population what includes some Europeans but many more from Mali, Morocco, Algeria, and the French West Indies. Now, with the colonies come to the metropolitan center, the teachers' own racism stares them in the face.

For all their professionalism, all their attention to detail, even all their caring for the welfare of the students, the school staff is absolutely blinkered to the contradictions between their world and the world of their immigrant students. They carry on with the traditions, the same books, the same punishments, the same procedures that have always meant French education. But even the meanings of their words, the culture they are hoping to pass on, are hopelessly disconnected from the culture and the web of meanings the students live in. Indeed, the teachers are trying to construct a culture that is fifty years old and will never exist again. They have no idea how to change for a global culture of the twenty-first century. While the staff worries about students who get in trouble or who may get deported, they are absolutely unreflective about the kind of teaching they're doing.

The school exhibits no curiosity about the cultures, the concerns, the passions of the students. It is all "come to me" teaching, with the European teacher as the authority in the front of the room. At the end of the film, Bégaudeau, who plays the teacher, asks his students to write down one thing that they will take away from the class—one book or idea or new perspective. After, as the kids file out, one girl comes to him and, as he looks at her expectantly, says, "I can't think of anything I learned." He's crestfallen, but so are we—school is supposed to uplift; teachers are supposed to make a difference in students' lives. The girl's comment is an indictment not just of Bégaudeau but of all colonial education, and of all teaching that denies dialogue or refuses to notice or appreciate the world from the students' perspectives.

But, indeed, a colonialist education philosophy demands the breaking of any potential student resistance, forcing compliance or at least passivity to an arbitrary authority. The project of the Paris school will be successful if it trashes the culture and self-respect of the students. What appears as annoying and juvenile rebellion, then, is often a kind of resistance—even if it is a resistance that is not strategic or even successful. The overwhelming truth *The Class* captures is the dilemma, the crisis, of education in new global communities. Clearly, the old white male curriculum of American schools won't cut it; clearly, the patronizing French colonialist education is not going to work.

Can we reconsider the project of education as a whole? Can we ask ourselves what an educated person is, what kind of world these students are living in, what options we are offering them? It's not simply a matter of making the top-down, white-centered French or American education more palatable or more successful with those whose cultures have been marginalized and attacked by colonialism, enslavement, or conquest. The answer lies in a pedagogy that decenters white, European authority and draws a new map, a new world, in which this new generation is allowed to define its own direction, its own educational needs and dreams.

Many powerful and effective educators are adapting and are inviting new voices and worlds into the classroom. Carol Lee's "cultural modeling," Django Paris's "culturally sustaining pedagogy," Gloria Ladson-Billings's "critical race theory," Rochelle Gutiérrez's "mathematics with Nepantla," and so many more all show the creative ways that cultural diversity enriches and deepens learning.[3]

Culture is an important window into a child, and effective teachers learn to become lifelong students of culture. This is an ongoing and potentially enormously satisfying challenge. Teachers can think of themselves as explorers and learners, with their workshop the students themselves, the families and neighborhoods, and ever wider circles embracing larger and larger communities.

Culture, of course, is more than holidays, more than artifacts. Culture includes all the surface objects and characteristics of a people—food, art, clothing, music, crafts, and so on. And culture embraces, as well, all the traditions and customs people create: their rituals, games, sports, dialects, habits, and ways of life. But on the deepest and most subtle level, culture also embodies a people's beliefs and values, their way of looking at and describing the world, their language practices. This might include their religion and philosophy, their shared outlook, their approaches to child rearing, mating, and relating. Culture covers it all.

We miss a lot, then, if we never look beyond the "what" of culture—the things, the objects—if we never get to the "how" and the "why." We stunt our growth with ideas of culture as curiosity, as bits of exotica that some people have while others do not. All human beings spend their lives weaving webs of significance, and culture is nothing more nor less than those webs. That is, culture encompasses everything beyond the biological aspect of being human. Exploring culture is beginning a bridge to something huge and complex and wonderful.

Frederick Douglass tells a remarkable story of learning to read as a subversive activity. As a slave, Douglass had no rights and meager opportunities. Reading among slaves was strictly forbidden, for it could open worlds and create unimaginable mischief. Besides, according to their overlords, slaves had no need of reading. They could be trained in the necessary menial and backbreaking work, and that was all. Yet his master's wife, believing him to be an intelligent youngster, undertook to teach Douglass how to read the Bible in hopes that he would come closer to God. When the master discovered the crime, he exploded: "It will unfit him to be a slave!"[4]

Authentic education will unfit anyone to be a slave. That is because education is bold, creative, illuminating—in other words, education is for self-activating explorers of life, for those who would become agents able to challenge fate, for doers and activists, for citizens. Training is for the enslaved, for loyal subjects, for tractable employees, for willing consumers, for obedient soldiers. Education tears down walls; training is all barbed wire.

And yet, what we call education is too often no more than training. We participate, then, in certification mills, institutions founded on notions of control and discipline, lifeless and joyless places where people serve time and master a few basic skills on their way to a plain piece of paper that justifies and sanctions the whole affair. Sometimes these places are merely mindless, and sometimes they are expressly malevolent.

Top-down educational strategies have a long history in the United States, alongside and then following the practice of withholding education altogether from slaves. They always take the form of working to "civilize the savages." The civilizing mission of education found its ugliest side in the Carlisle Indian School, founded by Colonel Richard Pratt in Pennsylvania during the same time as the Indian extermination wars in the US West. The goal of the school was to isolate students from nomadic life, to keep them under constant surveillance in order to police "savage" behavior, and to build values of individuality against tribal identification. Pratt testified before Congress in 1879, "A great general has said that the only good Indian is a dead one, and that high sanction of this destruction has been an enormous factor in promoting Indian massacres. In a sense, I agree with the sentiment, but only in this: that all the Indian there is in the race should be dead. Kill the Indian in him, save the man."[5]

The cost of education at an Indian boarding school was great—dignity, individuality, humanity, maybe even sanity. The payoff was rather small: a menial job, a marginal place in the social order. Students had to submit to humiliation, degradation, and mutilation simply to learn how to function at the lowest levels of society. No wonder most refused: the price was high, the benefit meager.

Pratt played a similar role to such reformers as General Samuel Armstrong, who founded Hampton Institute in 1868 for the uplifting (and civilizing) of Black workers in Virginia.[6] A few years after Hampton opened, Armstrong wrote, "This is no easy machine to run wisely, rightly. The darkies are so full of human nature and have to be most carefully watched over. They are apt to be possessed with strange notions. To simply control them is one thing, but to educate, to draw them out, to develop the germ of good possibilities into firm fruition, requires the utmost care." Both Pratt and Armstrong based their approach to school on a Hobbesian notion of violent human nature, the savage id that needs to be repressed. As a response, they proposed a Foucaultian panopticon of total surveillance in order to guard against native cultural practices. This is, in its unvarnished clarity, without the code words so well developed today, the essential principle of how an elitist, white, male pedagogy regards the outsider, the colonized, the less worthy.

Education psychologists such as Herbert Spencer and Stanley Hall in the early twentieth century proposed a crude social Darwinist theory of education, arguing that white men were the most evolved humans and needed support for the highest order of thinking, while students of color were only fit for menial tasks and needed to learn discipline in school. All women, too, were seen as unfit for higher education. Hall subscribed to the pseudoscience of the day, one embraced by the progressives and reformers as well, eugenics. This theory proposed that the "better," the more evolved humans needed support to expand and dominate, while the lesser races had to be controlled and civilized. The "culture of poverty" narrative, which began with American anthropologist Oscar Lewis in the 1950s and was solidified by Daniel Moynihan, a sociologist who became a US senator from New York, in the 1960s, was the late-twentieth-century version of the mandate to civilize the savages. The culture of poverty suggests that poor people have developed bad work habits, weak familial relations, and a childlike inability to defer gratification and therefore must be taken in hand and civilized, trained in the virtues of middle-class behavior.

This patronizing and dismissive philosophy is not something only of the quaint 1950s. These traditions are present in the twenty-first century in the new authoritarian education policies. The proliferation of special programs and charter schools aimed at "fixing" African American, Latinx, and immigrant students are rife with this civilizing language. It can be seen in the professional development trainings led by Ruby Payne, an educator and entrepreneur whose best known book is *A Framework for Understanding Poverty*, and in the curricula developed by foundations, charter schools, and state regulators.[7] Poor students, students from oppressed communities, are defined as suffering from bad habits formed in the culture of poverty. Various medicalized terms such as ADHD and ODD, as well as poor impulse control, define these students as "other" and their behavior as closer to id-driven animals.

Schools claim to be giving students key skills and knowledge, and yet many deny students the one thing that is essential to their survival: something to live for. All the units in drug awareness, gang prevention, and mental health together are not worth that single hopeful thing.

Highly paid consultants and entrepreneurs have eagerly entered the field to try to "fix" the problematic behavior of marginalized youth. Programs such as positive discipline, no-excuses discipline, and extensive suspension and expulsion have characterized the latest get-tough atmosphere. Student activity is closely monitored, and such practices as silently lining up in the hallway to walk between one place and another mimic prison practices.

Even classroom norms reflect this civilizing-the-savages mentality. At many KIPP schools, the practice of calling out "SAVE!" when a student is heard speaking community language forms, is common. "SAVE" stands for "Standard American Vernacular English," and the shout-out is meant to shame and silence students from speaking the language of their neighborhood, community, or home—all in the interest of locking students into the blessings of white middle-class English. Another practice is known as SLANT—an acronym for "Sit up, Lean forward, Ask and answer questions, Nod your head, and Track the speaker with your eyes." In other words, the smallest orientations of the body, even eye movement, are policed in the interest of imprinting behaviors identified with the white, middle-class kids.

An example of this kind of mentality, the authoritarian control approach to discipline for "those kids" is found in the training manual of the Relay Graduate School of Education, which marks as the first principle of classroom management that the so-called Demanding Teacher is "the ultimate authority in the classroom, in other words, your mindset is, I am a total badass." The fear of the "other" suffuses the entire approach.[8]

The practices designed to "civilize the savages" obliterate the rich contributions of global cultures, suppress the creativity of language practices in all communities, and miseducate youth. In struggling for a student-centered curriculum, for one that honors the powerful diversity of our world and recognizes the assets students bring to the class, teachers are enacting democratic education.

This means not only incorporating diverse world literature in order to engage and understand our diverse society but also exploring other cultural expressions—poetry, music, art, ritual, and drama—in order to gain the deepest experience in school. In addition, democratic teachers respect the multiple discourses and communicative practices of our students, their ways of approaching the epistemology of science and math, in order to discover the many ways in to deep educational experiences. At its best, learning in school is a creative experience, an active practice of joy and community engagement. It is, in short, the opposite of the dreary regimentation that the neo-reformers envision.

Thoughtful and sensitive teachers learn to respond to the deepest realities of children's lives. In powerful classrooms, children are simply allowed to love, respect, cherish, and retain what they bring to school—their language, for example, and their perceptions, their values. Teachers understand that even as they teach, they will also be taught; even as they help others develop, they will themselves change and grow. This involves a certain amount of plunging into the unknown, listening and hearing, not as a dismal chore but as a thrilling experience. It might mean soliciting or borrowing materials and ideas from parents—records, tapes, books, magazines, games, recipes, familiar plants and fruits to use in science and math, tapes of parents telling familiar stories or singing songs or simply chatting—creating a collection of "cultural artifacts" or even a small museum of culture.

Parents can give teachers important information about child-rearing practices. Perhaps some families feel strongly that children should show respect through silence, while others expect children to look adults in the eye and engage in some back and forth. Perhaps some people feel it is essential that women work outside the home and that housework should be shared, while others insist that women's cooking and being there in the home is an expression of cultural coherence. This is important information for teachers. It allows us to transform whatever sense of certainty and cultural superiority we might bring to school into a genuine search for the history and meaning behind specific practices.

Lisa Delpit argues that an old debate in education, the debate between a "skill" and a "process" approach, is really a sterile and a false debate.[9] Good teachers, she believes, incorporate all kinds of instructional strategies and are vigilant for "what works." She also points out that underneath the "skills" versus "process" debate is discomfort and difficulty in recognizing or acknowledging cultural differences and practices, especially what she calls "the culture of power."

The culture of power, she says, means that issues of power with specific rules for participation are enacted in classrooms and that those issues reflect power relationships in the larger society. For example, the culture of power requires a certain amount of assertiveness and a certain amount of deference—knowing *when* to do *what* can be the kind of subtle knowledge teachers enact but fail to really teach: "If you are not already a participant in the culture of power, being told explicitly the rules of that culture makes acquiring power easier" and "those with power are frequently least aware of—or least willing to acknowledge—its existence. Those with less power are often most aware of its existence"[10]

Delpit believes that children need to be taught the codes and rules for full participation and that that teaching can only happen if teachers authentically seek out and consult parents and other adults who share the cultures of the children. She argues for communicating across cultures, a bridge-building activity that requires teachers to look, to listen, to open themselves to new ways of seeing and being:

> We do not really see through our eyes or hear through our ears, but through our beliefs. To put our beliefs on hold is to cease to exist as ourselves for a moment—and that is not easy. It is painful as well, because it means turning yourself inside out, giving up your sense of who you are, and being willing to see yourself in the unflattering light of another's angry gaze. It is not easy, but it is the only way to learn what it might feel like to be someone else and the only way to start the dialogue.[11]

Each person is the expert on his or her own life, and the people with the problems are also likely to be the people with the solutions. This points us toward solidarity with the students we teach and their families, and away from smug superiority and patronization. It encourages us to study the history and reason within people's actions, to become explorers and ethnographers in the fullest sense. It becomes apparent, then, that multiculturalism is a political (as opposed to an anthropological) question, and that for teachers, it is a question of democracy as well.

When we as teachers recognize that we are partners with our students in life's long and complex journey, when we begin to treat them with the dignity and respect they deserve for simply being, then we are on the road to becoming truly worthy teachers.

"TEACHERS NEED TO FOCUS LESS ON THE ARTS, MORE ON STEM."

Too often schools are treated as feel-good centers with all manner of fun but irrelevant electives—from basket weaving to making up rap songs. These activities are welcome in after school and summer camp spaces, but public monies, especially in times of fiscal belt-tightening, should not be frittered away on this kind of fluff.

Or, to put it another way, our schools are failing to meet basic benchmarks in science and math, the fields that are vital to our economy and defense. The taxpayers who are footing the bill deserve more. Teachers must first cover the basics so our schools can supply the economy with the trained workers that have been identified as crucial. And that means less art and more science, technology, engineering, and mathematics—STEM.

REALITY CHECK

Art is not a distraction from the real business of school—far from it—nor is it a frivolous waste of time. A serious encounter with the arts unleashes critical qualities that are at the heart of an education for enlightened and engaged people: curiosity, imagination, critical investigation, initiative, problem solving, and improvisation. These are in fact the *arts of liberty*, the core values and conditions necessary for full and authentic participation in a democratic society. Working with the arts involves experimentation, observation and analysis, practice and reflection, discovery and surprise—indeed, the construction of a world as well as a self. Whatever subject matter or disciplinary areas a teacher shares—math, for example, or science, technology, literature, or history—artful teaching, at its best, always incites explorations.

Or, to put it in the memorable words of the dazzling Chicago poet Gwendolyn Brooks, who begins "The Chicago Picasso" with a question, "Does man love art?" and answers: "Man visits Art, but squirms. Art hurts. Art urges voyages."[1] As does teaching—in every realm.

The voyages art demands lie at the very heart of our humanness: journeys in search of new solutions to old problems, explorations of spirit spaces and emotional landscapes, trips into the hidden meanings and elaborate schemes we construct to make our lives understandable and endurable, flights hooked on metaphor and analogy, wobbly rambles away from the cold reality we now inhabit toward an indistinct but beckoning world beyond. These are the voyages that foreground the capacities and features that mark us as uniquely *human* beings.

But it's also true that art hurts. The capacity to see the world as if it could be otherwise creates yearning and liberates desire—we are freed (or condemned) to run riot. Art—necessarily subversive, unruly, and disruptive—challenges the status quo simply by opening considerations of alternatives; suddenly the taken-for-granted and the given world become choices and no longer habits and warrants, life (or death) sentences.

Art embraces the province of the possible, and that open territory is not always sweet and succulent—it can also contain monsters and horrors. "Art is not chaste," said Pablo Picasso. "Those ill-prepared should be allowed no contact with art. Art is dangerous. If it is chaste it is not art."[2] He distinguishes pretty decorations and castles in the clouds from the grit and grind, rough and tumble of art. Emily Dickinson asserted that "art lights the slow fuse of possibility."[3]

Imagination is more a process than a product, more "stance" than "thing," and engaging the student's imagination involves the dynamic work of mapping the world as such and leaning toward a world that might be but is not yet. Most of us, most of the time, accept our lot in life as inevitable—for decades, generations, even centuries. But when a revolution is in reach, when a lovelier life heaves into view, or when a possible world becomes somehow visible, the status quo becomes suddenly unendurable. We then reject the fixed and the stable, and begin to look at the world as if it could be otherwise, and we begin the important work of reweaving our shared world.

Cultivating imagination, and creating the conditions where more of us more of the time can wonder about our ability to create something else, to collectively conceive humane alternatives, asks us to be process oriented, more skeptical than certain, improvisational before formal, open to shifts and changes in a dynamic world.

The aesthetic is the opposite of the anesthetic: anesthesia is a drug that puts folks to sleep, while aesthetics is a treatment with the potential to wake us up and propel us out of bed again and again. It takes some courage to make or face strong art, life-saving art, or art that tells the unvarnished truth. The Beat poet Diane Di Prima said, "I have just realized that the stakes are myself; I have no other ransom money."[4]

We are, in spite of the existential feel of things and our own natural narcissism, *finite* beings plunging through an *infinite* space and gazing toward an expanding heaven. Learning to question, to experiment, to wonder and to wander, to construct and create—this is where art lives, and it is the sturdiest foundation upon which to build lives of participation and purpose for free people.

One of the disservices offered up by the narrow pragmatists in education, those who want to confine the curriculum to only those subjects that they think will be instrumental in advancing the economy, is that even on their own terms they're way off base. By proposing what "today's CEOs" are demanding from the labor force, they have accepted a shortsighted view, mainly a sparse vision of the present and a fantasy about the past. They have no idea where the economy, or the thriving of human society, is going, and they're shooting in the dark.

If you were to line up all the courses and curriculum of a high school in 1950 to what the CEOs demanded, you would be producing organization men, bureaucrats, factory workers, and bomb builders. Education policy makers did not emphasize computer technology, entrepreneurship, or international development. The only way new ideas, new futures, are produced is by allowing and encouraging people to think outside the taken for granted, to name new goals and to identify fresh challenges, solve new problems, and create the next horizons.

This is not to say that the arts should only be supported because they will produce the next start-ups or because they are the best way to assure US economic dominance. Pedro Noguera has pointed out that we particularly need the arts in inner cities because these communities need to nourish and build the imaginative capacities to develop and create new economic systems that have a place for them. A school system that promotes passivity, test prep aimed at getting the "right answer," only encourages the creation of tight technicians and passive rule-followers—people who would willingly synthesize genetically modified crops or operate distant drone-bombing sorties on a computer screen. People who think for themselves are dangerous—and they offer the only hope for our future.

But promoting and defending the arts in schools goes further than this and opens to the world of basic ethics—ethics concerning what it means to be human and how we all participate in culture. One of the first ethical principles of schooling has to be that each human being is unique and valuable and is living her or his life right now. Childhood is not just a time of preparation for a future life, the drudgery of training. Childhood is life itself. Children deserve a full and complex and satisfying life in the here and now. The joys of the arts, from literary to visual, from music to dance, are the birthright of every human being.

The arts are too often small and marginalized in schools, and this is a gathering catastrophe, not only for students and teachers but for our common future as well. The arts ought to be at the center and in every corner of an education for participation and democracy. Schools ban the arts from inside the walls at their peril. Young people will have culture; they will pursue beauty, whether it is inside or outside school. If the classroom is sterile, youth will break out to make music in the streets, to paint on the walls, to bust spoken word in hidden ciphers, and to dance in underground clubs. All these venues should exist but they also should be invited inside schools, through the permeable walls of a community-engaged curriculum. In "Boy Breaking Glass," Gwendolyn Brooks declares, in the voice of a delinquent, "I shall create! If not a note, a hole/ If not an overture, a desecration."[5]

In the United States, schooling favors the cool rationality and the distant objectivism associated with European legal scholarship—it's the formal reasoning of Apollo and the banishment of the passion and ecstasy of Dionysus. Behold the many ways an arts program, in its Dionysian ecstasy, resists and subverts the cool (and boring) classes of the rest of the day: intuition and feelings are honored; mistakes are welcomed as all creation comes from a series of missteps; the full person is present, the embodied and emotional and complex person, as opposed to the lonely logician; power is renegotiated as the teacher and student are contributing together to the project; an apprenticeship model of teaching replaces the top-down, "sage-on-the-stage" pedagogy.

Bertrand Russell once said that every person "is encompassed by a cloud of comforting convictions, which move with him [or her] like flies on a summer day."[6] The comforting convictions about schools include the bells and the public address system, of course, the classes and the schedules and the elaborate management schemes, but most important, the conviction that there is—and *must be*—a rigid hierarchy of teachers and learners in place.

The arts allow students to explore and create new and sustainable ways of living and thriving. Where school learning is too often derivative, generally looking passively at the actions and creations of others, the arts emphasize the production and reproduction of reality by students themselves. The arts explore the dangerous and exciting world of freedom, especially freedom of expression.

Students who resist school all day, who understand intuitively how it's not for them, often throw themselves powerfully into arts programs. As Maxine Greene points out, boredom in school is tied to meaninglessness, to hollowed-out constructs that are only dim approximations of reality.[7] But the arts engage students because they matter. Indeed, only by developing a vital arts program can we promote the kind of wide-awakeness that Paulo Freire describes, the kind of engaged *conscientização* (conscientization, the building of consciousness) that characterizes fully engaged, empowered participants in human society.[8] Life begins in wonder, and so does art; education too. Watch a newborn—five minutes old and at her mother's breast for the first time and already there are questions and explorations, a dialogue of discovery and surprise only just underway. Look at a toddler negotiating her apartment or a nearby park or the beach—all five senses are fully engaged, every discovery considered and touched and smelled and—oops!—into the mouth for a taste! And soon they are sorting and building, drawing on paper or walls if the materials are at hand, imagining stories and inventing words, and putting their handprints on everything. Every kid comes to school a question mark and an exclamation point.

Every teacher must decide whether to keep the questions and the passion alive—creating environments for exploration, for doing and making, for experimenting and hypothesizing and failing and succeeding—or to hammer the children into shape so that they leave her classroom, no longer as vital question marks or exclamation points, but as dull periods.

One of Paul Gauguin's most bizarre and oddly engaging works is a vast canvas filled with quasireligious symbolism and wild wanderings, its title scrawled across it in a fevered hand: *Where do we come from? What are we? Where are we going?*

Art asks those kinds of questions. At its best, education does too.

By developing arts education, we naturally create and enact horizontal classrooms, places where students are in authentic communication and necessary connection with each other. This is how adults live and work, how democracy works—it's never one person sitting alone but always people gathering together in associative living, active collaboration, the give and take of dialogue. This encourages the most powerful learning, the social construction of knowledge. In transformative classrooms and experiences, children become different than they were, and they do so voluntarily because of a need to create and to communicate with one another.

The arts need not be segregated and consigned only to the art classrooms or the extracurricular clubs. Many teachers are learning to apply what Lois Hetland calls the "Studio Habits of Mind"— learning skills that apply across disciplines and that can guide powerful planning and meaningful classroom performances.[9] These studio habits and practices are what characterize art class and art enterprises. They point the way to a more vital, meaningful, and revolutionary idea of schooling.

What would an arts-informed curriculum look like? First, artists learn to *engage and persist*. This means the capacity to approach a problem deeply, with full commitment, and to work on it over time. That is in contrast to the typical student, who has learned to get by with the minimum of work, to cut corners and fake it. Next they have to *observe* their world and other art closely, with fresh eyes. Art is often about making the familiar strange. And the best of education is the same.

After that, artists *envision*—how to reframe and imagine ways the world could be different, how to look at it anew. Then they *express*—they represent and create new realities; they create new worlds. In addition, artists *develop their craft*; they work over and over on skills and technique, bringing their vision and the representations they make into closer connection.

Artists learn to *reflect and critique*, to look back on what they have created, what others have created and evaluate it. They practice questioning and explaining artistic creations. Finally, artists *stretch and explore*, extending their work into new domains, crossing disciplinary and media boundaries, and engaging with communities for inspiration towards the next step.

All of these practices, these habits of studio thinking, also make for an inspiring curriculum in schools. The best teachers incorporate this kind of artistic thinking in their pedagogy and they regard teaching itself as an art—a practice of freedom and creativity that is always making new contributions to the world.

Stanford University's Design School has introduced the concept of "design thinking" into curriculum planning, an approach that incorporates arts sensibility into teaching.[10] Instead of the linear "backward planning," which presupposes that the endpoint is known by the teacher and the only task is to take the steps to get there, design approaches favor an open-ended, exploratory pedagogy. This, too, is a matter of learning from the arts.

The arts offer students an invitation to become the agents of their own stories, the authors of their own lives or the actors in their own films as opposed to some anonymous walk-on in someone else's worn-out and clichéd script.

Author, actor, composer—these roles allow youth to wield essential tools against propaganda, political agendas, dogma, and all manner of impositions and stereotypes. Art seeks honesty and authenticity, and that means it dives into disagreements, inconsistencies, confusion, challenges, turmoil, paradoxes, disputes, uncertainty, and every other kind of muddle. That makes art an ally of critical and engaged and vibrant minds. Art enhances a sense of being fully human, a work-in-progress born into the vortex of a dynamic world.

"THE TRULY GREAT
TEACHERS ARE HEROES."

We all know from hundreds of heartwarming stories that great teachers perform miracles. Every memorable teacher film for the last several decades—from *Blackboard Jungle* through *Stand and Deliver*, from *Dangerous Minds* to *Freedom Writers*—offers loads of inspiration and insight, as well as a successful model for teachers to follow. In every uplifting story, we see tough kids responding positively to a determined, hardworking teacher, someone willing to sacrifice everything in order to rescue these children and youth from the sewers of their circumstances (including their peers and their dreadful, dysfunctional families), and in the end we experience the payoff: triumph, transformation, redemption. The great ones, the teachers who truly make a difference for kids, work incredibly long hours, give freely of their time, forsake other interests and commitments, including family, and sometimes even their own health. They hold high standards and demand the best of their students. These hero teachers are the change-makers, helping these students to move up in the world, all the way to college.

Teachers work hard because of their deep hearts. Putting the kids first, they sacrifice and they connect. In fact, good pay would be an insult, as teaching is a calling for them, like becoming a priest or a nun.

REALITY CHECK

Teaching is a caring profession, it's true, like nursing or social work or elder care, and traditionally teaching has been female work. While the very earliest teachers in the United States were itinerant schoolmasters, the transition to mass education saw the feminization of the profession with layers of male supervision over them. This is a shameful part of American labor history. Women's "invisible" work in the home is defined as dwelling outside the money economy and is generally unpaid; women-dominated professions have been historically devalued, often cast as an extension of volunteerism, and therefore poorly compensated. Some years ago, nurses developed a more militant organizing and labor-union approach. Nurses today earn a more decent salary, averaging $70,000 to $90,000, while teachers—with unions that have not had the same level of militancy—are trapped in the narrative of sainthood, paid around $45,000 to $56,000.[1]

Horace Mann, the first proponent of universal public education, the common schools in Massachusetts, used praise for the virtues of women to marginalize them into low-paid and volunteer caring labor:

> As a teacher of schools, how she shames the wisdom of the lawgiver and the retributions of the judge, by saving where they sacrifice, and redeeming where they destroy! To hospitals for disease and suffering, to prisons for penal retribution, to receptacles for reformation from deepest abasement and guilt, how divinely does she come, her head encircled with a halo of heavenly light, her feet sweetening the earth on which she treads, and the celestial radiance of her benignity making vice begin its work of repentance through very envy of the beauty of virtue![2]

While Mann's language to the modern ear sounds sentimental and perhaps even ridiculous, the inheritors of this tradition exist in popular culture. The reign of dull and unhelpful slogans for effective teaching is deeply embedded in the culture and widely promoted by the corporate reform crowd, who double down on these already well-established but least helpful instructions for teachers: Have a big heart. But get tough and be firm.

In political debate, teachers are depicted variously as serious professionals worthy of the community's praise if not its bounty, or as under-skilled and unmotivated placeholders grown lazy in the sinecure of government employment. We are conduits of official curriculum—the stuff of classrooms—or creators and purveyors of some probably wacky or wicked ideas of our own creation, and here we inhabit a whole field of contention. Some focus on our dispositions and habits of thinking; others question our expertise and our proficiency; many seem giddily poised to spring upon our bleeding bodies. Teaching as work.

In popular culture, we are knaves or knights, both gods and monsters. The enduring image is of a solitary teacher-hero fighting valiantly to lift up poor or troubled kids, working diligently to save them from the sewers of their circumstances. Teaching as salvation and as drama.

And it's true: teaching is drama; it's work; it's both science and art. Still, none of these images holds much sustainable interest. None is wide enough or deep enough, none vital enough to capture the reality of teaching. None goes directly to the heart of the experience—to the intellectual demand, to the ethical purpose or the moral meaning, to the larger spirit that can animate the whole enterprise. What these narratives lack, even the seemingly benign, is a sense of the soul of teaching. It is this territory—teaching as a relentlessly moral endeavor, teaching as ethical action, messy, grand, and tangled—that cries out urgently to be explored.

The inadequate narrative occupies the standard teacher-movie plot, promoting a dominant idea of what good teaching is. In popular films like *Stand and Deliver* and *Lean on Me*, the teacher is an isolated hero (in other films a heroine) and a child-saver who must shake off naive and romantic notions in order to rescue the good juvenile delinquents. The hero teacher confronts wretched parents, cynical colleagues, dangerous gangs, and discouraged young people—and he (usually) prevails.

These themes are articulated perfectly in Richard Brooks's 1955 classic *Blackboard Jungle*, a film that manages to exploit perfectly the tinny patriotism and surface smugness of its day, while reflecting, and in a sense prefiguring, the underground conflicts and tensions about to burst to the surface in American society during that period. *Blackboard Jungle* says it all, beginning with a title that taps seamlessly into deep racial stereotypes and captures a pervasive sense of civilization in combat with savagery, of white chalk scraping along a black surface. It plays excitedly to all the received wisdom concerning teaching and schooling, as well as to the wider fears—racial and sexual—of a precarious middle class. Its portrait of the idealistic teacher struggling to save the delinquent boy with a good heart is imprinted in our cultural collective consciousness; it's a foundational myth. Much of what passes for common sense about teaching—and every popular teacher film since 1955—is simply derivative. The fact that the police were called in to control the violence in theaters across the country when *Blackboard Jungle* opened (a first!) set a pattern that itself has become a cliché.

The film opens with a prudish, if disingenuous, apology read against a military drumbeat:

> We in the United States are fortunate to have a school system that is a tribute to our communities and our faith in American youth.
>
> Today we are concerned with juvenile delinquency—its causes and its effects. We are especially concerned when this delinquency boils over into our schools.
>
> The scenes depicted here are fictional. However, we believe that public awareness is a first step toward a remedy for any problem. It is in this spirit and with this faith that *Blackboard Jungle* was produced.

But the filmmakers don't mean any of it.

The film thrusts the audience into an urban schoolyard where tough (mostly white) kids jitterbug and jostle one another to the pounding rhythms of Bill Haley and the Comets' "Rock Around the Clock." It's sexual, exciting, a bit anarchistic, amazingly melodramatic.

Enter Richard Dadier (Glenn Ford), a wide-eyed, shy, young Korean War veteran looking for a teaching job. To his delight, Dadier is hired on the spot, but when he turns hesitantly to the harsh and aloof principal with "just one question: the discipline problem," the response is definitive: "There is no discipline problem! Not as long as I'm principal." We are not reassured.

His fellow teachers mock the principal behind his back: "There's no discipline problem at Alcatraz either"; "They hire fools like us with college degrees to sit on that garbage can and keep them in school so women for a few hours a day can walk around the city without being attacked." Richard Dadier is awed, but can't resist a rookie's question: "These kids . . . they can't *all* be that bad. . . ."

Oh no? Opening day is anarchy. The new teachers sit blinking at the barbarians, while the assistant principal snarls and cracks the whip. The auditorium pulsates—it's a mob scene of pushing, punching, smoking, shouting. When the innocent Miss Hammond is introduced, the crowd goes into orbit, and with the camera playing on her ass, everyone—on and off screen—is invited to leer. The film is ambivalent later when she's attacked: she really shouldn't dress that way, it implies, or look that way, but at the same time, these boys are clearly animals—can't they draw a line between wolf whistles and rape? When Dadier saves Miss Hammond and captures her attacker, his students shun him.

Richard Dadier struggles on. He means well, and he cares, and within a certain framework, he even tries. He shows the kids a cartoon to accompany his homily on thinking for themselves; he encourages them to see how important English will be if they become mechanics or carpenters. He encourages Gregory Miller (Sidney Poitier), the good delinquent ("a little smarter, a little brighter") to play the piano and sing in the Christmas show. It's the Hollywood dream machine: Black folks sing and play, aspirations for working-class youth are appropriately low, and white liberals are loved for their good intentions. There's no hint that the obstacles and challenges these students face include structures of disadvantage, the harsh realities of race and class, or the existence of two worlds, separate and unequal. In fact, Richard Dadier tells Miller to get the chip off his shoulder and says that racism is "not a good excuse" for failure; "Dr. Ralph Bunche proved that."

Here's a short list of what Richard Dadier endures: he is mugged and badly cut by a group of delinquents in an alley; his best friend on the faculty has his priceless collection of jazz records smashed up by the kids; he and his pregnant wife are almost killed by kids drag racing; he is accused of racial prejudice after attempting to teach about the ignorance of name-calling; and his wife goes into premature labor after receiving anonymous notes and phone calls indicating that Miss Hammond and Dadier are having an affair. Through it all, Richard Dadier bends but never breaks. At his lowest point (with a new job offer in hand), his wife reminds him that "kids are people . . . most people are worthwhile. We all need the same things: patience, love, understanding." Her list, of course, is short, and it misses other possibilities, like justice, collective solutions, and the power to affect our lives.

Richard Dadier is wide-eyed much of the time, unable to process the depths to which human beings can sink. About to give up, he visits his old professor to seek advice. At the college during his visit, with the "Star Spangled Banner" playing in the background, Dadier watches well-mannered students attending well-run classrooms, and he questions how he can teach "kids who don't want to learn," who have "IQs of 66" and act like "wild animals." The sage old man reminds him that people want to be creative and that Dadier has been called to "sculpt minds" in a place where he is badly needed. "For every school like yours, there are a hundred like this. This school could use you; your school needs you."

Richard Dadier and the professor join in singing the last lines of the national anthem, and Dadier thanks his mentor: "I think I'll take another crack at my jungle."

Back in the jungle, Dadier's efforts are paying off. He works on Miller, urging him to use his influence to break the grip of the gangs: "I've been looking at your file," he says, "and you're a natural leader." When a troubled gang leader pulls a knife on Dadier, Miller backs his teacher and the tide turns. The whole class takes the bad delinquents to the principal's office, and Richard Dadier helps the class get on with the serious business of learning: copying sentences from the board.

Part of the attraction of a narrative like this is that it has some truth to it. Teachers take on the impossibly complex work of reaching and inspiring and connecting to 20 kids, 35 kids, sometimes 150 kids. The project of teaching is multifaceted and demanding, and most teachers do an incredible job of it. Teachers witness tragedies every day, yes, but also miracles—big ones and little ones. What teachers really want is a witness, someone to understand the tremendous transformations happening in their classrooms. And, it must be added, many of the people attending the teacher-hero movie may have memories of fantastic connection with and deep inspiration drawn from their own teachers.

The problem is that the Hollywood narrative, when reduced to the sound bite or played out in a tear-jerking movie, simplifies the task of teaching and reinforces the notion of the Christlike teacher. These versions have little room for the complexities of instruction, the adventures of a curriculum of inquiry, or the deep work that goes into community building. Instead, the hero teacher is an attractive genius who turns young people around with a few inspiring speeches. And she never, ever demands decent working conditions or more pay. That would be improper and a bit unseemly.

MADtv created the perfect critique of the teacher-hero narrative called "Nice White Lady."[3] The scene: A group of tough-looking and unruly Black and Latinx teenagers gathered together in a disheveled classroom where they lounge on the desks and admire their lethal-looking weaponry. The ominous, stentorian voiceover: "Inner-city high school is a dangerous place. A place where hope has lost out to hate, where your homework isn't about math, it's about staying alive." Cut to a Latinx student with maximum attitude, close-up, full face: "If you Black, Latino, or Asian, you will get shot—that's a fact." Voiceover: "There's only one thing that can make these kids learn—"

Before we finish that sentence, let's locate ourselves in the narrative thus far: We know that teenagers are trouble, that African American and Latinx kids are particularly problematic. More than indifferent and self-absorbed, they are prone to mindless violence. And while city schools are chaotic and dilapidated, there is a single, straightforward solution somewhere close at hand: "Only one thing that can make these kids learn . . ." And what is that miracle, that one thing? The narrator finishes with a flourish: "a nice white lady."

Most of us could have written that script ourselves. Our culture, after all, is steeped in cliché, and the plot points are all so predictable, the outcome so insistent, that it ends up overwhelming our own lived experiences, making us wonder why our efforts don't ever quite measure up, why the heroic outcome eludes us. The conclusion is never, what's wrong with this picture but, rather, what can I be doing wrong?

"Nice White Lady" lasts just over three minutes, but somehow packs in all the clichés: As a young, innocent Amy Little introduces herself to the jeering students, the narrator intones, "With the odds against her, she'll do the unthinkable." An older colleague, eager to temper her idealism and wake her up, barks, "Forget it! These are minorities—they can't learn, and they can't be educated." Amy Little won't be deterred: "With all due respect, sir, I'm a white lady— I can do anything."

She implores her students to let her teach them, but they resist, one girl giving her a standard street lecture: "What you think is going to happen here? You think you going to inspire me? Break through my tough-girl act and see the beauty that's within? Is that what you think?" She shoots the girl an intense and meaningful look, pulls out a pen and a notebook and pushes it toward her saying, "Write that down!"

Soon everyone is writing up a storm, weapons are holstered, and their troubles are gone. Before long, Amy and her students are dancing in the aisles as the narrator intones, "When it comes to teaching inner-city minorities, you don't need books and you don't need rules—all you need is a nice white lady."

Every part of "Nice White Lady" is well known, and all of it stands on a rampart of received wisdom and racist orthodoxy. All of it stands, as well, as an obstacle to effective teaching and meaningful effort.

The desire to help, always hierarchical and tied to privilege, typically feeds on sensationalism and images of the exotic, and often results, regardless of intent, in some form of colonial relationship. As Judith Halberstam writes in *The Queer Art of Failure*, "When we are taught that we cannot know things unless we are taught by great minds, we submit to a whole suite of unfree practices that take on the form of a colonial relation."[4] This is why "service" is such a miserable motivation for teachers and ought to be challenged and opposed in favor of solidarity: working with not for, learning from not about, moving horizontally not vertically. The stance of solidarity asks us to learn from one another—there is no outside expert to consult, no Lady Bountiful in the wings, no foundation or government grant that can replace the wisdom on the ground—and to note that while the world is not yet decolonized, we can each struggle to decolonize our own minds. As teachers we can resist the missionaries within ourselves while we find ways to work with the people.

Some of this sentiment is embodied in a poster directed at visitors that hangs today near the headquarters of the revolutionary Zapatista movement in Chiapas, Mexico: If you have come to help us, it says, please go home. If you have come to join us, welcome. Pick up a shovel or a machete and get busy.

Ella Baker, one of the leaders of the modern Black Freedom movement and the elder most revered in the 1960s by the young militants of the Student Nonviolent Coordinating Committee, promoted the idea of student volunteers working in the Freedom Schools and on voter-registration projects in Mississippi, Georgia, and Alabama. The work needed doing, and the volunteers were willing, but Baker was deeply skeptical about the help these students would actually bring to the sharecroppers and peasants of the South. She pointed out—in a radical reversal of the conventional wisdom that was typical of her—that the students from colleges and universities all over the country had everything to learn from the oppressed people themselves, and that the volunteers—with all their formal book-learning and their degrees and their professional futures—were the ones in deepest need of help. "The people you've come to help know better," she said.

So she urged them on, not in the posture of do-gooders but in the stance of seekers and learners. *Ella Baker and the Black Freedom Movement*, by Barbara Ransby, is a masterful study of a life devoted to participatory democracy and internationalism, community education, and grassroots organizing with the dispossessed.[5] Baker recognized and advocated the idea that the best teachers are first and foremost students of their students.

This reversal of power and privilege became a defining feature of the culture and the politics being built in the struggle against the racist Jim Crow system. The movement incubated and then sent forward its transcendent leaders—the visionary Reverend Martin Luther King Jr., the determined and courageous Rosa Parks, the intrepid organizer Bayard Rustin, the revolutionary Stokely Carmichael. But its character was shaped as well by the uncommon common people—Fannie Lou Hamer, Esau Jenkins, Bernice Robinson—pushing from the ground up, fueling a sense of urgency, and making connections between crummy schools, segregated facilities, and meager wages, for example, with a fatally flawed and fraudulent democracy: the rotting shack as an objective correlative for a rotting system. They had the problems, and they also had the solutions—they were the ones who kept the movement moving.

The philosopher Hannah Arendt argues:

> Education is the point at which we decide whether we love the world enough to assume responsibility for it and by the same token save it from that ruin which, except for renewal, except for the coming of the new and the young, would be inevitable. And education, too, is where we decide whether we love our children enough not to expel them from our world and leave them to their own devices, nor to strike from their hands their chance of undertaking something new, something unforeseen by us, but to prepare them in advance for the task of renewing a common world.[6]

Arendt provides a useful frame for considering teaching's moral heart. We can see that school is a natural site of hope and struggle—hope hovering around notions of a future, struggle busting out over everything about that future: the direction it should take, the shape it could assume, the meanings it might encompass. Who can participate? What do we want for the children? And for ourselves? What worlds might we dream into being? What tools, skills, and accumulated wisdom should we offer the young, the coming generation? What might they create for themselves? Each of these questions invites us to reflect, debate, consider, and make judgments from conflicting claims. We raise questions, doubts, and challenges about the aims and the content of education. We proceed into the ethical, the everyday universe and home address of thoughtful and caring teachers.

The real hero teacher is not a noisy performer or a larger-than-life savior. The real heroes show up and engage students; they are bold and modest, assertive but humble. They persevere, and they resist the narcissism that wants them on a pedestal as they readjust the spotlight to focus on the students. What does each one need? And just as important, what does each one bring?

The challenge for everyday teachers is to know that every student arrives in class as an *unruly spark of meaning-making energy on a voyage of discovery and surprise*; that each is unique, each a dynamic work in progress, unfinished, contingent, leaning forward. If a teacher embraces that diversity (as opposed to spending gobs of energy denying and suppressing it), the classroom will of necessity be seen as a work in progress as well, unfinished, ever changing, and contingent, filled with the messiness and wonder of humanity.

In schools for free people, obedience and conformity are pushed aside in favor of initiative and imagination, curiosity and questioning. On the side of a liberating and humanizing education is a pedagogy of inquiry, an approach that opens rather than closes the process of thinking, comparing, reasoning, and dialogue. It demands something upending and revolutionary from students and teachers alike: repudiate your place in the pecking order, it urges; remove that distorted, congenial mask of compliance. *You must change.*

Teachers who aspire to participate and contribute to the creation of free people who can participate fully in a free society embrace an elegant but straightforward ideal: every human being is a three-dimensional creature much like yourself; a person with hopes, dreams, skills, and experiences; each with a body, a mind, and a spirit; each with a history, a community, and agency that must somehow be valued, respected, and represented in your classroom and somehow taken into account in your teaching. This is a value to honor and embed deep within classroom routines, structures, culture, and environment—it's a value that challenges teachers to reject and resist actions that treat students as objects or gestures that erase, ignore, or silence their full humanity. This is easy enough to say, this simple injunction, but excruciatingly difficult to enact in the daily lives of schools or classrooms, especially in places where labeling students, sorting them into hierarchies of winners and losers, and managing their behaviors have become the commonplace markers of good teaching.

Recognition of the full humanity of each of our students is a kind of quiet, everyday heroism all its own. It's where we begin, and it's where we end.

Acknowledgments

This volume is simply the latest utterance in an ongoing conversation concerning the importance of public education, the power of public spaces to create and maintain a free society, and the collective duty of each generation to contribute to the possibility of a positive future for its children.

We acknowledge the many smart, hopeful, critical, caring, and generous people who have been part of that conversation for decades and who have led us to do this work. Thanks to the dazzling teachers who challenged and nourished us—often in the same gesture—inspired us and changed our lives, including Maxine Greene, Anna Richert, William Watkins, Leah Levinger, Nancy Balaban, Ray McDermott, Mike Rose, Lisa Delpit, Jabari Mahiri, and Erica Meiners.

We acknowledge the thoughtful and articulate scholars who pursued the evidence and pioneered and developed powerful arguments about the importance of public schools and the power of good teaching: Diane Ravitch, Pedro Noguera, David Berliner and Gene Glass, Kevin Kumashiro, Joel Westheimer, Joe Kahne, Lisa Delpit, Angela Valenzuela, Sonia Nieto, Alan Singer, and Gloria Ladson-Billings.

Special thanks to those colleagues and comrades who read parts of this manuscript in progress and offered helpful feedback: Wayne Au, Bree Picower, David Stovall, Valerie Kinloch, John Ayers, Ilene

Abrams, Mike Klonsky, Fred Klonsky, James Thindwa, and Jay Gillen. And to Boyd Bellinger for invaluable help in tracking down and documenting source materials.

And, finally, thanks to our awesome editors and staff at Beacon Press: Jill Petty, who brilliantly got the ball rolling, and also Helene Atwan, Maya Fernandez, Beth Collins, Susan Lumenello, Tom Hallock, Sanj Kharbanda, and Nicholas DiSabatino.

NOTES

INTRODUCTION: "Rotten Apples"

1. Haley Sweetland Edwards, "Rotten Apples: It's Nearly Impossible to Fire a Bad Teacher. Some Tech Millionaires May Have Found a Way to Change That," *Time*, November 3, 2014, cover.
2. Amanda Ripley, "How to Fix America's Schools," *Time*, December 8, 2008.
3. Elizabeth Green, "Can Good Teaching Be Learned?," *New York Times*, March 7, 2010, http://query.nytimes.com/gst/fullpage.html?res=9406E0D 6173BF934A35750C0A9669D8B63&pagewanted=all.
4. Evan Thomas, "Why We Must Fire Bad Teachers," *Newsweek*, March 5, 2010, http://www.newsweek.com/why-we-must-fire-bad-teachers-69467, accessed July 20, 2017.
5. Elizabeth Green, "Building a Better Teacher," *New York Times Magazine*, March 7, 2010, http://www.nytimes.com/2010/03/07/magazine/07 Teachers-t.html.
6. Steven Brill, "The Rubber Room: The Battle over New York City's Worst Teachers," *New Yorker*, August 31, 2009, http://www.newyorker.com /magazine/2009/08/31/the-rubber-room.

MYTH 1: "Teachers' Unions Are the Biggest Obstacle to Improving Education Today."

1. Donald Trump, *The America We Deserve* (Los Angeles: Renaissance Books, 2000).
2. Bradford Richardson, "Christie: Teachers Union 'Single Most Destructive Force' in Education," *Hill*, January 9, 2016, http://thehill.com/blogs/ballot -box/gop-primaries/265324-christie-teachers-union-single-most -destructive-force-in.
3. Lyndsey Layton, "Chris Christie to Teachers Union: You Deserve a Punch in the Face," *Washington Post*, August 3, 2015, https://www.washingtonpost .com/local/education/chris-christie-to-teachers-union-you-deserve-a -punch-in-the-face/2015/08/03/86358c2c-39de-11e5-8e98-115a3cf7d7ae _story.html.

4. George Skelton, "Teacher Union Bosses Have Forgotten Civic Lessons," *Los Angeles Times*, May 23, 2001, http://articles.latimes.com/2002/may/23/local/me-cap23, accessed May 7, 2017.

5. "Right-Wing Radio Host: Teachers Unions Are 'Much More Dangerous' Than Al Qaeda," *ThinkProgress*, February 20, 2007, https://thinkprogress.org/right-wing-radio-host-teachers-unions-are-much-more-dangerous-than-al-qaeda-396be2d4f747, accessed May 9, 2017.

6. Andrew Sullivan, "Quote for the Day," *Atlantic*, November 13, 2008, https://www.theatlantic.com/amp/article/208661, accessed May 9, 2017.

7. Robert Pear, "Education Chief Calls Union 'Terrorist,' Then Recants," *New York Times*, February 23, 2004, http://www.nytimes.com/2004/02/24/us/education-chief-calls-union-terrorist-then-recants.html, accessed May 9, 2017.

8. "Right-Wing Radio Host: Teachers Unions Are 'Much More Dangerous' Than Al Qaeda."

9. Matthew DiCarlo, "The Real Effect of Teachers Union Contracts," *The Answer Sheet* blog, *Washington Post*, October 25, 2010, http://voices.washingtonpost.com/answer-sheet/guest-bloggers/how-states-with-no-teacher-uni.html.

10. National Center for Education Statistics, *The Nation's Report Card: Reading 2011* (NCES 2012–457) (Washington, DC: Institute of Education Sciences, US Department of Education, 2011), https://nces.ed.gov/nationsreportcard/pdf/main2011/2012457.pdf.

11. OECD, PISA 2015 Results in Focus (2016), https://www.oecd.org/pisa/pisa-2015-results-in-focus.pdf.

12. Andrew Coulson, "The Effects of Teachers Unions on American Education," *Cato Journal* 30, no. 1 (Winter 2010).

13. W. E. B. Du Bois, *Black Reconstruction in America: An Essay Toward a History of the Part Which Black Folk Played in the Attempt to Reconstruct Democracy in America, 1860–1880* (New York: Harcourt Brace, 1935), 638.

14. Jonathan Zimmerman, "Why Is American Teaching So Bad?," *New York Review of Books*, December 4, 2014, http://www.nybooks.com/articles/2014/12/04/why-american-teaching-so-bad, accessed May 9, 2017.

15. Jean Guarino, "Teachers' Pests in the 1800s," *Chicago Tribune*, September 9, 1981, http://archives.chicagotribune.com/1981/09/09/page/27/article/teachers-pests-in-the-1800s, accessed May 9, 2017.

16. Dana Goldstein, *The Teacher Wars: A History of America's Most Embattled Profession* (New York: Anchor Books, 2015), 85.

17. Ibid.

18. Daniel H. Perlstein, *Justice, Justice: School Politics and the Eclipse of Liberalism* (New York: Peter Lang Publishing, 2004).

19. Aamer Madhani, "Chicago Teachers Union Members Authorize Strike," *USA Today*, September 26, 2016, https://www.usatoday.com/story/news/2016/09/26/chicago-teachers-union-members-authorize-strike/91118748/.

20. Elizabeth Todd-Breland in correspondence with the authors.

21. National Coalition of Education Activists, "Social Justice Unionism: A Call to Education Activists," *Rethinking Schools* 9, no. 1 (Fall 1994), http://rethinkingschools.aidcvt.com/special_reports/union/sjun.shtml.

MYTH 2: "You Can't Fire the Bad Ones."

1. Ted Olson, in discussion with David Boies and Charlie Rose, *Charlie Rose*, PBS, June 19, 2014, https://charlierose.com/videos/8159.

2. The case of *Vergara v. California* in 2014 held that several key job protections for teachers were so harmful that they deprived students of their constitutional right to an education. LA County Superior Court judge Rolf Treu sided with the plaintiffs, saying the tenure system resulted in educational malpractice that "shocks the conscience." The effect of the rules, he said, was to allow ineffective teachers to keep their jobs and subject students— especially poor and minority ones—to inferior schooling that could stunt their futures. In 2016, a three-judge appellate panel in Los Angeles saw the evidence and the law differently in a unanimous opinion. "Plaintiffs failed to show that the statutes themselves make any certain group of students more likely to be taught by ineffective teachers than any other group of students." Howard Blume, Joy Rosmovits, and Sonali Kohli, "In a Win for Unions, Appeals Court Reverses Ruling That Threw Out Teacher Tenure in California," *Los Angeles Times*, April 14, 2016, http://www.latimes.com/local/lanow/la-me-ln-court-rejects-bid-to-end-teacher-tenure-in-california-marking-huge-win-for-unions-20160414-story.html.

3. Caroline Porter and Melanie Trottman, "Teachers Unions Under Fire: Educators Plan to Fight Back After California Ruling Gutting Tenure Emboldens Critics," *Wall Street Journal*, September 4, 2014, https://www.wsj.com/articles/teachers-unions-under-fire-1409874404.

4. Arne Duncan, "Partners in Reform," remarks to the National Education Association, July 2, 2009, https://www2.ed.gov/news/speeches/2009/07/07022009.html.

5. Randi Kay, "All Teachers Fired at Rhode Island School," CNN, February 24, 2010, http://www.cnn.com/2010/US/02/24/rhode.island.teachers.

6. Brian Montopoli, "Obama Official Applauds Rhode Island Teacher Firings," *CBS News*, February 24, 2010, http://www.cbsnews.com/news/obama-official-applauds-rhode-island-teacher-firings.

7. Pete Wilson, "State of the State Address," remarks by the governor of California, January 9, 1995, http://governors.library.ca.gov/addresses/s_36-Wilson07.html.

8. Chris Christie, "State of the State Address," remarks by the governor of New Jersey, January 11, 2011, http://www.state.nj.us/governor/news/addresses/2010s/approved/20110111b.html.

9. Joy Resmovits, "Michelle Rhee's StudentsFirst Will Merge with Education Advocacy Group 50Can," *Los Angeles Times*, March 29, 2016, http://www

.latimes.com/local/education/la-me-edu-michelle-rhee-studentsfirst
-50can-20160329-story.html.

10. Michelle Rhee, interview with Julie O'Connor, *Star Ledger*, December 19,
2010, http://www.nj.com/njvoices/index.ssf/2010/12/ask_michelle_rhee
_there_is_no.html.

11. Sam Dillon, "A School Chief Takes on Tenure, Stirring a Fight," *New York
Times*, November 12, 2008, http://www.nytimes.com/2008/11/13/education
/13tenure.html.

13. Donald J. Trump, "Donald J. Trump Remarks on Creating a New and Better
Future for America's Inner Cities," prepared remarks, August 16, 2016,
transcript available at http://www.politico.com/story/2016/08/full-text
-donald-trumps-speech-on-227095.

13. Rhode Island Public Radio, "Central Falls High School, Three Years After a
Mass Firing," December 31, 2013, http://ripr.org/post/central-falls-high
-school-three-years-after-mass-firing.

14. Diane Ravitch, "What Was the Evidence in the Vergara Case? Who Wins?
Who Loses?," *Diane Ravitch's Blog: A Site to Discuss Better Education for All*,
June 11, 2014, https://dianeravitch.net/2014/06/11/what-was-the
-evidence-in-the-vergara-case-who-wins-who-loses.

15. Howard Blume, Joy Resmovits, and Sonali Kohli, "In a Win for Unions, Appeals Court Reverses Ruling That Threw Out Teacher Tenure in California,"
Los Angeles Times, April 14, 2016, http://www.latimes.com/local/lanow
/la-me-ln-court-rejects-bid-to-end-teacher-tenure-in-california
-marking-huge-win-for-unions-20160414-story.html.

16. Steve Owens, "Keeping Great Teachers in the Classroom," *Teacher* (blog),
Education Week, September 22, 2010, http://www.edweek.org/; Eric
Westervelt, "Where Have All the Teachers Gone?," *NPREd*, March 3, 2015,
http://www.npr.org/.

17. Alan Singer, "Why Tenure for Teachers Is Important," *Huffington Post*, May
25, 2011, http://www.huffingtonpost.com/alan-singer/why-tenure-for
-teachers-i_b_461540.html.

MYTH 3: "Teachers' Unions Represent a Flock of 'Go Slow/Status Quo' Sheep."

1. David Leonhardt, "Hillarynomics: Big Policy Questions for Clinton," *New
York Times*, March 13, 2015, https://www.nytimes.com/2015/03/14/upshot
/hillarynomics-big-policy-questions-for-clinton.html, accessed May 9, 2017.

2. Ruben Navarrette, "Reformer's Defeat Is Bad News for Public Schools in
DC, and Everywhere," *Beaumont (TX) Enterprise*, October 19, 2010, http://
www.beaumontenterprise.com/opinions/columns/article/RUBEN
-NAVARRETTE-Reformer-s-defeat-is-bad-news-815779.php, accessed
May 9, 2017.

3. Newsweek Staff, "Jonathan Alter on Obama and Education," *Newsweek*, July
11, 2008, http://www.newsweek.com/jonathan-alter-obama-and-education
-92615, accessed May 9, 2017.

4. Marcus Winters, "In Chicago, the Education Status Quo Makes Its Stand," Manhattan Institute, September 14, 2012, http://www.manhattan-institute .org/html/chicago-education-status-quo-makes-its-stand-3842.html, accessed May 9, 2017.

5. Carlo Rotella, "Class Warrior: Arne Duncan's Bid to Shake Up Schools," *New Yorker*, February 1, 2010, http://www.newyorker.com/magazine/2010 /02/01/class-warrior.

6. "Romney's Education Speech," transcript, *The Answer Sheet* blog, *Washington Post*, May 23, 2012, https://www.washingtonpost.com/blogs/answer -sheet/post/romneys-education-speech-text/2012/05/23/gJQAUAtpkU _blog.html, accessed May 9, 2017.

7. Antonio Villaraigosa, "Why Are Teachers Unions So Opposed to Change?," op-ed, *Wall Street Journal*, July 20, 2014, https://www.wsj.com/articles /antonio-villaraigosa-why-are-teachers-unions-so-opposed-to-change -1405893828.

8. Eric Bradner, "Conway: Trump White House Offered 'Alternative Facts' on Crowd Size," CNN, January 23, 2017, http://www.cnn.com/2017/01/22 /politics/kellyanne-conway-alternative-facts/index.html; Max Greenwood, "Trump Tweets: The Media Is the 'Enemy of the American People,'" *Hill*, February 17, 2017 http://thehill.com/homenews/administration/320168 -trump-the-media-is-the-enemy-of-the-american-people.

9. Michael Winerip, "Hard-Working Teachers, Sabotaged When Student Test Scores Slip," *New York Times*, March 4, 2012, http://www.nytimes.com/2012 /03/05/nyregion/in-brooklyn-hard-working-teachers-sabotaged-when -student-test-scores-slip.html.

MYTH 4: "Good Teaching Is Entirely Color-Blind."

1. Parents Involved in Community Schools v. Seattle School District No. 1 et al., 551 US 701 (2007).

2. Roberts opinion, in League of United Latin American Citizens, et al., Appellants, v. Rick Perry, Governor of Texas, et al. (2006), https://www.law .cornell.edu/supct/html/05-204.ZX3.html.

3. James Baldwin, "A Talk to Teachers," *Saturday Review*, December 21, 1963, 42.

4. *2013–2014 Civil Rights Data Collection: A First Look* (Washington, DC: US Department of Education, Office for Civil Rights, 2016), https://www2.ed.gov /about/offices/list/ocr/docs/2013-14-first-look.pdf, accessed May 9, 2017.

5. http://rickayers.blogspot.com/.

6. Bureau of Labor Statistics, "Unemployment Rate and Employment-Population Ratio Vary by Race and Ethnicity," *Economics Daily*, January 13, 2017, https://www.bls.gov/opub/ted/2017/unemployment-rate-and -employment-population-ratio-vary-by-race-and-ethnicity.htm, accessed May 14, 2017.

7. Richard Rothstein, *The Color of Law: A Forgotten History of How Our Government Segregated America* (New York: W. W. Norton, 2017).

8. Upton Sinclair, *I, Candidate for Governor: And How I Got Licked* (1935; Berkeley: University of California Press, 1994), 109.

9. National Governors' Association, *Closing the Achievement Gap* (2005).

10. Django Paris and Samy Alim, *Culturally Sustaining Pedagogies: Teaching and Learning for Justice in a Changing World* (New York: Teachers College Press, 2017).

11. Carol D. Lee, *Culture, Literacy, and Learning: Taking Bloom in the Midst of the Whirlwind* (New York: Teachers College Press, 2007).

13. Jonathan Kozol, *The Shame of the Nation: The Restoration of Apartheid Schooling in America* (New York: Crown, 2005).

13. Gloria Ladson-Billings, "From the Achievement Gap to the Education Debt: Understanding Achievement in US Schools," *Educational Researcher* 35, no. 7 (2006): 9.

14. Katie Reckdahl, "A Call for More Black Men to Become Teachers," *Atlantic*, December 15, 2015, https://www.theatlantic.com/education/archive/2015/12/programs-teachers-african-american-men/420306/.

15. Katie Reckdahl, "Leading by Example: Black Male Teachers Make Students Feel Proud," *Hechinger Report*, December 2015, http://hechingerreport.org/leading-by-example-black-male-teachers-make-students-feel-proud/.

16. Melinda D. Anderson, "Why Schools Need More Teachers of Color—for White Students," *Atlantic*, August 6, 2015, https://www.theatlantic.com/education/archive/2015/08/teachers-of-color-white-students/400553/; L. Casey and Albert Shanker Institute, *The State of Teacher Diversity in American Education* (Washington, DC: Albert Shanker Institute, 2016), http://www.shankerinstitute.org/resource/teacherdiversity.

17. Ladson-Billings, "From the Achievement Gap to the Education Debt," 8.

18. W. E. Burghardt Du Bois, "Does the Negro Need Separate Schools?," *Journal of Negro Education* 4, no. 3 (July 1935): 328–35; Newton Edwards, "A Critique: The Courts and the Negro Separate School," *Journal of Negro Education* 4, no. 3 (July 1935): 442–55.

19. Carter G. Woodson, *The Mis-Education of the Negro* (1933; New York: AMS Press, 1972).

20. Lewis Steel, quoted in Harvie Wilkinson, *From Brown to Bakke: The Supreme Court and School Integration: 1954–1978* (New York: Oxford University Press, 1981), 67.

MYTH 5: "Teachers Have It Easy."

1. Valerie Strauss, "Kasich: 'If I Were King in America, I Would Abolish All Teachers Lounges Where They Sit Together and Worry About How Woe Is Us,'" *The Answer Sheet* blog, *Washington Post*, August 19, 2015, https://www.washingtonpost.com/news/answer-sheet/wp/2015/08/19/kasich-if-i-were-king-in-america-i-would-abolish-all-teachers-lounges-where-they-sit-together-and-worry-about-how-woe-is-us.

2. Andrew G. Biggs and Jason Richwine, "Assessing the Compensation of Public School Teachers," *AEI*, November 1, 2011, https://www.aei.org /publication/assessing-the-compensation-of-public-school-teachers, accessed May 9, 2017.
3. Matt McCall, *The Willis Report*, Fox Business Network, July 13, 2011.
4. Ruben Navarrette Jr., "Firing All the Teachers Was Justified," CNN, March 5, 2010, http://www.cnn.com/2010/OPINION/03/05/navarrette.teacher .firings, accessed May 9, 2017.
5. "Average Salary for All K–12 Teachers," *PayScale Human Capital*, updated June 3, 2017, http://www.payscale.com/research/US/All_K-12_Teachers /Salary.
6. Alissa Quart, "Teachers Are Working for Uber Just to Keep a Foothold in the Middle Class," *Nation*, September 7, 2016, https://www.thenation .com/article/teachers-are-working-for-uber-just-to-keep-a-foothold -in-the-middle-class.
7. Linda Darling-Hammond, Roberta Furger, Patrick M. Shields, and Leib Sutcher, *Addressing California's Emerging Teacher Shortage: An Analysis of Sources and Solutions* (Palo Alto, CA: Learning Policy Institute, 2016).
8. Westervelt, "Where Have All the Teachers Gone?"
9. Sarah Hulett, "Teaching Teachers to Teach: It's Not So Elementary," *NPREd*, NPR, October 24, 2015, http://www.npr.org/sections/ed/2015/10/24 /437555944/teaching-teachers-to-teach-its-not-so-elementary, accessed May 9, 2017.
10. Green, "Building a Better Teacher."
11. Quoted in ibid.
13. Ibid.

MYTH 6: "High-Stakes Standardized Tests Improve Student Achievement and Effectively Detect Inferior Teachers."

1. "Baby's Brain Begins Now: Conception to Age 3," Urban Child Institute, http://www.urbanchildinstitute.org/why-0-3/baby-and-brain, accessed July 20, 2017.
2. Sean McAdam, "What Happens When Common Doesn't Address Everyone," in Brett Gardiner Murphy, ed., *Inside Our Schools: Teachers on the Failure and Future of Education Reform* (Cambridge, MA: Harvard Education Press, 2017).
3. American Statistical Association, "Using Value-Added Models for Educational Assessment," April 8, 2014, https://www.scribd.com/document /217916454/ASA-VAM-Statement-1.
4. Eduardo Porter, "Grading Teachers by the Test," *New York Times*, March 27, 2016, https://www.nytimes.com/2015/03/25/business/economy/grading -teachers-by-the-test.html.

5. Paul Offit, *Pandora's Lab: Seven Stories of Science Gone Wrong* (New York: National Geographic, 2017), 103.

6. Nicholas Lemann, *The Big Test: The Secret History of the American Meritocracy* (New York: Farrar, Straus & Giroux, 1999), 34.

7. Jesse Hagopian, "A Brief History of the 'Testocracy,' Standardized Testing and Test-Defying," *Truthout*, March 25, 2015, http://www.truth-out.org/progressivepicks/item/29847-a-brief-history-of-the, accessed May 9, 2017.

8. Elizabeth Kolbert, "Big Score: When Mom Takes the SATs," *New Yorker*, March 3, 2014, http://www.newyorker.com/magazine/2014/03/03/big-score, accessed May 9, 2017.

9. Hagopian, "A Brief History of the 'Testocracy,' Standardized Testing and Test-Defying."

10. John Dewey, *The Influence of Darwin on Philosophy and Other Essays* (New York: Henry Holt and Co., 1910), 19.

11. Ladson-Billings, "From the Achievement Gap to the Education Debt," 3–12.

13. *Newsweek* staff, "America's Best High Schools 2012," May 20, 2012, http://www.newsweek.com/americas-best-high-schools-2012-how-we-compiled-list-64857.

13. David C. Berliner and Gene V. Glass, *50 Myths & Lies That Are Threatening America's Public Schools* (New York: Teachers College Press, 2014), 59.

14. Richard Rothstein, "If You Cheat to Escape a Corrupt Accountability System, Who Is Really to Blame?," *The Answer Sheet* blog, *Washington Post*, April 5, 2015, https://www.washingtonpost.com/news/answer-sheet/wp/2015/04/05/if-you-cheat-to-escape-a-corrupt-accountability-system-who-is-really-to-blame.

15. Valerie Strauss, "Why Not Subpoena Everyone in D.C. Cheating Scandal—Rhee Included?" *Washington Post*, April 12, 2013, https://www.washingtonpost.com/news/answer-sheet/wp/2013/04/12/why-not-subpoena-everyone-in-d-c-cheating-scandal-rhee-included/; John Merrow, "Michelle Rhee's Reign of Error," *Learning Matters*, April 11, 2013, http://takingnote.learningmatters.tv/?p=6232.

16. Rachel Aviv, "Wrong Answer," *New Yorker*, July 21, 2014, http://www.newyorker.com/magazine/2014/07/21/wrong-answer.

17. Monty Neill, Lisa Guisbond, and Bob Schaeffer, *Failing Our Children: How "No Child Left Behind" Undermines Quality and Equity in Education* (Cambridge, MA: FairTest/National Center for Fair and Open Testing, May 1, 2004), http://nepc.colorado.edu/publication/failing-our-children-how-no-child-left-behind-undermines-quality-and-equity-education.

MYTH 7: "While Teachers and Their Unions Use Poverty as a Convenient Smokescreen for Their Own Failures, It's Become Obvious that Grit and Merit Can Overcome Every Disadvantage."

1. Eva Moskowitz, "Schools Can Help All Kids—Poverty Is No Excuse," op-ed, *New York Post*, July 30, 2014, http://nypost.com/2014/07/30/the-poverty-myth-lame-excuse-for-failing-schools.

2. Trip Gabriel, "From Gingrich, an Unconventional View of Education," *The Caucus* blog, *New York Times*, November 19, 2011, http://thecaucus.blogs .nytimes.com/2011/11/19/from-gingrich-an-unconventional-view-of -education/

3. Pam Fessler, "Is There Truth in Gingrich's Remarks on the Poor?," National Public Radio, December 7, 2011, http://www.npr.org/2011/12/07 /143301568/a-look-at-gingrichs-comments-about-the-poor.

4. Mike Klonsky, "The Year They Began Calling Poverty and Homelessness an 'Excuse,'" *Huffington Post*, December 29, 2010, http://www.huffingtonpost .com/michael-klonsky-phd/the-year-they-begain-call_b_801931.html.

5. Tim Walker, "Shameful Milestone: Majority of Public School Students Live in Poverty," *NEA Today*, January 16, 2015, http://neatoday.org/2015/01/16 /shameful-milestone-majority-public-school-students-now-live-poverty.

6. National Center for Education Statistics, *The Nation's Report Card*.

7. Bernadette D. Proctor, Jessica L. Semega, and Melissa A. Kollar, *Income and Poverty in the United States: 2015* (Washington, DC: US Government Printing Office, 2016), https://www.census.gov/content/dam/Census /library/publications/2016/demo/p60–256.pdf.

8. "Measuring Poverty," National Center for Children in Poverty, http://www .nccp.org/topics/measuringpoverty.html, accessed July 20, 2017.

9. UNICEF Office of Research, *Child Well-Being in Rich Countries: A Comparative Overview*, Innocenti Report Card 11 (Florence, Italy: UNICEF Office of Research, 2013), 7.

10. "Child Poverty," National Center for Children in Poverty, http://www.nccp .org/topics/childpoverty.html, accessed June 7, 2017.

11. Mark Gruenberg, "AFT's Weingarten: School Reformers Ignore 'Elephant in the Room,'" *People's World*, October 31, 2013, http://www.peoplesworld.org /article/aft-s-weingarten-school-reformers-ignore-elephant-in-the-room.

13. Luke Towler, "Linda Darling-Hammond: Time for the U.S. to Learn the Right Lessons from High-Performing Nations," *NEA Today*, October 20, 2014, http://neatoday.org/2014/10/20/linda-darling-hammond-time-for -the-u-s-to-learn-the-right-lessons-from-high-performing-nations.

13. Paul Gorski, "Five Stereotypes About Poor Families and Education: The Trouble with the 'Culture of Poverty' and Other Stereotypes About People in Poverty," *The Answer Sheet* blog, *Washington Post*, October 28, 2013, http://www.washingtonpost.com/blogs/answer-sheet/wp/2013/10/28 /five stereotypes-about-poor-families-and-education.

14. Paul Gorski, "The Myth of the Culture of Poverty," *Educational Leadership* 65, no. 7 (2008): 32–36.

15. William H. Watkins, *The Assault on Public Education: Confronting the Politics of Corporate School Reform* (New York: Teachers College Press, 2012).

16. David C. Berliner, *Poverty and Potential: Out-Of-School Factors and School Success* (Boulder, CO: National Educational Policy Center, 2015), http:// nepc.colorado.edu/publication/poverty-and-potential.

17. Gruenberg, "AFT's Weingarten."

18. Angela Duckworth, *Grit: The Power of Passion and Perseverance* (New York: Scribners, 2016).

19. Gloria Ladson-Billings, "Now I Need to Have Grit?," *Black & Smart: The Place for Thinking Black Folks*, April 22, 2015, https://blackandsmart .wordpress.com/2015/04/22/now-i-need-to-have-grit.

MYTH 8: "Teachers Are Made More Visible and Accountable in Charter Schools, More Competitive Through Voucher Programs, and Irrelevant with the Advent of Teacher-Proof Cyber Schools."

1. Trump, *The America We Deserve*.

2. Kate Zernike, "Betsy DeVos, Trump's Education Pick, Has Steered Money from Public Schools," *New York Times*, November 23, 2016, https://www .nytimes.com/2016/11/23/us/politics/betsy-devos-trumps-education -pick-has-steered-money-from-public-schools.html.

3. Wisconsin Education Association Council, "Researcher 'Stunned' by High Rate of Voucher School Failures in Milwaukee," June 16, 2016, http://weac .org/2016/06/16/researcher-stunned-by-high-rate-of-voucher-school -failures-in-milwaukee/.

4. Diane Ravitch, "Vouchers Don't Work: Evidence from Milwaukee," *Diane Ravitch's Blog: A Site to Discuss Better Education for All*, March 29, 2013, https://dianeravitch.net/2013/03/29/vouchers-dont-work-evidence -from-milwaukee.

5. Gordon Lafer, "Do Poor Kids Deserve Lower-Quality Education Than Rich Kids? Evaluating School Privatization Proposals in Milwaukee, Wisconsin," Economic Policy Institute, April 24, 2014, http://www.epi.org/publication /school-privatization-milwaukee; Ben Joravsky, "Today's Lesson: Charters Do Not Outperform Unionized Schools," *Chicago Reader*, October 3, 2012, http://www.chicagoreader.com/chicago/chicagos-unionized-public -schools-outperform-charter-schools/Content?oid=7559748.

6. "Statement Regarding the NAACP's Resolution on a Moratorium on Charter Schools," NAACP, October 15, 2016, http://www.naacp.org/latest /statement-regarding-naacps-resolution-moratorium-charter-schools, accessed May 9, 2017.

7. Richard D. Kahlenberg and Halley Potter, "The Original Charter School Vision," *New York Times*, August 30, 2014, https://www.nytimes.com /2014/08/31/opinion/sunday/albert-shanker-the-original-charter -school-visionary.html.

8. Gary Miron, William J. Mathis, and Kevin G. Weiner, review of *Separating Fact and Fiction: What You Need to Know About Charter Schools*, by National Alliance for Public Charter Schools, National Educational Policy Center, February 23, 2015, 10, http://nepc.colorado.edu/thinktank/review -separating-fact-and-fiction.

9. Valerie Strauss, "In California's Charter World, a Tangled Web of For-Profit Companies and Nonprofit Schools," *The Answer Sheet* blog, *Washington Post*,

October 14, 2016, https://www.washingtonpost.com/news/answer-sheet/wp/2016/10/14/in-californias-charter-world-a-tangled-web-of-for-profit-companies-and-nonprofit-schools/?utm_term=.593d2b40aec0.

10. Peter Cunningham, "Is School Integration Necessary?," *US News & World Report*, August 15, 2016, https://www.usnews.com/opinion/articles/2016-08-15/segregated-schools-may-not-be-that-bad.

11. As quoted in Steven M. Singer, "No New Charter Schools—NAACP Draws Line in the Sand," *Gadfly on the Wall Blog*, July 30, 2016, https://gadflyonthewallblog.wordpress.com/2016/07/30/no-new-charter-schools-naacp-draws-line-in-the-sand, accessed May 9, 2017.

13. Based on Diane Ravitch, *Reign of Error: The Hoax of the Privatization Movement and the Danger to America's Public Schools* (New York: Alfred A. Knopf, 2013).

13. Valerie Strauss, "Democrats Make Education Revisions to 2016 Platform—and a Key Reformer Is Furious," *Answer Sheet* blog, *Washington Post*, July 12, 2016, https://www.washingtonpost.com/news/answer-sheet/wp/2016/07/12/democrats-make-key-education-revisions-to-2016-platform-and-a-key-reformer-is-furious/.

14. Pedro Noguera, "Why Don't We Have Real Data on Charter Schools?," *Nation*, September 24, 2014, https://www.thenation.com/article/why-dont-we-have-real-data-charter-schools.

MYTH 9: "Anyone Can Be a Teacher."

1. Pete Wilson, "State of the State Address," January 9, 1995, California State Library online, accessed June 26, 2017.

2. Wendy Kopp, *One Day, All Children: The Unlikely Triumph of Teach for America and What I Learned Along the Way* (New York: PublicAffairs, 2011), xi.

3. Linda Darling-Hammond et al., "Does Teacher Preparation Matter? Evidence About Teacher Certification, Teach for America, and Teacher Effectiveness," *Educational Policy Analysis Archives* 13 (October 2005), doi: http://dx.doi.org/10.14507/epaa.v13n42.2005.

4. T. Jameson Brewer and Kathleen deMarrais, *Teach for America Counter-Narratives: Alumni Speak Up and Speak Out* (New York: Peter Lang Publishing, 2015).

5. Paul T. Decker et al., *The Effects of Teach for America on Students: Findings from a National Evaluation* (Princeton, NJ: Mathematica Policy Research, 2004).

6. Barbara Miner, "Looking Past the Spin: Teach for America," *Rethinking Schools* (Spring 2010), https://www.rethinkingschools.org/articles/looking-past-the-spin-teach-for-america.

7. Julian Vasquez Heilig and Su Jin Jez, *Teach for America: A Review of the Evidence* (Boulder, CO: Education and the Public Interest Center/Education Policy Research Unit, 2010), http://nepc.colorado.edu/files/PB-TeachAmerica-Heilig.pdf.

8. Patricia Schaefer, "After 25 Years, Teach for America Results Are Consistently Underwhelming," *Nonprofit Quarterly*, September 11, 2015, https:// nonprofitquarterly.org/2015/09/11/after-25-years-teach-for-america -results-are-consistently-underwhelming.

9. Miner, "Looking Past the Spin."

10. Doug McAdam and Cynthia Brandt, "Assessing the Effects of Voluntary Youth Service: The Case of Teach for America," *Social Forces* 88, no. 2 (2009): 945–70, https://eric.ed.gov/?id=EJ872459.

11. Point/Counterpoint, "My Year Volunteering as a Teacher Helped Educate a New Generation of Underprivileged Kids vs. Can We Please, Just Once, Have a Real Teacher," *Onion*, July 17, 2012, http://www.theonion.com /multiblogpost/my-year-volunteering-as-a-teacher-helped-educate -a-28803.

MYTH 10: "Teachers Follow Popular Fads and Political Correctness Rather Than Teaching the Basics."

1. Glenn Beck, *An Inconvenient Book: Real Solutions to the World's Biggest Problems* (New York: Threshold Editions, 2009).

2. Florida Education Omnibus Bill, HB 7087, Florida House of Representatives, 2006, http://www.myfloridahouse.gov/Sections/Documents/load doc.aspx?FileName=_h7087e3.doc&DocumentType=Bill&BillNumber =7087&Session=2006.

3. State of Arizona, Forty-Eighth Legislature, SB 1108, 2008, https://www .azleg.gov/legtext/48leg/2r/bills/5B1108p.pdf.

4. State of Arizona House of Representatives Forty-Ninth Legislature, HB 2281, 2010, https://www.azleg.gov/legtext/49leg/2r/bills/hb2281s.pdf.

5. Christine Sleeter, "Ethnic Studies and the Struggle in Tucson," *Education Week*, February 15, 2012, http://www.edweek.org/ew/articles/2012/02/15 /21sleeter.h31.html.

6. Karen Herzog, "Walker Proposes Changing Wisconsin Idea—Then Backs Away," *Milwaukee Journal Sentinel*, February 4, 2015, http://archive .jsonline.com/news/education/scott-walkers-uw-mission-rewrite-could -end-the-wisconsin-idea-b99439020z1-290797681.html/.

7. David Coleman, "Bringing the Common Core to Life," speech to the New York State Department of Education, Albany, April 28, 2011, available on YouTube, https://www.youtube.com/watch?v=Pu6lin88YXU.

8. Casey Quinlan, "College Board Caves to Conservative Pressure, Changes AP US History Curriculum," *ThinkProgress*, July 30, 2015, https://thinkprogress .org/college-board-caves-to-conservative-pressure-changes-ap-u-s -history-curriculum-236d89a40bba.

9. Catherine Gewertz, "Republican National Committee Condemns New AP History Framework," *Curriculum Matters* blog, *Education Week*, August 11, 2014, http://blogs.edweek.org/edweek/curriculum/2014/08/college_board _statement_on_ap.html.

10. "US and World Population Clock," US Census Bureau, https://www.census .gov/popclock/.

11. Bureau of Justice Statistics, https://www.bjs.gov/.

13. "Life Expectancy at Birth (Years), 2000-2015," World Health Organization, http://gamapserver.who.int/gho/interactive_charts/mbd/life_expectancy /atlas.html.

13. "How Many People Died in World War 2?," *History on the Net*, http://www .historyonthenet.com/how-many-people-died-in-world-war-2/, last updated November 23, 2014, accessed July 20, 2017.

14. "Documenting Numbers of Victims of the Holocaust and Nazi Persecution," *Holocaust Encyclopedia*, https://www.ushmm.org/wlc/en/article.php ?ModuleId=10008193.

15. David Swanson, "War Is Not Going to End on Its Own," *World Beyond War*, http://worldbeyondwar.org/war-going-end/, accessed August 2, 2017.

16. Nick Turse, "'So Many People Died': How Afghanistan and Iraq Echo Vietnam," *Mother Jones*, January 9, 2013, http://www.motherjones.com/politics /2013/01/civilian-suffering-afghanistan-and-vietnam-kill-anything -that-moves/.

17. Charles Dickens, *Hard Times* (orig. pub. 1854; London: J. M. Dent & Sons, 1954).

18. Jay Gillen, *Educating for Insurgency: The Roles of Young People in Schools of Poverty* (Oakland, CA: AK Press, 2014).

MYTH 11: "Teacher Activists Are Troublemakers."

1. Julia Glum, "Central Park Five Controversy: NYC Teacher Jenna Lee-Walker Fired Because School Feared Black Students?," *International Business Times*, January 8, 2016, http://www.ibtimes.com/central-park-five-controversy -nyc-teacher-jenna-lee-walker-fired-because-school-2256795.

2. Bertolt Brecht, *Galileo* (1952), trans. Charles Laughton, ed. Eric Bentley (New York: Grove Press, 1966).

3. W. E. B. Du Bois, *The Education of Black People: Ten Critiques, 1906–1960*, ed. Herbert Aptheker (orig. pub. 1973; New York: Monthly Review Press, 2001), 42.

4. Freeman Dyson, *The Scientist as Rebel* (New York: New York Review Books, 2006), 4–5, 7.

5. Michael E. Dantley and Linda C. Tillman, "Social Justice and Moral Transformative Leadership," in *Leadership for Social Justice*, ed. Catherine Marshall and Maricela Oliva (Upper Saddle River, NJ: Pearson, 2010), 19–34.

6. Edward Said, *Representations of the Intellectual: The 1993 Reith Lectures* (New York: Pantheon Books, 1994), quotes from this book on pp. 11–12, 23, 6, 35, xviii.

MYTH 12: "Discipline Is the First Priority for Every Teacher, and It Is Especially Essential for Teachers in Urban Schools with Large Numbers of Black Students."

1. Trump, *The America We Deserve*

2. Bill O'Reilly, *The O'Reilly Factor*, Fox News, January 12, 2006.

3. Trump, *The America We Deserve*.

4. Ed Brockenbrough, "'The Discipline Stop': Black Male Teachers and the Politics of Urban School Discipline," *Education and Urban Society* (2014): 1–24.

5. Christopher Emdin, "Why Black Men Quit Teaching," op-ed, *New York Times*, August 27, 2016, https://www.nytimes.com/2016/08/28/opinion /sunday/why-black-men-quit-teaching.html.

6. Monique W. Morris, "The Black Girl Pushout," interview by Melissa D. Anderson, *Atlantic*, March 15, 2016, https://www.theatlantic.com/education /archive/2016/03/the-criminalization-of-black-girls-in-schools/473718.

7. Leticia Smith-Evans and Janel George, *Unlocking Opportunity for African American Girls: A Call to Action for Educational Equity* (New York: NAACP Legal Defense and Educational Fund and National Women's Law Center, 2014), http://www.nwlc.org/sites/default/files/pdfs/unlocking_opportunity_for _african_american_girls_final.pdf.

8. "Oppositional Defiant Disorder," *Diagnostic and Statistical Manual of Mental Disorders*, 5th ed. (Arlington, VA: American Psychiatric Publishing, 2013).

9. Gail Fernandez and Robert Myers, "Oppositional Defiant Disorder," *Child Development Institute*, https://childdevelopmentinfo.com/child-psychology /oppositional-defiant-disorder, accessed May 9, 2017.

10. "Oppositional Defiant Disorder. A Guide for Families by the American Academy of Child and Adolescent Psychiatry," *American Academy of Child & Adolescent Psychiatry*, 2009, https://www.aacap.org/App_Themes/AACAP /docs/resource_centers/odd/odd_resource_center_odd_guide.pdf, accessed May 9, 2017.

11. Lauren Mizock and Debra A. Harkins, "Diagnostic Bias and Conduct Disorder: Improving Culturally Sensitive Diagnosis," *Child and Youth Services* 32 (2011): 243–53.

12. Jerome Kagan, "What About Tutoring Instead of Pills?," *Der Spiegel*, August 2, 2012, http://www.spiegel.de/international/world/child-psychologist -jerome-kagan-on-overprescibing-drugs-to-children-a-847500.html.

13. Enrico Gnaulati, *Back to Normal: Why Ordinary Childhood Behavior Is Mistaken for ADHD, Bipolar Disorder, and Autism Spectrum Disorder* (Boston: Beacon Press, 2014).

14. Quoted in Valerie Strauss, "Beating 'Compliance Acquiescence Disorder' in School," *The Answer Sheet* blog, *Washington Post*, October 5, 2012, https:// www.washingtonpost.com/news/answer-sheet/wp/2012/10/05/beating- compliance-acquiescence-disorder-in-school/?utm_term=.36cf63a8633e.

15. Ta-Nehisi Coates, *The Beautiful Struggle: A Memoir* (New York: Speigel and Grau, 2009), 170.

16. Ibid., 26.

17. Ibid., 36.

18. Quraysh Ali Lansana, "Male Bonding," in *Reluctant Minivan* (Tulsa: Living Arts Press, 2014).

MYTH 13: "Teachers Need to Set High Standards and Drive Kids Hard."

1. Vicki Abeles, "Modern Education Is Making Our Kids Sick," commentary, *Dallas Morning News*, January 5, 2016, http://www.dallasnews.com/opinion /commentary/2016/01/05/vicki-abeles-modern-education-is-making -our-kids-sick.

2. Jerusha Conner, "Sleep to Succeed," *US News & World Report*, July 22, 2015, https://www.usnews.com/opinion/knowledge-bank/2015/07/22/teens -need-more-sleep-to-succeed-in-school.

3. American Psychological Association, "American Psychological Association Survey Shows Teen Stress Rivals That of Adults," news release, February 11, 2014, http://www.apa.org/news/press/releases/2014/02/teen-stress.aspx.

4. Brian J. Mistler et al., *The Association for University and College Counseling Directors Annual Survey* (Indianapolis: Association for University and College Counseling Directors, 2012), 174, http://files.cmcglobal.com/Monograph _2012_AUCCCD_Public.pdf.

5. American Psychological Association, *Stress in America: Are Teens Adopting Adults' Stress Habits?* (Washington, DC: American Psychological Association, 2014), https://www.apa.org/news/press/releases/stress/2013/stress -report.pdf.

MYTH 14: "Teachers Are Poorly Served by the Universally Dreadful Teacher-Education Programs Currently Available."

1. Fareed Zakaria, "When Will We Learn," November 28, 2011, https://fareed zakaria.com/2011/11/28/when-will-we-learn.

2. Nancy Gibbs, "Honor Thy Teacher," *Time*, October 24, 2014, http://time .com/3533566/honor-thy-teacher.

3. Jason Richwine and Andrew G. Biggs, *Assessing the Compensation of Public-School Teachers* (Washington, DC: Heritage Foundation, 2011), http://www .heritage.org/education/report/assessing-the-compensation-public -school-teachers.

4. Dana Goldstein, "Fact-Checking Joel Klein: Is It True Most Teachers Think Credentialing Is Useless?," *Dana Goldstein* blog, May 18, 2011, http://www .danagoldstein.com/2011/05/fact-checking-joel-klein-is-it-true-most -teachers-think-traditional-training-is-useless.html, accessed June 12, 2017.

5. Kevin Kumashiro, *Bad Teacher: How Blaming Teachers Distorts the Bigger Picture* (New York: Teachers College Press, 2012).

6. "Help Teachers Before They Get to Class," editorial, *New York Times*, October 14, 2016, https://www.nytimes.com/2016/10/15/opinion/help-teachers -before-they-get-to-class.html, accessed March 14, 2017.

7. Westervelt, "Where Have All the Teachers Gone?"; Gary Barnes, Edward Crowe, and Benjamin Schaefer, The Cost of Teacher Turnover in Five School Districts: A Pilot Study (Arlington, VA: National Commission on Teaching and America's Future, 2007), https://nctaf.org/wp-content/uploads/2012/01 /NCTAF-Cost-of-Teacher-Turnover-2007-full-report.pdf.

8. Jill Tucker, "SF Offers Rare Signing Bonuses amid Big Teacher Shortage," *San Francisco Chronicle*, July 6, 2016, http://www.sfchronicle.com /education/article/SF-offers-rare-signing-bonuses-amid-big-teacher -8344621.php.

9. "Child Poverty," National Center for Children in Poverty, http://www .nccp.org/topics/childpoverty.html.

10. Nikole Hannah-Jones, "Choosing a School for My Daughter in a Segregated City: How One School Became a Battleground over Which Children Benefit from a Separate and Unequal System," *New York Times*, June 9, 2016, https:// www.nytimes.com/2016/06/12/magazine/choosing-a-school-for-my -daughter-in-a-segregated-city.html.

11. Jeff Chang, *We Gon' Be Alright: Notes on Race and Resegregation* (New York: Picador Books, 2016).

12. Ravitch, *Reign of Error*.

13. US Department of Education, "Education Department Releases Final Teacher Preparation Regulations," news release, October 12, 2016, https:// www.ed.gov/news/press-releases/education-department-releases-final -teacher-preparation-regulations.

14. National Education Policy Center, "Proposed Federal Regulations Likely to Harm Education," news release, January 12, 2015, http://nepc.colorado .edu/newsletter/2015/01/review-proposed-teacher-preparation.

15. Edward J. Fuller, "Shaky Methods, Shaky Motives: A Critique of the National Council of Teacher Quality's Review of Teacher Preparation Programs," *Journal of Teacher Education* 65, no. 1 (January–February 2014): 63–77, http://jte.sagepub.com/content/65/1/63.

16. "Help Teachers Before They Get to Class," editorial, *New York Times*.

17. Marilyn Cochran-Smith et al., *Holding Teacher Preparation Accountable: A Review of Claims and Evidence* (Boulder, CO: National Education Policy Center, 2016), http://nepc.colorado.edu/publication/holding-teacher -preparation-accountable-a-review-of-claims-and-evidence, accessed March 14, 2017.

MYTH 15: "Too Many Bad Teachers Have Created a Public School System That Is Utterly Broken, and the Only Solution Is to Wipe the Slate Clean and Start Over."

1. Nick Anderson, "Education Secretary Duncan Calls Hurricane Katrina Good for New Orleans Schools," *Washington Post*, January 30, 2010, http://www.washingtonpost.com/wp-dyn/content/article/2010/01/29 /AR2010012903259.html, accessed May 9, 2017.

2. Erica Green, "Betsy DeVos Calls for More School Choice, Saying Money Isn't the Answer," *New York Times*, March 29, 2017, https://www.nytimes .com/2017/03/29/us/politics/betsy-devos-education-school-choice -voucher.html.

3. Kevin Carey, "Dismal Voucher Results Surprise Researchers as DeVos Era Begins," *New York Times*, February 23, 2017, https://www.nytimes.com

/2017/02/23/upshot/dismal-results-from-vouchers-surprise-researchers
-as-devos-era-begins.html.

4. Naomi Klein, *The Shock Doctrine: The Rise of Disaster Capitalism* (New York: Henry Holt, 2007).

5. Andrew Vanacore, "New Orleans May Become First Major City with All-Charter Public School System," *New Orleans Advocate*, December 10, 2016, http://www.theadvocate.com/new_orleans/news/education/article _2cf99eb6-bf28-11e6-89e1-7fbc99a44ab4.html.

6. Nathan Barrett and Douglas Harris, "Significant Changes in the New Orleans Teacher Workforce," policy brief, Education Research Alliance for New Orleans, August 24, 2015, http://educationresearchalliancenola .org/files/publications/ERA-Policy-Brief-Changes-in-the-New-Orleans -Teacher-Workforce.pdf.

7. Raynard Sanders, "The New Orleans Reformed Public School System: National Model?," Bank Street College of Education Occasional Paper Series 27, part II (2012), https://www.bankstreet.edu/occasional-paper-series/27 /part-ii/new-orleans-reformed-public-school-system.

8. Mikhail Zinshteyn, "New Orleans Schools: A Nexus of Poverty, High Expulsion Rates, Hyper-Security, and Novice Teachers," *American Independent*, July 21, 2011, http://americanindependent.com/194488/new-orleans -schools-a-nexus-of-poverty-high-expulsion-rates-hyper-security-and -novice-teachers.

9. Charles J. Hatfield, "Comparison of 2014 LEAP Results for RSD-NO to Other Louisiana Public School Districts (Revised)," August 15, 2014, http://www.researchonreforms.org/html/documents/Comparisonof2014 LEAPResultsforRSD-NOtoOtherLouisianaPublicSchoolDistricts-Rev.pdf.

10. Raynard Sanders, "The New Orleans Reformed Public School System: National Model?," Bank Street Occasional Papers, 2012, https://www.bank street.edu/occasional-paper-series/27/part-ii/new-orleans-reformed -public-school-system/; and personal correspondence.

11. Liz Brown and Eric (Rico) Gutstein, *The Charter Difference: A Comparison of Chicago Charter and Neighborhood High Schools* (Chicago: Collaborative for Equity and Justice in Education, 2009), http://ceje.uic.edu/wp-content /uploads/2013/11/CharterDifference.pdf.

13. Chicagoland Researchers and Advocates for Transformative Education (CReATE), Factsheet on Charter Schools (Chicago: CReATE, 2012), https:// www.dropbox.com/s/y38db4yt5bl2yt4/CReATE%20Factsheet%20on% 20Charter%20Schools%20November%202012.pdf.

13. George E. Curry, "Take a Recess from Closing Public Schools," *Washington Informer*, May 27, 2013, http://washingtoninformer.com/take-a-recess -from-closing-public-schools/.

14. Stephanie Farmer et al., "CReATE Research Brief on School Closures," 2013, http://blogs.roosevelt.edu/sfarmer/files/2013/02/CReATE-BRIEF -5-School-Closures.pdf.

15. Grover J. "Russ" Whitehurst and Matthew M. Chingos, *Class Size: What Research Says and What It Means for State Policy* (Washington, DC: Brown Center on Education Policy, Brookings Institution, 2011), https://www.brookings.edu/wp-content/uploads/2016/06/0511_class_size_whitehurst_chingos.pdf.

16. Marisa de La Torre and Julia Gwynne, *When Schools Close: Effects on Displaced Students in Chicago Public Schools* (Chicago: Consortium on Chicago School Research, 2009), http://ccsr.uchicago.edu/sites/default/files/publications/CCSRSchoolClosings-Final.pdf, accessed March 14, 2017.

17. De la Torre and Gwynne, *When Schools Close*, 2.

MYTH 16: "Teachers Are Unable to Deal Adequately with the Disciplinary Challenges Posed by Today's Youth, and We Need More Police in Our Public School Buildings to Do the Job and Maintain Law and Order."

1. Lucinda Gray, Laurie Lewis, and John Ralph, *Public School Safety and Discipline: 2013–14* (Washington, DC: US Department of Education, 2015), https://nces.ed.gov/pubs2015/2015051.pdf.

2. Emma Brown, "Police in Schools: Keeping Kids Safe, or Arresting Them for No Good Reason?," *Washington Post*, November 8, 2015, https://www.washingtonpost.com/local/education/police-in-schools-keeping-kids-safe-or-arresting-them-for-no-good-reason/2015/11/08/937ddfd0-816c-11e5-9afb-0c971f713doc_story.html.

3. Hawes Spencer, "Child Handcuffed and School Policies Questioned," *Radio IQ*, December 9, 2014, http://wvtf.org/post/child-handcuffed-and-school-policies-questioned; Andrew Buncombe, "Ahmed Mohamed Demands $15m Compensation and Written Apology After Homemade Clock Arrest," *Independent*, November 25, 2015, http://www.independent.co.uk/news/people/ahmed-mohamed-demands-15m-compensation-for-homemade-clock-arrest-a6745706.html.

4. Melinda Anderson, "When Schooling Meets Policing," *Atlantic*, September 21, 2015, https://www.theatlantic.com/education/archive/2015/09/when-schooling-meets-policing/406348.

5. Alexis Karteron and New York Civil Liberties Union, "Do the Police Belong in Our Schools?," *New York Times*, April 22, 2013, http://www.nytimes.com/2013/04/23/opinion/do-the-police-belong-in-our-public-schools.html.

6. Jawanzaa Kunjufu, *Countering the Conspiracy to Destroy Black Boys*, vol. 2 (Chicago: African American Images, 1986), 32.

MYTH 17: "Teachers Need to Stick with Teaching the Great Lessons of Western Civilization in Order to Civilize Youth and Mold Them into the Good Citizens of the Future."

1. E. D. Hirsch Jr., *Cultural Literacy: What Every American Needs to Know* (New York: Vintage Books, 1988), 14.

2. William Bennett, *The Book of Virtues* (New York: Simon & Schuster, 1996).

3. Lee, *Culture, Literacy, and Learning*; Django Paris, "Culturally Sustaining Pedagogy: A Needed Change in Stance, Terminology, and Practice," *Educational Researcher* 41, no. 3 (2012): 93–97; Gloria Ladson-Billings and William Tate, "Toward a Critical Race Theory of Education," *Teachers College Record* 97, no. 1 (1995): 47–68; Rochelle Gutiérrez, "What Is Nepantla and How Can It Help Physics Education Researchers Conceptualize Knowledge for Teaching?" in *Proceedings of the 2008 Annual Meeting of the Physics Education Research Conference*, ed. Charles Henderson, Mel S. Sabella, and Leonardo Hsu (Edmonton, Alberta, 2008).

4. From Frederick Douglass, *Life of an American Slave* (Boston: Anti-Slavery Office, 1845), chapter VI, available at http://utc.iath.virginia.edu/abolitn /abaufda8t.html.

5. Richard H. Pratt, "Official Report of the Nineteenth Annual Conference of Charities and Correction (1892)," in *Americanizing the American Indians: Writings by the "Friends of the Indian," 1880–1900*, ed. Francis Paul Prucha (Cambridge, MA: Harvard University Press, 1973), 260.

6. William Watkins, *The White Architects of Black Education, 1865–1954* (New York: Teachers College Press, 2001).

7. Ruby Payne, Aha Process, Inc., http://www.ahaprocess.com/book-ruby/.

8. Carol Burris, "Some Scary Training for Teachers," *The Answer Sheet* blog, *Washington Post*, July 25, 2012, https://www.washingtonpost.com/blogs /answer-sheet/post/some-scary-training-for-teachers/2012/07/25 /gJQAzXyJAX_blog.html.

9. Lisa Delpit, "Skills and Other Dilemmas of a Progressive Black Educator," *Harvard Educational Review* 56, no. 4 (1986): 379–86; Lisa Delpit, "The Silenced Dialogue: Power and Pedagogy in Educating Other People's Children," *Harvard Educational Review* 58, no. 3 (1988): 280–99.

10. Delpit, "The Silenced Dialogue," 282.

11. Ibid., 297.

MYTH 18: "Teachers Need to Focus Less on the Arts, More on STEM."

1. In D. H. Melhem, *Gwendolyn Brooks: Poetry and the Heroic Voice* (Lexington: University of Kentucky Press, 1987), 179.

2. Herbert Kohl and Tom Oppenheim, eds., *The Muses Go to School: Inspiring Stories About the Importance of Arts in Education* (New York: New Press, 2014), 63.

3. Maxine Greene, "The Slow Fuse of the Possible," *Teachers & Writers Magazine* 32, no. 5 (2001).

4. Diane Di Prima, "Revolutionary Letter #1," *Revolutionary Letters* (Berkeley, CA: Wingbow Press, 1978).

5. Gwendolyn Brooks, "Boy Breaking Glass," in *Blacks* (Chicago: Third World Press, 1987), 438.

6. Bertrand Russell, "Dreams and Facts," 1919.

7. Maxine Greene, *Releasing the Imagination: Essays on Education, the Arts, and Social Change* (San Francisco: Jossey-Bass, 2000).

8. Paulo Freire, *Pedagogy of the Oppressed* (New York: Continuum, 1968).

9. Lois Hetland et al., *Studio Thinking: The Real Benefits of Visual Arts Education* (New York: Teachers College Press, 2007).

10. "K12 Lab Network," Stanford Design School, https://dschool.stanford.edu /programs/k12-lab-network.

MYTH 19: "The Truly Great Teachers Are Heroes."

1. Alia Wong, "What If America's Teachers Made More Money?," *Atlantic*, February 18, 2016, https://www.theatlantic.com/education/archive/2016 /02/what-if-americas-teachers-made-more-money/463275.

2. Horace Mann, *A Few Thoughts on the Powers and Duties of Woman: Two Lectures* (Syracuse, NY: Hall, Mills & Co., 1853), 37.

3. "Nice White Lady," *Madtv*, Fox TV, 2007, YouTube, https://www.youtube .com/watch?v=ZVF-nirSq5s.

4. Judith Halberstam, *The Queer Art of Failure* (Durham, NC: Duke University Press, 2011), 14.

5. Barbara Ransby, *Ella Baker and the Black Freedom Movement: A Radical Democratic Vision* (Chapel Hill: University of North Carolina Press, 2005).

6. Hannah Arendt, "The Crisis in Education," 1954, available at http:// la.utexas.edu/users/hcleaver/330T/350kPEEArendtCrisisInEdTable.pdf.

About the Authors

WILLIAM AYERS is Distinguished Professor of Education and Senior University Scholar at the University of Illinois at Chicago (retired) and the author of numerous books about schools and education, including *Teaching Toward Freedom*, *A Kind and Just Parent*, *and To Teach*, along with the memoirs *Fugitive Days and Public Enemy*.

CRYSTAL T. LAURA is associate professor of educational leadership and codirector of the Center for Urban Research and Education at Chicago State University. She is the author of *Being Bad: My Baby Brother and the School-to-Prison Pipeline*.

RICK AYERS is associate professor of education at the University of San Francisco in the Urban Education and Social Justice Cohort and the USF coordinator of the San Francisco Teacher Residency. He is the author of *Studs Terkel's "Working": A Teaching Guide*, *An Empty Seat in Class*, *Great Books for High School Kids*, and, with William Ayers, *Teaching the Taboo*.